D1592638

The Middle-Class City

The Middle-Class City

Transforming Space and Time in
Philadelphia, 1876–1926

John Henry Hepp, IV

PENN

University of Pennsylvania Press
Philadelphia

Copyright © 2003 University of Pennsylvania Press
All rights reserved
Printed in the United States of America on acid-free paper

10   9   8   7   6   5   4   3   2   1

Published by
University of Pennsylvania Press
Philadelphia, Pennsylvania 19104-4011

Library of Congress Cataloging-in-Publication Data
Hepp, John Henry, IV.
   The middle-class city : transforming space and time in Philadelphia, 1876–1926 / John Henry
Hepp, IV.
      p. cm.
   Includes bibliographical references and index.
   ISBN 0-8122-3723-4 (acid-free paper)
   1. Middle class—Pennsylvania—Philadelphia—History.   2. Cities and
towns—Pennsylvania—Philadelphia—Growth. 3. City
planning—Pennsylvania—Philadelphia—History. 4. Department
stores—Pennsylvania—Philadelphia—History. 5. Urban
transportation—Pennsylvania—Philadelphia—History. 6. Newspaper
reading—Pennsylvania—Philadelphia—History. 7. Philadelphia (Pa.)—History. 8.
Philadelphia (Pa.)—Social life and customs. I. Title.

HT690.U6H46 2003
974.8'11041—dc21

2003041001

Contents

Preface

       Historians have often viewed the reaction of the American middle class to the sweeping changes wrought by industrialization and urbanization as negative or, at best, ambivalent. The classic interpretation of the late nineteenth and early twentieth centuries sees this period as a political "search for order" by the bourgeoisie. My book examines transformations in everyday middle-class life in Philadelphia between 1876 and 1926 to discover the cultural roots of this search for order. By looking at the complex relationships among members of that city's bourgeoisie and three largely middle-class commercial institutions (newspapers, department stores, and railroads), it finds that the bourgeoisie consistently reordered its world along new, rational lines during the late nineteenth century. At first, these changes were largely internal to the middle class, only affecting institutions that it used and controlled. Later, during the early twentieth century in particular, the bourgeoisie began to expand this new cultural sense of order to encompass politics as well.

       In Philadelphia, these changes in middle-class world view were less inspired by a fear of the future than by a faith in continued progress. Although this confidence was not always unbounded and was occasionally tinged with a sense of nostalgia, the city's bourgeois men and women saw the region's transformation as positive. They believed, by and large, that the Philadelphia of tomorrow would be better than that of their day, which in turn was an improvement on the city of twenty years before. This is not surprising, as they were, for the most part, beneficiaries of these changes. Not only could they see tangible economic, scientific, and technological advancement with, at least for many of them, few costs, but their class was largely a product of this new order.

*   *   *

Writing is a highly collaborative process. In the course of this work's long gestation period, I ran up a lot of debts: emotional, financial, and intellectual. Now is the time to repay some of them, however inadequate these words may be.

First and foremost, special thanks are due my family: my grandparents (the people who first introduced me to late nineteenth- and early twentieth-century Philadelphia), my parents, my long-suffering wife, Julie, and most recently my son John (who has developed at quite a young age a love for department stores, newspapers, and trains). Without them and their interests in history, this project would have never happened.

Next, special credit is owed to my friends and colleagues at the University of North Carolina at Chapel Hill. Peter Filene, William Barney, Peter Coclanis, Jacquelyn Hall, and John Kasson were all supportive, challenging, and engaged throughout the entire process. In addition, many others suffered through parts of the work and helped me think more clearly about key concepts: Stacey Braukman, Gavin Campbell, Sean Doig, Natalie Fousekis, Gary Frost, Kelly Hughes, Kathy Newfont, Steven Niven, Mike Ross, Robert Tinkler, and Michael Trotti.

A large number of archivists and librarians at a variety of institutions helped me throughout my research. There are too many to list but a few went well beyond the call of duty. Linda Stanley, formerly of the Historical Society of Pennsylvania, helped me negotiate that archive's rich collections and regularly pointed out items that I may have otherwise missed. Virtually the entire staff of the Free Library of Philadelphia's Print and Picture Collection went out of their way to give me incredible access to their holdings. Finally, special thanks are due to Douglas B. Rauschenberger (of the Haddonfield Public Library) and Katherine Mansfield Tassini (of the Historical Society of Haddonfield), who made special arrangements for me to have greater access to the Historical Society's collections.

More recently, the faculty at Wilkes University have been very supportive of my writing. My colleagues in History—Joel Berlatsky, Harold Cox, Dennis Hupchick, Jack Meyers, and Jim Rodechko—and English—Darin Fields and Jennifer Nesbitt—have helped me negotiate the often tortuous path of teaching four courses a semester while finishing a book.

In addition to my family, I must thank four organizations for providing funding at key points in the research and writing process. The History Department (through its research grants) and the Graduate School (via its research and writing fellowships) of the University of North Carolina at Chapel Hill provided significant support. The New Jersey Historical Commission gave me a research grant that allowed me to follow a number of leads in New Jersey at a crucial time in my research. Finally, Wilkes University provided a needed grant to help turn my book into a reality.

My final thanks go to my editor at the University of Pennsylvania Press, Robert Lockhart, the readers, and the editorial board for helping in a myriad of ways to shape the final product. It has been a fun adventure and I look forward to doing it again in the future.

Introduction: A Revised and Enlarged Philadelphia

When this book was first issued, in 1883, it gave a faithful presentation of the Philadelphia of that day. . . . But we would not ignore the fact that there is a revised and enlarged Philadelphia. . . . Perhaps no American city, within sixteen years, has undergone a greater change. . . . The concentration of trade has made the high building a necessity. Where once twenty buildings stood side by side, now they are constructed one upon the other. . . . The railway engine no longer halts on the outskirts of the city, but is driven close to our very doors. . . . The old cobble-stone is fast becoming a recollection, and, with two hundred and fifty miles of asphalt, it is, perhaps, the best-paved city in the world. In addition to this, there is an electric railway system which is unexcelled by any other city. The suburbs have been beautified beyond description, and localities once inaccessible now contain some of the most attractive homes.[1]

Philadelphia underwent an impressive physical reconstruction in the five decades from 1876 to 1926, doubling in population, extending farther north, south, and west from the original urban core, and reaching ever farther skyward. Never again would Philadelphia go through a period of such sustained growth. Equally important, but much less obvious than these physical changes to the region during this period, was the creation of new visions of the city by Philadelphians. In his tribute to civic progress, J. Loughran Scott hints at these new images by his use of the term "revised" to describe the metropolis, as this word implies thoughts in addition to deeds. Not only did the Victorian city grow in size and its buildings in height but its residents changed how they viewed it. These new urban images—broadly shared along class lines—resulted in multiple Philadelphias occupying the same physical space. The city of the elite, who lived on Rittenhouse Square or the Main Line, summered in Maine or Europe, and lunched at the Philadelphia Club, was a far different urban vision from that of the working classes, in which life often revolved around a single neighborhood or town. Philadelphia's aristocracy could afford to use every transportation and technological innovation to remake and to expand their world. By the turn of the century, elite Philadelphians were a part of a national upper class. Their city not only included exclusive shops, all the latest gadgets, and servant-filled homes, but was part of a national—and increasingly international—network of wealth and privilege. For working-class Philadelphians, home, work, and shopping, indeed much of everyday life, often was bounded by a few blocks. Throughout the nineteenth century, high transport fares made the streetcars and trains luxuries for most workers and their families and the traditions of the walking city remained strong well into the twentieth century in largely working-class sections like Kensington and Manayunk. Yet these different Philadelphias coexisted within one region, often overlapping in areas like Center City (the map in figure 1 identifies some of these locations).[2]

But the Victorian Philadelphia story was more than a tale of just two cities. Between these two Philadelphias lay the subject of this study: the metropolis of the middle class. Members of the bourgeoisie could afford to ride the trains and trolleys daily, so they had more freedom to construct their city than did their working-class counterparts (although not, of course, as much as the elite). The middle class used this latitude to make their version of Philadelphia during the late nineteenth and early twentieth centuries. The bourgeois city was logical and rational and well-cataloged: everything and everyone had its place in this Philadelphia. What inspired this search for order was the application of science—as the Victorian middle class understood the term—to everyday life. Following the leads of Isaac Newton and Francis Bacon, the bourgeoisie carefully arranged and classified their world.[3]

This scientific worldview pervaded late nineteenth- and early twentieth-century middle-class society. Behind it was a faith in continued progress that drove the bourgeoisie throughout western Europe, the United States, and many European colonies worldwide to embrace change. This search for order by the middle class was more than a simple reaction to the effects of industrialization and urbanization, and it was more than a fearful drive for paternalistic control. Science allowed the late nineteenth- and early-twentieth century bourgeoisie to revisualize and to remake their environment.[4]

What follows is a case study in the use of science to reconstruct—both mentally and physically—the urban environment by one city's middle class. The women and men of late nineteenth- and early twentieth-century Philadelphia were no more rational or better educated than their counterparts in New York or Baltimore or Glasgow or Berlin or Melbourne. What happened

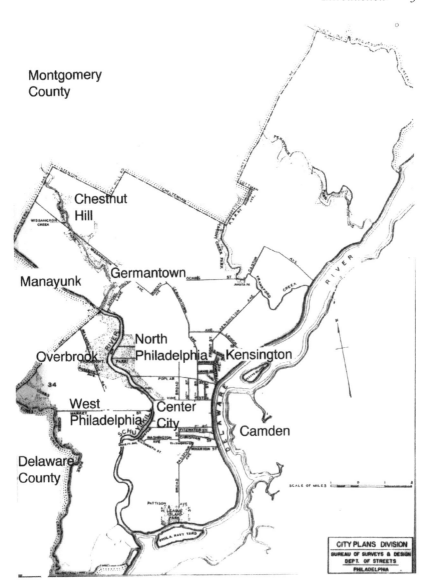

Figure 1. Map of Philadelphia. Base map courtesy of the Philadelphia City Archives.

in the Quaker City took place throughout Westernized society at about the same time. Bourgeois Philadelphia's search for order was not unique. In many ways, the city's true value to the scholar lay in its typicality. But the study of a large yet second-tier city like Philadelphia also has significant advantages. Unlike in a national capital, where the structures and plans often reflect national ambitions and pretensions, those of an industrial and commercial center like Philadelphia tend to mirror more local—and often middle-class—considerations. In addition, cities like Philadelphia, Chicago, and Glasgow underwent some of their greatest growth during the late nineteenth and early twentieth centuries, and the culture of that period can be more easily seen in them, than in cities that developed earlier (like London or Rome) or later (like Detroit or Los Angeles). Finally, Philadelphia has the added advantage that topography did not restrict or channel its growth in any significant way, unlike New York. Philadelphia was not only typical, in many ways it was also exemplary, of Victorian bourgeois culture.[5]

To find dramatic evidence of this new middle-class vision of Philadelphia, one only needs to look a few blocks from the bourgeois row homes of West and North Philadelphia to Fairmount Park. For six months in 1876, the city held a massive fair in its park to celebrate the one hundredth anniversary of the American Declaration of Independence. The Centennial Exposition drew more than eight million visitors who paid the expensive fifty-cent admission to see the carefully classified exhibits of science, commerce, technology, art, and agriculture from around the globe. Formally commemorating history, the fair also focused on the entry of the United States into the modern industrial world. Although Americans compared their show with prior international fairs in Paris, London, and Vienna, and found the native version superior in many regards, it was not a perfect vision. The Centennial—like the city and the nation in 1876—was a confusing melange of substance and glitter, commerce and science, public and private, enlightenment and deception. In all, the exhibition set the stage for the next five decades of Philadelphia's and America's development.[6]

The Centennial was an ideal prelude to the remainder of the nineteenth century. This period, usually known today as the Gilded Age (from the title of a Mark Twain satire), was a time of great economic and political adjustment for Americans. Many of these same tensions could be found at the exhibition in Fairmount Park. During this period, the nation came to terms, often violently, with the political effects of industrial capitalism. As wealth and economic power became more concentrated, visions of a classless republic faded for many. At the Centennial, the egalitarian rhetoric of a fair for all Americans was betrayed by the high entrance fee and the decision to close on Sundays, both measures effectively denying easy access to most working-class Philadelphians. The sectional differences that continued to plague the country also affected the exhibition; western states limited the federal government's financial involvement and many southern states refused to participate at all. Many displays at the fair celebrated the growing middle-class culture of consumption with a panoply of goods and gadgets for the respectable home or office. The grand buildings and avenues of the grounds hinted at the coming planned reconstruction of parts of many major cities into ceremonial public spaces (see figure 2 for a view of one of the exhibition's grand avenues) while the shoddy, unchecked development of restaurants, hotels, and amusements just outside the gates perhaps more accurately mirrored the consequences of unfettered growth for the urban fabric. But even within the fence, most of the Centennial's buildings nicely extended Mark Twain's Gilded Age metaphor because they were inexpensive, temporary construction made to look—from a distance—far more imposing and permanent than they were in fact.[7]

The Centennial presaged not only the Gilded Age but also the Progressive Era of the early twentieth century. A period viewed by political historians as a reaction to the excesses of the Gilded Age, the Progressive Era was a time of middle-class reform. A faith in science and progress allowed many people to believe that rational planning and governmental regulation coupled with private initiatives could channel the dynamic forces of capitalism into less threatening forms and head off class warfare. Not only did the carefully designed grounds and monumental structures of the Centennial hint at the City Beautiful movement but, more importantly, the entire arrangement of exhibits extended the realm of science into everyday life. By the Progressive Era, many middle-class Americans believed that the application of scientific methods could solve most of society's problems.[8]

At the heart of the Centennial was its careful, hierarchical classification of exhibits. The system was designed by a geologist (trained in a discipline that employed "scientific classification" or taxonomy), and initially the fair was to be divided into ten departments, with each department further subdivided into ten groups and one hundred classes. This elaborate decimal system would have allowed almost all human achievement to be placed in one of ten thousand classes. What was finally adopted for use at the fair was a modified version of this plan, with seven departments, each with differing numbers of groups and classes. This still impressive arrangement allowed each item exhibited to be assigned a three-digit number that immediately

Figure 2. The well-organized grounds of the Centennial Exhibition. Courtesy of the Print and Picture Collection, Free Library of Philadelphia.

identified class, group, and department. For example, the water color entitled "Interior of the Sistine Chapel" by H. M. Knowles shown by Britain was placed in class 411 ("water color pictures"), which was under group 41 ("painting") and department IV ("art").[9]

The Centennial's system of classification did not work as well in practice as it did in theory, highlighting the difficulty of developing an effective taxonomy. The Chief of the Bureau of Awards (the man in charge of the judging process) afterwards protested: "The classification of articles . . . omitted some of the most important groups of products in the Exhibition, including tea, coffee, tobacco, spices, and the whole line of cereals, rendering it necessary to assign . . . the omitted products to groups which were already overburdened." He also complained that "the obscurity of some of the lines of classification adopted . . . increased the liability . . . of articles falling through between contiguous but not always conterminous groups." Although this application of science to everyday life was far from an unmitigated success, the numeric classification of exhibits at the fair represented an important trend in late nineteenth- and early twentieth-century middle-class America: the search for new ways to order the world on a more rational basis. The taxonomy adopted at the Centennial was an early example of the application of science to the problems of society.[10]

Often historians have viewed the reaction of the American middle class to the sweeping changes wrought by industrialization and urbanization during this period as negative or, at best, ambivalent. Some scholars have found strong strains of anti-modernism throughout Victorian bourgeois culture. Others have concluded that the middle-class home was an insulated, yet ineffective, haven against the turbulent city. Still others have highlighted the escape to the suburbs of some bourgeois men and women. The classic political interpretation of the late nineteenth and early twentieth centuries sees this period as a "search for order" by the middle class. Overly simplified, this argument finds that by the 1870s the United States was a distended society in which modern social and economic forces brutally undermined the autonomy of small towns and neighborhoods. In reaction to these changes, the bourgeoisie created a bureaucratic state with the intent to curb (what they perceived as) the growing disorder. Although this interpretation does an admirable job of explaining the broad structural changes in late nineteenth- and early twentieth-century America, its focus on politics leaves out many similar cultural transformations. When these shifts in everyday life are added to the mix, they do more than complicate it; they call into question the driving forces behind this middle-class search for order.[11]

This work examines the changes in everyday middle-class life between 1876 and 1926 to discover the roots of this broader cultural search for order. What this case study of Philadelphia shows is that the women and men of that city's bourgeoisie consistently reshaped their world and thrived in a society that was transformed along rational lines starting in the late nineteenth century. At first, these changes were largely internal to the bourgeoisie, affecting only institutions that they used and controlled. Later, during the early twentieth century, the middle class began to expand this new cultural sense of order to encompass politics as well. This study suggests that it was primarily a middle-class faith in progress and the future, not a fear of contemporary society, that drove these changes.[12]

To uncover these cultural transformations, I look at three quintessentially bourgeois commercial enterprises: department stores, newspapers, and urban transit (streetcars and commuter railroads). These three areas touch on much of the broad panoply of everyday life: consumption, communication, and movement. Because of relatively high prices and low working-class wages, all three developed a largely middle-class clientele in the late nineteenth century. My examination of these institutions has uncovered a consistent reorganization of space and time in all three, beginning in the late nineteenth century. To put it simply, space and time became more precisely organized and increasingly subject to human definition and control. These changes took place not only within the organizations I study but on the streets of the city and throughout bourgeois life in general. Historians have found a desire for exacting classification and organization nearly everywhere in Victorian bourgeois society, both in not-for-profit enterprises like public libraries, museums, and universities and in businesses. These changes took place in public spaces (office and factory buildings) and in private ones (the middle-class home). Scholars have noted this new bourgeois worldview in education (in the creation of universities and new disciplines—the social sciences—and in methodology), in architecture (in both the layout of middle-class homes and more complex commercial structures), in business (careful classification was the "science" in scientific management), in knowledge (library cataloging), and in the presentation of time (timepieces and timetables).[13]

Within the three specific middle-class commercial enterprises that I have examined in Philadelphia, this increased specialization of space and new dominion over time are abundantly clear. The department store was more than just an expanded dry goods emporium; it was an entirely new way of organizing and presenting merchandise for sale. The arrangement of the store, in both management structure and interior layout, manifested the classification of people and things. Its very name highlights the importance of departmentalization to the process. Retail managers also extended control over time. It was during this period that they invented the retail calendar, with its "White Sales" and similarly created events. The complex interiors of the urban railroad stations likewise reflected this specialization in space, while the railways' schedules placed in printed form the modernization of time. Victorian newspaper editors carefully defined the layout of their journals; they created sports and business pages, women's columns, and dedicated spaces for international, national, and local news.

By actively using all three of these commercial institutions, the women and men of Philadelphia's middle class not only mentally reconstructed their metropolis but also helped to physically reshape the city between 1876 and 1926. Commuter trains and streetcars had the most dramatic—and direct—effects on the landscape as they allowed the bourgeoisie to define specialized areas in the region. Middle-class men and women took these vehicles to the Jersey shore and Willow Grove Park for amusement; to Center City for work, shopping, and entertainment; to the ballparks on the industrial fringe for sports; to Fairmount Park for recreation; and to the neighborhoods and the suburbs for home and rest. The steel rails of these "bourgeois corridors" allowed the middle class to categorize space in the metropolis and to reconstruct their vision of the region. The department stores served as middle-class havens of order in the heart of the city. Drawing bourgeois women and men to downtown from places like West Philadelphia, Germantown, and Haddonfield, the stores helped define a shared culture—based on consumption—throughout the region. Newspapers not only brought well-organized news and entertainment to middle-class homes and offices throughout the metropolis, but they also carried the retail advertisements and theatrical announcements that helped entice middle-class men and women to Center City via train and streetcar.[14]

Throughout late nineteenth-century bourgeois life in Philadelphia, space became better classified and time more precise and increasingly divorced from nature. By the early twentieth century the bourgeois world was well ordered and middle-class Philadelphians were willing to use their political power to force their vision of the city on recalcitrant others. At the same time, the economic forces that had helped create middle-class Philadelphia in the late nineteenth century started to undermine it. Ironically, the classifications developed by the Victorian bourgeoisie allowed many of the once exclusively middle-class commercial institutions (like department stores and newspapers) to reach broader markets as the culture of consumption expanded. Areas that had been almost solely bourgeois in the late nineteenth century became increasingly multi-classed in the early twentieth.

*   *   *

By the late nineteenth century, every problem in the middle-class world seemed ripe for a scientific solution. The Victorian bourgeoisie used the term "science" so often that many historians today no longer take the term seriously and treat the word as little more than a synonym for "good" or "new." Nevertheless, middle-class women and men were being scientific—at least as far as they defined the term—in their reconstruction of society. To understand what they meant by science and what they thought they were doing, we have to go back to the early nineteenth century and look at what constituted science then. It was this conceptualization of science that the bourgeoisie learned in school and then applied to their world in the late nineteenth century.[15]

Today, educated men and women are reasonably confident of what they mean when they use the term "science." It is, according to the *Oxford English Dictionary*, "in modern use, often treated as synonymous with 'Natural and Physical Science', and thus restricted to those branches of study that relate to the phenomena of the material universe and their laws. . . . This is now the dominant sense in ordinary use." What the early twenty-first-century middle class recognizes as science is almost exclusively experimental: physics, chemistry, and biology.[16]

In the nineteenth century, the bourgeoisie was equally sure of what they meant by the term "science" and it incorporated more methodologies than just experimentation. Much of what we now call "technology" was then considered science, so engineering marvels like the steam locomotive, the massive iron and glass buildings of the Centennial, and the Brooklyn Bridge were all examples of scientific progress to Victorians. In addition, many nineteenth-century sciences, in particular the life sciences, had not adopted the experimental process that we today associate with science but had retained the rational models developed by Bacon and Newton during the Scientific Revolution. Perhaps the most significant scientific advancement of the nineteenth century, at least in popular culture, was made by Charles Darwin using one of these alternative methodologies. Darwin's theory of evolution, which so sparked the bourgeois imagination, was based on taxonomy. One historian of science has written that "[t]he search for systematic schemes of classification [had] dominated the life sciences during the seventeenth and eighteenth centuries," and that same search for order captured the Victorian bourgeoisie in the nineteenth.[17]

The Darwinian revolution in popular middle-class thought was two-fold. What has been well studied is how the theory of evolution became part of the bourgeois world view, along with a related concept known as Social Darwinism. But what has largely been missed is that besides offering a general theory, Darwin also offered an example of a scientific methodology to an increasingly well-educated middle class. This methodology—taxonomy— was reinforced by science courses offered in Victorian high schools and colleges. In addition, new disciplines, like the "social sciences," and existing ones, such as the law, borrowed this methodology from the sciences and created detailed classifications of human behavior during this period. By the start of the twentieth century, taxonomy was commonplace throughout middle-class society.[18]

Because our conception of science has changed and because members of the middle class used the term so often during the late nineteenth and early twentieth centuries, it is easy to overlook this metaphor as the basis of the bourgeoisie's reconstruction of their world. Just as the middle class began to apply taxonomy throughout everyday life, the scientific community shifted away from classification to experimentation as its paradigm. Historians of other fields, well versed in their generations' understandings of science, often seem unaware of the earlier traditions. As but one example, a legal historian recently claimed that "Langdell's [a leading late-nineteenth-century law professor and the inventor of the casebook method of legal study] proudest boast was that the law was a science, and his method was scientific. But his model of science was not experimental, or experiential; his model was Euclid's geometry, not physics or biology." That analysis misses the point; the model Langdell used was scientific at the time he used it. But we do not have to take Langdell at his word; we can look at what he created with his "scientific" approach to legal education: a detailed, hierarchical outline of the law. Langdell is but one example of this broad Victorian obsession with classification.[19]

Another example should help make this scientific metaphor as it relates to middle-class culture somewhat less esoteric. As Chapter 7 will develop in more detail, historians have viewed Philadelphia's late nineteenth-century hinterland as a classic statement of the American railroad suburb. Historians claim that a variety of motives both pushed and pulled the Victorian bourgeoisie from the city to the country: a long-standing American distrust of cities; an equally durable rural ideal; the availability of cheap land and transport; the development of inexpensive construction techniques (the balloon-frame house); and racial and ethnic prejudice. My work indicates that Philadelphia—at the time the nation's third-largest city—did not suburbanize in conformity with this model until well into the twentieth century. What the city's nineteenth-century middle class did do, however, was to develop a greater specialization in the use of land throughout the Victorian metropolis. In other words, they created a taxonomy of space. Changing bourgeois residential patterns—both within the city and without—were simply one manifestation of this larger redefinition of urban geography. When we look in detail at what happened, suburbanization ceases to be a discrete phenomenon and becomes part of a larger cultural matrix.[20]

If this new bourgeois wordview was as commonplace as I argue, why have historians failed to link it with the broader changes in turn-of-the-century society? Quite simply, because until recently taxonomy remained a familiar and effective (though not "scientific") way of organizing knowledge. The Library of Congress cataloging system, for example, is little more than an even more detailed version of the one Dewey developed. It was not until the proliferation of powerful personal computers that classification and hierarchy ceased to be the primary ways to access large amounts of data. Mid-twentieth-century intellectuals were trapped in the same mental world as their grandparents and great-grandparents because modern society continued to use the same system of organization. With new ways of managing information, the late twentieth- and early twenty-first-century middle class has created new metaphors for everyday life based upon popular understandings of how computers work and with them new ways of visualizing themselves and their world. This shift in mental paradigms exposes the bases of the old ways of thinking.[21]

The goal of this work is quite simple: to take middle-class women and men seriously when they claimed to be employing science to remake their world in the late nineteenth and early twentieth centuries. The rewards for doing so are ample: the culture of the turn-of-the-last-century bourgeoisie makes far more sense as a whole and the politics of the Progressive Era become much more connected with broader trends in society.

To recapture fin-de-siècle middle-class Philadelphia, I employ a variety of sources and techniques drawn from both social and cultural history. Initially, I tried to view this now-vanished world through the eyes of its inhabitants: the men and women of the late nineteenth- and early twentieth-century urban bourgeoisie. Only after assimilating their understanding of their city could I do what they could not: step back and analyze their metaphors for space and time and interpret how these mental images affected their physical environment. By applying this broader understanding of culture to relationships among the members of the middle class and the three commercial enterprises that are the focus of this study, we should be able to discover bourgeois culture in the rhythms of everyday life. The power of this study, then, comes from looking at three separate institutions, finding the many similarities among them, and seeing that these businesses were more than simply the creations of their owners and managers; their cultural meaning derived from their roles as shared symbols of a society.[22]

Take, for example, the case of the Victorian department store. In 1877, when John Wanamaker converted his men's clothing store to Philadelphia's first department store, he was neither terribly rich nor powerful. It is difficult to argue that he or his store could impose anything upon its customers. In a city with hundreds of retail establishments, shoppers could easily go elsewhere if they did not like what Wanamaker was doing and how he was doing it. Instead we can see the fantastic success of the Wanamaker store and its counterparts as reflecting the shopping rituals and values of their customers. As Wanamaker and his competitors served a largely middle-class market, it is the values of the bourgeoisie that we can find in those early department stores.[23]

My starting points for recreating this shared culture are the diaries, memoirs, oral histories, and letters left by the middle-class women and men of the region. I use dozens of these sources to follow bourgeois Philadelphians as they rode trains and trolleys, read newspapers, and shopped at department stores. These first-hand accounts serve as individualized guidebooks to the metropolis: highlighting for each person activities that were typical and unique, everyday and extraordinary. I analyze this information both quantitatively (how often people used particular facilities) and qualitatively (how people perceived the institutions). To place these men and women in broader context, I turn to census data and city directories. The manuscript census and the directories create a better understanding of the precise settings in which the historical actors lived while the published census figures establish the societal framework.[24]

After determining when and how middle-class Philadelphians used the three commercial institutions, I shift the focus of my study to these establishments. By examining the surviving business records, I develop an understanding of the changing nature of space and time within and around the firms. I use photographs, floor plans, maps, newspaper articles, printed ephemera, and surviving objects to help reconstruct the physical settings of these enterprises. It is the combination of these corporate records and artifacts with the human accounts that make the following recreations of everyday bourgeois life possible.[25]

*   *   *

Before we can explore this world made by the Philadelphia middle class, we must define whom we mean when we use that always slippery term. According to the historian Karen Lystra, " 'middle class' refers not only to economic and occupational levels but also to cultural characteristics: concepts of privacy, the self, and standards of social behavior. . . . These men and women used such concepts to separate themselves from those they considered inferior, to build social hierarchies, and to measure their own 'class' performance."[26]

Essentially "class" is an economic notion that has important cultural overlays. Defining any social class begins with its position in the economic system, and traditionally, American scholars have used two approaches to do this. One looks at the relationship between members of the class and the means of production. The other focuses (somewhat more prosaically) on issues of income and wealth. The first approach, derived from Karl Marx, recognizes the existence of (but usually dismisses the long term importance of) the bourgeoisie (as that term is used in this work). For Marx and many Marxist scholars, the middle class was and is an intermediate group that simply is not a key part of the capitalist mode of production and will disappear over time. In the other approach, class conflict does not exist and the seemingly permeable barriers of earned income and accumulated wealth are all that (largely statistically) divide one social stratum from another. But both approaches deal inadequately with the specifics of the historical experience. The concept of "false consciousness" may aid the social scientist Marx in explaining why a worker at the Baldwin Locomotive Works viewed himself as a member of the bourgeoisie, but it does not help the historian understand that person's worldview. Equally troubling for scholars wedded to the income/wealth approach are those people who exhibited working-class beliefs and attitudes but earned more than some members of the middle class.[27]

What a cultural view adds to either of these economic definitions of class is a way to deal with the seeming aberrations and (hopefully) to treat them within the historical framework. It allows historians to focus upon what might be called (with apologies to Marx) the "class consciousness" of the group. This would consist of the activities, beliefs, and institutions that members shared and often used to differentiate themselves from others in a society. Thus a poorly paid clerk would be lower-middle class because he adopted bourgeois norms. The danger of a purely cultural approach would be the ease of creating a tautology; one could declare something a middle-class standard and then use it to delimit the bourgeoisie. That is why it is important to use economics as a starting point and then apply culture to refine the definition.[28]

Another advantage of this cultural analysis (particularly for the bourgeoisie of late nineteenth and early twentieth centuries) is that it helps to integrate women more fully into the story. Because many middle-class women did not work for pay outside the home during this period, studies that focus on employment often undervalue female contributions to society. Not only did women constitute half the bourgeoisie but, as other cultural studies have shown, they played extremely important roles in shaping the Victorian middle-class world.[29]

Finally, maintaining a sensitivity to the multitude of divisions that existed within the turn-of-the-century bourgeoisie is important. In addition to the commonly used dichotomy of "new" versus "old," there existed various economic layers: upper, middle, and lower. Because this is a broad-based look at middle-class culture, throughout most of this work, such differences are ignored. What this study focuses upon is the shared bourgeois culture. This should not be seen as a rejection of the many important fissures within the middle class. The bourgeois experience in the city would vary greatly depending upon whether one was male or female, white or black, Protestant or Roman Catholic or Jewish, native-born or immigrant, but there was also a common culture and it is this shared world that is at the center of this study.[30]

The resulting working definition of the middle class for this study focuses on employment (or an individual's relationship to the means of production), annual income, accumulated wealth, self-description, and lifestyle. Philadelphia's bourgeoisie at the end of the nineteenth century consisted of hundreds of thousands of people located throughout the region. The men often worked in white-collar clerical, managerial, or professional jobs. Others owned shops (or small businesses) or were skilled craftsmen. A majority of the married women did not work for pay outside the home but often had important volunteer positions. Some women were college educated and some (mostly single but a few married) had entered the professions. Although annual incomes varied greatly (throughout most of the period they could range from less than $500 for junior clerks to more than $5,000 for professionals), most middle-class males earned a regular income (often termed a "salary") that was sufficient to buy or to rent a home located away from the work site, to commute by mass transit, to engage in the culture of consumption, and to put a small amount in the bank. Accumulated wealth also ranged widely: some members of the bourgeoisie barely made ends meet on their salary whereas others had investments (particularly in the cases of small business owners) worth tens of thousands of dollars. For the purposes of this study, if a person acquired significant property, he or she was no longer considered middle class. Most had some formal education, and as the period progressed, more attended high school and went on to college. Many were Protestant: mainly Baptist, Episcopalian, Friend, Lutheran, Methodist, or Presbyterian. Some were Roman Catholic or Jewish. A vast majority were white, but there was a small African-American middle class in the city. Most (regardless of race or religion, and, by 1920, sex) were registered Republican. Many employed servants, although this declined toward the end of the period. Though some lived in heterogenous neighborhoods, others were helping to form the first middle-class enclaves both inside and outside the city limits. In Philadelphia proper, members of the bourgeoisie lived around (but not on) Rittenhouse Square and in West Philadelphia, Germantown, and North Philadelphia. In the Pennsylvania hinterland they lived in Montgomery and Delaware Counties: Cynwyd, Jenkintown, and Lansdowne. In New Jersey, they lived in the little towns strung along the railroad and trolley lines in Burlington, Camden, and Gloucester Counties: Collingswood, Glendora, and Haddonfield.

These middle-class Philadelphians shared activities; these were the rituals that helped to define bourgeois culture. They read the "breezy" *Philadelphia Inquirer* or the more serious *Public Ledger* in the morning and *The Evening Bulletin* at night. They shopped at the major Center City department stores: John Wanamaker, Strawbridge & Clothier, Gimbel Brothers, N. Snellenburg, and Lit Brothers. If they lived in North or West Philadelphia they rode the streetcars. If they lived farther from downtown, they used the frequent trains of the Atlantic City Railroad, Baltimore & Ohio Railroad, Pennsylvania Railroad, Philadelphia & Reading Railway, or West Jersey & Seashore Railroad to and from work, shopping, and entertainment.

Applying this definition to the women and men who are at the heart of this work proved, for the most part, not to cause many problems. In the course of this study, no person was excluded because I felt he or she was likely working class; in fact, only three of the historical actors even raised this possibility (highlighting what social historians have long known: how few working-class diaries survive in archives). In two of these cases, evidence within the diaries points to a largely middle-class lifestyle; in the other, little is evident about the writer but his uncle was a successful lawyer. Much more common was to exclude men and women because they were elite and not upper-middle class. Wealth, income, and *Social Register* status eliminated dozens of possible guides. There were a few difficult cases here but two specific examples should help illustrate how I drew this line. Eugenia Barnitz was clearly from a very wealthy family. Although her memoirs do not mention income or property, she was raised in large homes on the fringes of aristocratic sections of the city. Her father was a "factory manager" (according to the manuscript census) and she shopped at some of the elite stores in Center City (along with their more pedestrian counterparts). In the end, based largely on the totality of her activities, she seemed to be at the very upper end of the middle class and she was included in the survey. A nineteenth-century Philadelphia lawyer, Josiah Granville Leach, was excluded from the survey because, although in many ways he seemed to conform to bourgeois norms, his wife made regular trips to Europe and eventually he was listed in the *Social Register*. Leach might have been an example of a middle-class person who, in the polite terms of the Victorian bourgeoisie, "married well," but excluding him seemed safer.[31]

By the centennial year of 1876, middle-class Philadelphians were, by and large, confident, content, and complacent. Their city had expanded in wealth and population throughout the nineteenth century, and although steadily losing its long competition with New York City, it remained a national center of finance, publishing, and manufacture. As they prepared for their world's fair, middle-class Philadelphians also began to reinvent their metropolis. To understand the rhythms of this city, we can follow John L. Smith, a Philadelphia mapmaker, as he rode a horse-drawn streetcar to the Centennial grounds. After that prelude, our study of how bourgeois Philadelphians scientifically reconstructed their society can begin in earnest.

Part I examines the evolution of late nineteenth-century middle-class culture in Philadelphia. During the last few decades of that century, the vast economic changes associated with industrialization created a large and powerful bourgeoisie throughout the Europeanized world. In Philadelphia, the women and men of the middle class used their newfound wealth and influence to create a new image of the city along rational, scientific lines. They did this by traveling throughout the region by streetcar and train, shopping at the new department stores, and reading their daily newspapers. As developed in Part II, starting about the turn of the century, the expansion of the market to include more members of the working classes caused these once almost exclusively middle-class institutions to become increasingly multi-classed.

Ironically, this transformation from the Victorian bourgeois market to the early twentieth-century mass market was in part made possible by the very rational, ordered commercial structures that had so reflected the values of the Victorian middle class. Within the bourgeoisie's reactions to these changes can be found the roots of the Progressive Era's search for political order.

PART I

Late Nineteenth-Century Philadelphia

Prelude: I Went Out to the Centennial

Wednesday, June 14, 1876: I went out to Centennial in afternoon & I looked around in Machinery Hall—Art Gallery & Main B. & went home.[1]

This was not John L. Smith's first visit to the Centennial. He, like thousands of other Philadelphians, had toured the grounds regularly even before the fair had opened. Smith also was one of the lucky people who had jammed themselves inside the main building a month earlier when President Ulysses S. Grant (a hero to Smith, a thirty-year-old mapmaker whose life had been largely defined by his service in the Union Army) started the great Corliss steam engine to inaugurate the exposition. But that day had been very busy and crowded, unlike most days since at the Centennial. To help better understand the rhythms of everyday middle-class life in Philadelphia in 1876, we can follow John Smith on a more typical day as he takes a horse-drawn streetcar from his shop downtown out to the exhibition grounds in Fairmount Park.

That morning Smith left the house he shared with his mother in middle-class North Philadelphia and went to his store at 27 South Sixth Street (located a block from the old State House in the commercial center of Philadelphia). He spent the morning at work but business had been, in his words, "dull" even though he found the city "full of strangers." That afternoon, the combination of slow sales and near-perfect weather drew Smith to Fairmount Park for another visit to the Centennial. Like many other middle-class Philadelphians, Smith made multiple trips to the fair that summer. In Smith's case, it was very cheap entertainment, for, as an exhibitor, he could enter the grounds for free.

After lunch, Smith left his quiet shop in the hands of his clerks. Out the front door and into the crowds on Sixth, Smith walked one-half block north to the corner of Market Street to catch one of the frequent cars of the West Philadelphia Passenger Railway Company. The Market Street line of this firm ran directly from the railroad ferries on the Delaware River through downtown to Fairmount Park. Standing near the corner, he glanced across the street at the massive men's clothing store of Wanamaker & Brown as a sea of humanity flowed around him. He was on the city's busiest street, in the heart of its commercial district. The sounds of the street vendors, the horses, the wheels of the carts and street cars, the many construction projects, and all the people filled his ears while the aroma of the vendors' foods combined with the other smells of the city—the horses and their residue, the unwashed wool clothes and their occupants—filled his nose. Smith likely noticed few of these sights, sounds, and smells that day; they were simply the background to everyday life in one of the world's largest cities.

As he waited, Smith, a loyal Republican, probably thought about the big news in the *Public Ledger* that day: speculation over the likely nomination of James Blaine. Or he may have pondered what a beautiful day it was: low humidity, temperature in the eighties. In a few weeks would come Philadelphia's hot and sticky summer. Or perhaps he wondered why John Wanamaker had opened an additional store a few blocks to the west when he had such a beautiful store here. Regardless of Smith's thoughts, he did not have long to develop them, as the cars on this line ran every few minutes. His attention was diverted by the driver bringing the team of horses to a stop. He waited as people stepped off the car and was happy to see that it was not too crowded. He would get a seat today; sometimes he had to stand for almost the whole journey. After he boarded, he paid the conductor his seven-cent fare and settled in for the thirty-minute ride to the gates of the exhibition. Traffic would be heavy and the pace slow until at least Twelfth Street, which was then the western extremity of downtown.

Smith, a keen observer of the city's progress, probably stared out the open window of the car seeking further evidence of the numerous "improvements" along the route. Smith loved to explore all the city's changes with friends; he was quite a civic booster and Philadelphia's continuing progress thrilled him. Market Street was the commercial spine of the metropolis; it was lined with a variety of business enterprises from the Delaware to the Schuylkill River. Its one-hundred-foot width, originally designed by William Penn to accommodate market stalls (and hence its name), allowed it to be filled with tracks for both the local and long distance railways, adding to its busy air. Heading west, Smith could see a number of the city's tallest commercial structures (all about five or six stories in height): at Seventh, the publishing house of J. B. Lippincott; at Eighth, the massive dry goods emporium of Hood, Bonbright & Company; and at Eleventh, the Bingham House, Philadelphia's leading hotel. Smith's interest rose as he approached Thirteenth Street, for there he could see two of Philadelphia's larger and more recent developments: the massive (and elaborately decorated) clothing store of John Wanamaker (the merchant's third in the city) and the construction site of the new Public Buildings in Centre Square.

Between Centre Square and the Schuylkill River the commercial buildings became smaller and more utilitarian and of less interest to Smith. As the car plodded westward, Smith may have been lulled to sleep by the combination of the rhythm of the horses' shoes on the stone street and the warmth inside the small, slow-moving, ill-ventilated car. His attention likely rose again after crossing the river. Just past Thirty-first Street he could see the recently opened depot of the city's most powerful corporation (and an occasional client): the Pennsylvania Railroad. In a few hours, a special train would leave the station inaugurating service on the city's newest steam railroad, the grandly named Philadelphia, Newtown and New York Railroad that actually only went eleven miles to Fox Chase. Smith hoped to catch a glimpse of the train and reminded himself that he should ride the new line soon. He likely thought about all the improvements the new line would bring to a still largely rural section of the city.

After passing the depot, he was about two-thirds of the way through his journey in terms of time. Most of the land between the depot and the park was filled with the respectable middle-class homes of West Philadelphia, very similar to—although a bit more commodious than—the one he and his mother shared in equally bourgeois North Philadelphia. As the streetcar neared the Centennial grounds, Smith viewed with some distaste the large number of temporary buildings housing hotels, restaurants, bars, and inexpensive amusements that lined the streets just outside the gates. It was not just their size and gaudiness that caused these structures to stand out but also their construction: in an almost exclusively brick- and stone-built city, they were made of wood. Smith did not view this tacky temporary "city" as an improvement; not only were these down-market hotels and amusements poor substitutes for their downtown counterparts but visitors staying in West Philadelphia were less likely to patronize Center City businesses like his own.

The car came to a stop at the terminus outside the main gates at Elm

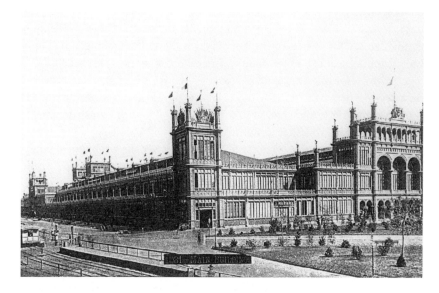

Figure 3. The Main Building of the Centennial. Courtesy of the Print and Picture Collection, Free Library of Philadelphia.

and Belmont Avenues. The massive fan of tracks was designed to handle dozens of street cars simultaneously and was part of the elaborate transportation system built especially for the fair. On opening day, Smith had been one of the estimated 200,000 riders who had tested the limits of this terminus. Thankfully, there were far fewer passengers today. After leaving the car, Smith threaded his way through the cars, horses, and people and walked past the main entrance (as it was for paying customers only). A half-block west was the smaller and less busy entry to Machinery Hall. Smith had his exhibitor's ticket punched by the attendant and went through the turnstile that both controlled ingress and counted the visitors. He spent the afternoon touring the major buildings and examining whatever caught his eye (figure 3 shows the Main Building). He thoroughly enjoyed himself and vowed to return again. After a long day, he went out through the main gates and took a car on the Girard Avenue line to within a few blocks of his mother's house.[2]

Chapter 1

The Most Traversed City by Railways in This Country, If Not the World

Philadelphia, containing one hundred and twenty-nine square miles, is, doubtless, the most traversed city by railways in this country, if not the world. It has more than 600 miles of track on its streets, upon which are carried over 100,000,000 passengers annually. These figures do not include the steam roads, with over one hundred regular stations, and an ever-increasing business. All of these lines of travel form a network of thoroughfares through the limits of the city, and extend to its furthest outskirts.[1]

As this excerpt from an 1887 guidebook to Philadelphia makes clear, the horse-drawn streetcars that John L. Smith road to the Centennial were just a small part of a complex urban transportation system that developed in the city during the second half of the nineteenth century (see figure 4 for a contemporary streetcar). Although the exact mix of steam trains, streetcars, and subways varied from city to city, the rapid expansion of transport facilities that happened in Victorian Philadelphia took place throughout the major cities of the Europeanized world at approximately the same time. The steel rails of these transit lines became "bourgeois corridors" that knit together the various strands of the emerging middle-class metropolis during the late nineteenth century. The vehicles were safe, usually comfortable, bourgeois spaces in the city, as were the homes, the department stores, the amusement parks, and the offices that these rail lines connected with each other.

These bourgeois corridors are what made both the reality and the perception of Philadelphia as a massive middle-class metropolis possible. For many modern students of Victorian Philadelphia, it is this interplay between reality and perception that makes the late nineteenth-century city so fascinating. The middle-class city was in part reality because there were simply so many areas spread throughout the region that were used largely (but never

Figure 4. The intersection of Broad Street with Germantown and Erie Avenues in 1883. Courtesy of the Print and Picture Collection, Free Library of Philadelphia.

exclusively) by the bourgeoisie. But it was also a perception, an image held by many members of the middle class of an exclusively bourgeois city, their city. One native-born playwright recalled that "most of the people in Philadelphia are in one class. One great big stretch of middle class." He and so many other members of the bourgeoisie missed the complex and heterogeneous nature of the city because of the seamlessness of the flow from one largely middle-class location to another along these corridors. This tension between the reality of bourgeois space in the multi-classed metropolis and the perception of the middle-class city is behind all the journeys that follow. This tension is also our key to understanding why the Victorian metropolis was so fragile: it was as much a product of the mind as it was of bricks and mortar.[2]

Because these corridors were a part of the bourgeois city, middle-class women could use them on largely equal terms with their male counterparts to exploit the many resources of the metropolis. Bourgeois women traveled alone by day and night, no longer needing male escorts. The same cars that carried John L. Smith also took Eliza N. Smith of West Philadelphia (no relation) and her daughters throughout the region. Whether to Wanamaker's for shopping, various schools for work, the Witherspoon Building for charity board meetings, or Delaware County for flowers, the female Smiths were frequent users of the bourgeois corridors. Without the freedom of movement brought about by the trains and the streetcars, many largely female spaces in the city—like the large department stores—could not have developed as they did.[3]

What set the bourgeois tone of these steel corridors in the late nineteenth century was unregulated capitalism. Throughout most of the Victorian period, the steam and street railways in Philadelphia (and the rest of the United States) were free to operate their services and to set their fares largely as they chose. Unlike in Britain, where the state-mandated parliamentary and workmen's trains meant members of the working classes had some access to the rail facilities, the high charges of most American companies essentially limited everyday ridership on the trains and streetcars to the bourgeoisie and above.[4]

After the Centennial year, this growing array of transportation options helped middle-class Philadelphians remake their mental maps of the city and its region. How individuals chose to use those options—separate home from work, shop at a big dry goods store downtown rather than a smaller one closer to home—is what shaped Philadelphia's new spatial order. Trains and streetcars did not dictate the rationalization of Victorian Philadelphia; their middle-class riders did. They used the transport facilities to develop distinctly middle-class locations in and around the metropolis, and these places reflected bourgeois culture. Urban geography, as represented by both city blocks and larger tracts, increasingly became specialized in use because bourgeois women and men slowly (and largely unconsciously) created a taxonomy of space for their city. Because this new Philadelphia of specialized spaces was created by hundreds of thousands of individual decisions, tracing its roots can be difficult. But what is so striking about the Victorian bourgeoisie's world is that in so short a time it became so rationally classified largely without coercive governmental action. This suggests that there was shared belief behind all these individual decisions. This faith in rational classification became commonplace throughout middle-class society, and by the new century bourgeois Philadelphians had both mentally and physically transformed the texture of their city's landscape and the rhythms of their lives through their use of money and technology in accordance with this sentiment.[5]

This comprehensive reconstruction along rational lines of "their" Philadelphia by the late nineteenth-century middle class represented an unprecedented intellectual victory over the physical world. Although there had been previous attempts at imposing order on smaller parts of the urban fabric, from like-minded firms clustering together to noxious producers moving away from those likely to complain, none were as impressive as that undertaken by the women and men of the middle class in the late nineteenth century. Not only did bourgeois Philadelphia encompass a vast region but it happened so subtly, or perhaps so "naturally" to the Victorians, that most contemporaries failed to connect the changes. Journalists, guidebook authors, and diarists all noted the individual transformations in the city—the tall buildings, the trolleys, the residential neighborhoods, and the like—but failed to see the underlying relationships. By the start of the twentieth century, the collective efforts of the Victorian middle class had created a detailed classification of space in the metropolis that would rival any present-day land use plan. To find this map, however, a scholar cannot go to City Hall, for formal zoning regulation would not come to Philadelphia until the 1930s, but must instead turn to the written words left behind in numerous diaries and letters. By following these bourgeois men and women as they went about their metropolis, the contour of the bourgeois city—where there was a place for everything and everything was in its place—slowly begins to appear through the rituals of everyday life.

Before we can understand the transportation dynamics of Victorian Philadelphia, we must consider a bit of its history. As late as the middle of the nineteenth century, Philadelphia (along with the other major cities of the Westernized world) had been a "walking city" for all but the elite. Only a very small percentage of the population could afford the horse and carriage that allowed for a significant separation of home from work. In 1850 the average worker lived within six-tenths of a mile of his or her workplace. The only modes of urban transport then available were omnibuses and a small number of steam railroad local trains. Both were relatively expensive and neither offered extensive service.[6]

In 1854, the Pennsylvania legislature took the first step toward creating the modern metropolis when it merged Philadelphia county (and its many political subdivisions) into the city. Although governmental fiat could create a unified political entity, it could not alter social reality. For years Philadelphia would continue to function as a series of large and small towns rather than as a single community because there was no form of reliable, inexpensive transport available. Two transportation changes occurred following the creation of the expanded city in 1854 that allowed for its effective consolidation by 1876: increased local train service and the development of the horse-drawn streetcar. Neither was a great technological leap forward, but both helped to transform the geography of the city for those who could afford their fares: the middle class and above.[7]

Since the opening in 1832 of the city's first steam passenger railway company, technological change had been evolutionary—rather than revolutionary—in the railroad industry. Steam locomotives became bigger and more powerful, passenger coaches longer and more comfortable, and track heavier and more durable, but the basic technology remained largely unchanged. The importance of the steam passenger railway to intracity transportation grew slowly (and unevenly) during the Victorian age, but by the 1880s Philadelphia had a large network of lines that both served the city and connected the metropolis with its hinterland in New Jersey and Pennsylvania.[8]

Far more important for the city was the introduction of horse-drawn streetcars in 1858. Entrepreneurs combined two existing technologies—the body and motive power of the omnibuses and the track of the railroads—to create a new form of transport. The rails gave a smoother ride for passengers than the rough, stone-paved streets and the combination of metal wheels on metal rails made for less friction so the horses could both haul greater loads and accelerate faster. These two advantages helped to ensure the rapid decline of omnibus usage on any route with enough patronage to justify the higher capital investment of laying the rails for the streetcars. By 1880, horse-drawn street railways served almost all populated areas within the city limits and carried 99 million passengers annually.[9]

By the 1880s, middle-class Philadelphians had a more than adequate system of horse-drawn streetcars and steam-hauled commuter trains to serve their transportation needs in both the booming metropolis and its expanding hinterland in Pennsylvania and New Jersey. The lines of the various privately owned streetcar companies occupied every major street (and many minor ones) in Center City and extended southward, westward, and northward from the original urban core along the Delaware River into the adjoining neighborhoods. In addition to these routes centered on the business district, there were a large number of local lines operating in the other densely populated portions of the city like West Philadelphia. The steam trains served not only the city but also the larger region. The 1870s and 1880s were a period of transition for the railroads; some lines had quite intensive service whereas others still had surprisingly few trains. For example, on its Chestnut Hill branch in 1876, the Philadelphia & Reading offered thirty round trips a day between Center City and Germantown, over twice as many as the Pennsylvania Railroad provided to suburban Bryn Mawr. In addition to having the most service, the Philadelphia & Reading lines serving northwest Philadelphia also had special-fare trains in order to encourage daily commuting. Overall, however, the steam trains were not used by many middle-class Philadelphians for their daily commute in 1880 simply because all of the downtown terminals were a long walk or horse car ride from the business district. By 1893, both major rail systems serving the city had relocated their main facilities to Center City and the daily commute by steam train became more viable for members of the bourgeoisie who could afford the fares.[10]

The electric trolley, introduced in the mid-1890s after a brief and unsuccessful flirtation with cable cars, quickly became the typical mode of middle-class transport and eventually the symbol of the late Victorian era. The advent of the trolley caused great excitement in the city as it was a technological marvel; science, in the form of electricity, replaced brute force, in the form of horses, on the streets of the city. In just five years, from 1892 to 1897, trolleys replaced all the horse-drawn streetcars and cable cars in the city. One person caught up in this technological fervor was Mary B. Smith of West Philadelphia, then in her early twenties. She noted in her diary the opening of almost every newly electrified line in the city, including those that were miles from her home and that she probably never used, such as the Twelfth and Sixteenth Streets line in January 1894. Mary's enthusiasm grew as the wires and poles that were the physical manifestation of this techno-logical marvel came closer to her home. She, her parents, and her siblings would often ride the new trolleys just to sample modernity, taking for the first time routes that had existed as horse-powered lines for years. Here is her record of the day electric service arrived on the line closest to her house: "Trolley cars started on Woodland Avenue. Papa and Lathrop took a ride on them as far as Paschalville. Papa and Mamma took same ride in evening."[11]

Mary's excitement over the arrival of the trolley was typical of middle-class Philadelphians. Leo Bernheimer, then a high school student living in North Philadelphia, noted in his diary (emphasis in the original): "*I rode down in the trolley car* this morning for the *first time*." Trolleys and the locations they served quickly became emblematic of bourgeois Victorian Philadelphia.[12]

By the centennial year, Philadelphia boosters were justifiably proud of their city's transit infrastructure. One guide boasted that the metropolis had "the best system of street [railway] transportation in the Union. . . ." A decade later, a similar guide enlarged the claim and Philadelphia was "the most tra-versed city by railways in this country, if not the world." Middle-class women and men used these bourgeois corridors in a variety of ways and for a multi-tude of reasons in the late nineteenth century and, largely without realizing it, helped to radically reshape their vision of the region. We can rediscover this Victorian middle-class metropolis amongst the jumbled streets of the multi-classed city by following bourgeois Philadelphians as they traveled by train, omnibus, streetcar, and trolley. By the 1880s, such trips encompassed a series of middle-class areas in the region: residential neighborhoods, down-town, the surrounding countryside, and the New Jersey coast. In the 1890s, these journeys would add new destinations: suburban homes and amuse-ment parks.[13]

The regular travels of John L. Smith nicely illustrate the commute by streetcar of tens of thousands of middle-class Philadelphians in the two de-cades between the Centennial and the coming of the trolley. In 1880, he lived with his mother in North Philadelphia, and about two and one-quarter miles separated his home from his South Sixth Street shop. He could walk the dis-tance in about an hour, and he did at times, but he usually took the streetcar. Slightly over one-third of the streetcars' patronage consisted of regular com-muters like Smith. Many white members of the "old" middle class—small business-owners and professionals—started to separate their homes from their workplaces at mid-century. Also, like Smith, the vast majority of these

Victorian commuters were not suburbanites; they lived within the expansive limits of the city. The largely middle-class neighborhood of North Philadelphia was well served with routes, so Smith had a number of options. It is likely that he usually took the Philadelphia Railway Company's Ridge Avenue route as it offered the most direct service (on one of the few diagonal streets to disturb the city's extension of William Penn's grid) with only short walks at both ends of the ride. On mornings that he was willing to hike the few blocks to Columbia Avenue, he could take a red car of the Philadelphia Traction Company that would leave him within a half block of his office. Philadelphia Traction also offered a number of other routes that came close to Smith's house that connected with their main east-west lines to Center City.[14]

Another bourgeois neighborhood well served by the streetcars was West Philadelphia. J. Harper Smith, coal merchant and father of diarist Mary, lived with his family in an Italianate semi-detached house at 509 Woodland Terrace, which was on the fringes of development in the 1880s. He worked in rented office space downtown. The nearest line to the family home was the Darby Branch of the Philadelphia Traction Company, which ran on Woodland Avenue, one-half block away to the south. In horsecar days, Smith probably never used this line for his commute to work as he would have had to change cars to reach downtown. The Darby Branch was one of those local lines that served the neighborhoods and operated as a shuttle between Darby and Thirty-Second and Market Streets in West Philadelphia. A five block walk north would take him to Philadelphia Traction's Chestnut Street line and cars that would leave him almost at the door of his office. When the Darby Branch was electrified in 1894 and the service extended into downtown, he likely switched to the more convenient trolleys. Had he and his family lived a few blocks to the north in the more densely populated area, they would have had as many transit options as John Smith did in North Philadelphia.[15]

Every day, middle-class students used the same corridors to travel throughout the region, and their trips helped to further define the bourgeois metropolis. Most grammar school students walked to school as the institutions drew from the surrounding neighborhood. Mary Smith's younger brother Lathrop had only to walk a couple blocks to attend the Newton School in West Philadelphia. Once students moved beyond grammar school to attend Central High School, Girls High School, or the Normal School, and (possibly later) the University of Pennsylvania, they usually needed some type of urban transport to reach the facilities. One such student was Leo G.

Bernheimer, who often rode the streetcars between his home in North Phila-delphia and his classes at Central. Following his graduation from high school, Bernheimer continued to live at home while he attended law school at the University of Pennsylvania in West Philadelphia. He usually rode to Penn as it was quicker than walking. Early in his first semester he noted that his ride from campus to home "in Lombard (via South) and up 8th [took] about 45 minutes or 50 [compared to] about 75 walking there." But the cars were not always faster; sometimes delays, missed connections, and traffic jams significantly slowed the trip. Leo complained one morning that he had arrived at college "late though I started soon enough not to be" because of "coal wagons" impeding the trolleys. In the course of his student career, he took just about every possible combination of routes between his home and the campus.[16]

As Leo Bernheimer's experiences indicate, in general, the horse-drawn streetcars only slightly increased the commuting range. The cars were typi-cally (but as Bernheimer learned, not always) faster than walking. In addi-tion, because the inter-company transfer privileges varied, sometimes the most direct route could not be taken without paying a second fare. Finally, many streetcar commuters liked to walk whenever possible (or necessary) to save money. The streetcars and later the trolleys helped to develop the inner ring of bedroom communities but could not greatly extend the metropolis. The steam railroads, however, allowed the middle class to radically alter the urban landscape because of the trains' higher speeds and greater distances between stops.[17]

Starting in the 1870s, continuing through the 1880s, and accelerating in the 1890s, steam railroad commuter trains played an important role in the city's transportation mix. The old "city" terminals of the 1870s were simply too far from the business district to be of much use to daily commuters. As the combination of new stations and an expanded commercial core rectified this problem, the steam roads increased services, cut fares, and added sta-tions to build ridership. In 1875, the Philadelphia & Reading introduced "workmen's trains" on some of its branches that reduced the fares (on speci-fied trips) to nearly that of the streetcars (for example, between stations in the city and the downtown termini the railroad charged between seven and ten cents compared to the six-cent horsecar fare). The competition between the Philadelphia & Reading and the Pennsylvania Railroads also helped to spur service improvements in the city and both the Pennsylvania and New Jersey suburbs. New areas in the city and its hinterland were opened for residential use as steam commuter trains radically altered time and space

relationships in the region. For example, to go from Center City to Germantown by streetcar could take one hour and forty minutes while it required
just thirty minutes on a Philadelphia & Reading train. Overbrook, located at
the city limits in far West Philadelphia, underwent rapid development in the
late nineteenth century because it was only fifteen minutes from Center City
by train, significantly closer (in time) than much of the intervening area that
was linked to downtown solely by trolley. The wealthy "suburb in the city" of
Chestnut Hill and its bourgeois neighbors of Mount Airy and Germantown
also underwent massive growth in the late nineteenth century largely because steam railroads made them convenient to Center City. Germantown
and Chestnut Hill were particularly well served by frequent trains of both
the Pennsylvania and Reading systems.[18]

One regular Germantown commuter was Edwin C. Jellett. His first job
outside of the neighborhood in 1886 was as a clerk at a steel mill. Initially, he
usually walked from his home to the works and only took the Reading when
he was tired or the weather was bad. As time went by (and his pay increased),
Edwin rode the train more often. By 1888, he was buying monthly or season
(quarterly) tickets for the railroad, illustrating that he had all but given up on
walking and that he had firmly entered the middle class (for the monthly
tickets cost $5.25 and the quarterly $14.15, payable in advance). In September
1888, Edwin moved from the plant to the main office downtown and spent
the remainder of his life commuting to various white-collar jobs in Center
City. Except for a few periods immediately after the introduction of electric
trolleys in the 1890s, he stayed a loyal rider of the Philadelphia & Reading.[19]

The streetcars, trolleys, and trains allowed the white middle class to begin to withdraw their homes from heterogeneous walking city to bourgeois
neighborhoods like Germantown, West Philadelphia, and North Philadelphia. Racial discrimination restricted the housing options of the city's
African-American bourgeoisie and, although they were active users of the
trains and streetcars, middle-class blacks generally lived in more class heterogeneous neighborhoods than their white counterparts. For the white bourgeoisie, the middle-class home on the middle-class street in the middle-class
neighborhood became a reality well before Philadelphia began to suburbanize in significant numbers around the turn of the century.[20]

For these white bourgeois neighborhoods to exist, their residents
needed easy access to places other than just work and school. They had to
buy food, clothes, and sundries and, after commuting, shopping was the
most frequent activity for which middle-class Philadelphians used the streetcars and trains. Over one-quarter of all streetcar riders in 1880 were shop-

pers. The streetcars and the trains not only helped make the Center City department store possible but they also allowed other shopping nodes to thrive: the local equivalents of Center City's Market Street in Germantown and West Philadelphia.[21]

Middle-class men and women frequently used the trolleys and trains to shop at the large retail establishments of Center City. Starting in the 1870s, these palaces of consumption drew customers not only from the residential neighborhoods and the early suburbs but from throughout the nation. This retail area was especially busy and festive during the Christmas season; in 1877 John L. Smith noted the "Splendid" display windows on Chestnut Street and the "Great Many Persons out . . . Shopping for Christmas." A few years later another shopper, Edwin Lehman of West Philadelphia, described in greater detail the excitement he found in the display windows at two early department stores ". . . a Christmas scene at Sharpless window of St. Nicholas with his pack full of toys on his back in a sleigh + driving for reindeer—he is descending a hill + the winter scene around him is beautiful. There are also other pretty windows—Wanamaker has one of flower stalks + flowers trailing along the side of this window—composed entirely of silk [handkerchiefs] of [different] colors—also a mantel and a looking glass—the frame and decorating of mantel piece being all made of pocket + other hdkfs. of different colors—making a very odd + novel display." By the end of the century, visiting the large department stores became as much a part of a trip to Philadelphia as touching the Liberty Bell in the lobby of the old State House.[22]

The department store zone that anchored this retail district was a relatively compact area that developed in the 1880s and 1890s as the central business core extended westward. By the turn of the century, all the major merchants had picked sites along an L-shaped, eight-block-long corridor (figure 5). Convenient to the trains and streetcars and surrounded by specialty stores and restaurants, shoppers and visitors flocked by the tens of thousands every day to this retail district. It was a very rare day in the 1890s when at least one member of Mary Smith's family did not take the trolley from West Philadelphia to go shopping in Center City.[23]

The locations of the street railway lines (and to a lesser extent, the steam railroad depots) are what shaped this retail zone. The city's main east-west car lines on Market, Chestnut, and Arch streets brought shoppers from the New Jersey ferries, from many of the outlying train depots, and from the middle-class residential areas of West Philadelphia. On Eighth Street, one axis of the department store district, ran the only double-tracked north-

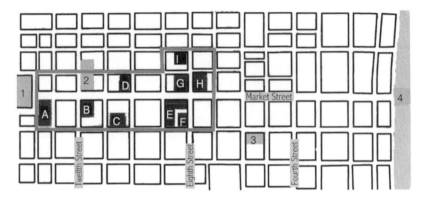

Figure 5. The Center City department store district in 1901. Based on a 1876 John L. Smith map of Center City in collection of author.

Key:

A	John Wanamaker	Thirteenth and Market
B	Nathan Snellenburg	Twelfth and Market
C	Joseph Darlington	Tenth and Chestnut
D	Blum Brothers	Tenth and Market
E	Gimbel Brothers	Ninth and Market
F	Partridge & Richardson	Eighth and Chestnut
G	Strawbridge & Clothier	Eighth and Market
H	Lit Brothers	Eighth and Market
I	Marks Brothers	Eighth and Arch
1	City Hall	Broad and Market
2	Reading Terminal	Twelfth and Market
3	Old State House	Fifth and Chestnut
4	Market Street ferry	

south street railway in the central business district. This line connected Center City with the bourgeois sections of North Philadelphia and Germantown. Where these two transit corridors crossed, at Eighth between Arch and Chestnut, by 1900 could be found five of the city's largest department stores: Gimbel Brothers, Lit Brothers, Marks Brothers, Partridge & Richardson, and Strawbridge & Clothier.

The street and steam railroads did not just expand the customer base for the major Center City stores but they also spurred the development of a number of neighborhood shopping districts. The result was a series of nodes throughout the city, none as large as the central business district, but nonetheless important to local shoppers. These smaller shopping precincts first began to develop in the late nineteenth century as space in the heterogeneous "walking city" started to become more specialized in use. Local shopping evolved from corner stores scattered throughout the neighborhood to shops grouped along major thoroughfares. In West Philadelphia, Lancaster Avenue became a regional shopping center, as did Girard Avenue in North Philadelphia and Main Street in Germantown. Main Street in Germantown not only had streetcar service but also was served by two steam railroad lines. In the late 1880s, Mrs. Tucker C. Laughlin regularly took the train from her home in Chestnut Hill to the stores in Germantown. On a Friday he had off from school, Leo Bernheimer spent the morning shopping for his mother in North Philadelphia: "This morning I was first to the Globe market; then to 13th and Columbia Av., and then to the Girard Avenue market."[24]

The trains and trolleys helped people to create these various retail districts not just by bringing customers to the shops but also by hauling the merchandise to the businesses and the purchases home. This largely unseen network of freight trains and express trolleys, along with the mail trains and trolleys, tied the expanding metropolis together as one market and linked it to the national one. They made it possible for Mrs. Tucker C. Laughlin in Chestnut Hill to have a carpet sweeper delivered from Wanamaker's, her new stove brought from North Philadelphia, and her buttermints to arrive safely. They also allowed for strawberries grown in Florida to be sold on the streets of Philadelphia during a blizzard.[25]

None of these shopping locations—whether Wanamaker's in Center City or a shoe store on Main Street in Germantown—served exclusively the middle class. The men and women of the bourgeoisie shared the streets and the stores (and the trains and trolleys) with both the elite and the working classes. Many of these businesses, however, consciously pitched themselves at the new "mass" market, which during the Victorian era consisted largely of the middle class. The downtown dry goods stores were in the forefront of this and, as we shall explore in more detail later, evolved into key nodes in the "bourgeois city." The reality of many middle-class men and women shopping in certain locations coupled with the bourgeois tone and marketing of the stores helped to reinforce their perception of the bourgeois city.[26]

Beyond work, school, and shopping, middle-class Philadelphians used the streetcars and the trains to reach a variety of locations at which they hoped to have fun. Recreation could take many forms: visiting an amusement park or museum, exploring the city or region, calling on relatives or friends, or simply riding the train or trolley to escape the heat or boredom.

Through these journeys of leisure, middle-class men and women helped to further expand and define their space in the region.[27]

Middle-class men and women used the trolleys and the trains to visit the various cultural institutions that began to develop in late nineteenth-century Philadelphia. Many of these, such as the theater district and the Academy of Fine Arts, were in Center City, while others were located in Fairmount Park (an area particularly well served by public transit because the Centennial had been held there), and still others, such as sporting venues and amusement parks, tended to be located along rail lines in the fringes of the city.

The area with the greatest concentration of cultural and entertainment attractions was Center City, and middle-class Philadelphians went there often during the late nineteenth century to be amused, enlightened, or informed. The fringes of the business and retail districts quickly developed into the city's leading culture zone. Mary Smith's parents and siblings were regular theatergoers; they would take the same streetcar routes that her father used to commute to work to see a play in the evening. Members of her family also took the trolley to attend the art shows and other special exhibitions that took place in the large halls located in Center City. The Smiths' frequent weekend and evening visits to downtown cultural institutions were typical of many other middle-class women and men who lived in West and North Philadelphia and could quickly and easily reach Center City by streetcar. For people living farther away, in Germantown, the suburbs, and the outlying portions of the region, the steam trains provided the same access. Edwin Jellett from Germantown regularly used both the Reading's and Pennsylvania's Chestnut Hill trains to hear opera at the Academy of Music or to attend various shows downtown. These excursions to Center City were an important part of Jellett's social life; for the twenty-five-cent train fare and the admission fee, he could meet other young middle-class Philadelphians.[28]

Other special events also brought bourgeois Philadelphians from the neighborhoods to downtown by trolley and train. The regular occurrence of such celebrations helped establish central Philadelphia as a ceremonial space for the entire region. In the days of politics as spectacle, both parties staged parades and mass meetings in Center City. Edwin Jellett took the train in after supper on September 23, 1884, in order to stand "in front of the Union League" on Broad Street "to see the Republican Parade." He spent the entire evening at the parade, reaching home at 1:30 A.M. on the last train. Events like the Constitution Centennial in 1887 and the "Peace Jubilee" in 1898 (celebrating the end of the Spanish-American War) drew great crowds to Center City.

One middle-class man living in lower North Philadelphia wanted to go to the latter but failed "as the cars could not accommodate the people" by the time they had arrived at his street.[29]

After Center City, the next most popular set of destinations for relaxation for middle-class men and women were the various parks in and around the city. Fairmount Park, the large municipally owned green space along the Schuylkill River, offered a number of possible destinations. Although clearly a space shared with the women and men of the working classes, Fairmount Park maintained its bourgeois tone in part because of proximity: in the late nineteenth century, middle-class neighborhoods faced all the major entrances to the park. Starting in the 1890s, there were also a number of commercial amusements parks. Many of these were owned by the trolley companies to encourage patronage on their lines. Philadelphia never had one very intensively developed location like Coney Island in New York City but instead had a number of smaller sites located throughout the region. In general, all these enterprises offered the same types of services: rides, food, picnic sites, and music. More basically, they all offered an escape from the brick-and-stone row-house world of middle-class Philadelphia to a land of green grass and trees. Philadelphia, like most industrial cities, was dirty and crowded and the parks offered some momentary relief from the less enchanting conditions of everyday urban life.[30]

Finally, during the 1890s the trolley cars themselves were another popular middle-class destination. On beautiful days in the spring and fall many women and men used the trolleys to explore the city and region. For example, after supper one Sunday, Leo Bernheimer took the trolley to Germantown just to see a new place. During the hot days and nights of the summer, middle-class Philadelphians used the streetcars to cool off. Eugenia Barnitz took open trolleys with her friends to Willow Grove Park as a teenager in the late 1890s. Because of the high fares that effectively limited working-class ridership, the cars themselves were a safe, middle-class space in the city.[31]

In the late nineteenth century, the steam trains (and to a lesser extent the trolleys) also linked middle-class Philadelphians more firmly to the city's hinterland and the nation as a whole. People rode the railroads for both business and pleasure. Professionals and tourists visited New York and Washington for the day and took extended trips to Pittsburgh and New England. Towns along the New Jersey coast became destinations for thousands of middle-class men and women on hot summer days. The rail lines were not just "metropolitan corridors" but bourgeois ones as well in which middle-class men and women sped through the countryside from one bourgeois space to another in comfort and modernity. Not only was Atlantic City part of the world of Philadelphia's bourgeoisie but so too were the trains of the Pennsylvania and the Philadelphia & Reading that connected the two communities. The illustration in figure 6 of a well-dressed woman being deferentially served by a Pennsylvania Railroad conductor is a window into this world.[32]

At the most mundane level, the trains and trolleys allowed middle-class Philadelphians to explore for a day the countryside around the city. The women of the West Philadelphia Smith family, for example, often used the trolleys to collect flowers to decorate their home. Edwin Jellett and his friends regularly took day trips to the Pennsylvania and New Jersey countryside in order to "botanize." Jellett was a particularly active user of the region's transportation system; he filled his Sundays with trips to Montgomery County, Pennsylvania; Burlington, New Jersey; and dozens of other locations throughout the area in the late nineteenth century. Others, like the mapmaker John L. Smith, took the trains and trolleys to follow the expansion of the metropolis; nothing seemed to make him happier than to record "the many improvements" he found in some outlying district.[33]

The trains permitted many middle-class Philadelphians to spend part or all of their summers in the late nineteenth century "boarding" in the surrounding countryside. Escaping the heat of the city for the rural hinterland had long been common for the city's elite, but the frequent train service meant that middle-class families could now join the summer exodus and still work or shop in the city. Edwin Jellett spent many of his vacations near Schwenksville in Montgomery County. Mary Smith's family spent a month of the summer of 1896 on a farm just outside Hatboro. Her father commuted to the city on the trains of the Philadelphia & Reading and she, her older sisters, and their mother occasionally went into Center City to shop. Although the Smith family returned to their home in the city, the convenience of the train service first sampled in these summer stays may have helped convince other middle-class Philadelphians of the advantages of suburban living.[34]

There were many popular summer destinations for bourgeois Philadelphians along the New Jersey shore. From Cape May to Asbury Park, the coast was dotted with towns that catered to city dwellers escaping the heat of the metropolis for the cool sea breezes. Both the Pennsylvania and the Philadelphia & Reading systems linked these shore communities with Philadelphia. By the 1890s, some of the fastest trains in North America plied the rails between Camden (linked by ferry to Philadelphia) and Atlantic City. Both railroads operated express trains with extra-fare Pullman parlor cars, cheap

Figure 6. The bourgeois corridor. Courtesy of the Pennsylvania State Archives, Pennsylvania Historical and Museum Commission.

excursion trains for day-trippers, early morning locals full of anglers and Philadelphia newspapers, and "cottagers trains" at the start and end of the "season" to convey families and their possessions to and from the shore. The season for the shore started in late May and continued through early September with its peak in July and August. As was common in many late nineteenth-century businesses, the Pennsylvania and the Reading engaged in an odd mixture of competition and collusion; although they met annually to set fares and rules for excursion traffic, they battled for passengers by offering faster trains, better equipment, and even bribes to Atlantic City hoteliers and cab drivers.[35]

During the last few decades of the nineteenth century, the trains and the streetcars allowed middle-class Victorian Philadelphians to travel easily throughout the metropolis and to refine their visions of the city and its region. In this way, a new, better-ordered, more controlled relationship developed between middle-class Philadelphians and their metropolis. The trains and trolleys, however, were not perfect and this comfortable relationship could be undermined. Both nature, in the form of adverse weather, and man, in the form of accidents and strikes, could disrupt the city's transportation system. During the late nineteenth century, snowstorms often shut down Philadelphia. Steam train and streetcar accidents, though usually less disruptive to the city as a whole, were far more likely and more deadly occurrences. Starting in the 1890s, strikes against the streetcar companies became more common and often interrupted the flow of travel in the city for middle-class Philadelphians.

The worst snowstorm during this period was the "Blizzard of '88" that brought the city to a standstill for a number of days in early March. Although the city only officially received ten inches of snow, the combination of low temperatures and high winds halted all transportation in the region. One Philadelphian recalled, "During the blizzard of 1888, not even four horses could pull the [street]cars up that hill terminating at Poplar Street. Transportation [in the city] stopped." William Hemsing recorded conditions along the Philadelphia & Reading's line to Bethlehem. On Monday, March 12, the second day of the storm, he observed: "The storm still continues. . . . The telegraph wires are down and the local freight was delayed here all day. . . . The train that passes here at 10 A.M. with three parlor and sleeping coaches and two others, with two engines, one broken, reached here about six o'clock. I watched them as they passed up the road and soon heard that they were stuck in the cut." Fifty-eight men from Lansdale worked for nearly two days to dig the stuck train out of the drifting snow. Finally, on Wednesday, Hemsing noted that "The unfortunate train at last started off in a snowstorm at 11:30 this morning nearly fifty hours late." It was not until Thursday that service returned to normal: "Today all the passenger trains are running nearly on time. They had two engines for every train this morning, but this evening it is better. . . . We got all our papers today." In the city, William Armstrong, an engraver, also recorded the unusual conditions: "Snow drift on the track Penna. R.R. near Wynnewood is 10 + 15 feet deep. All communication to New York is stop't except by telephone." Trains also were halted in southern New Jersey by the storm; Chalkley Matlack "saw the smoke of an engine at the Maple Shade Station [on Tuesday morning from his farm] and had my suspicions aroused that a train was probably blocked there, . . . discovered it had been since the preceding morning and that there was little likelihood of it getting away soon."[36]

Even less dramatic snowstorms disrupted the horse-drawn streetcars in the city. One morning in 1880, John Smith noted that it had "Blowed + snowed all night" and the "Car horses [were] having a Rough time." Later that year, he walked to work during a snow storm because "I waited for a Car [and when one finally arrived, saw] such a gang Hanging on I made up my mind that If I wanted to get down town I would have to walk." John Wilson, an engineer, voluntarily postponed a business trip to Reading one day in 1883 because of snow, only to have the lack of streetcar service the next day further delay the journey. A heavy snowstorm right before Christmas caused "trade [to be] very poor for this season" at Septimus Winner's music store, largely because the "cars and travel [were] almost closed up."[37]

Although the cable cars and the trolleys were less affected by snow than were the horse cars, storms could interfere with service and, in the case of the electric trolleys, down the overhead electrical lines that supplied the power. During a heavy snow in 1895, Leo Bernheimer noted that most of the trolleys and horse cars had stopped and the "cable being almost the only cars going." During a storm in 1899, Mary Smith observed that "Heavy snow all day long. . . . Street cars and steam roads completely blocked by evening. Market Street and Lancaster Avenue cars only ones running in West Philadelphia."[38]

Nature was not the only force that could halt the smooth flow of Philadelphia's transportation system and middle-class Philadelphians' travels. Far more common were streetcar accidents. Many were fairly minor; they might disrupt service but caused no major injuries to passengers or crews. During the Centennial, one newspaper reporter witnessed three "narrow escapes" involving streetcars in just ninety minutes. All three he blamed on the "incautioness and carelessness on the part of the passengers," a sentiment certainly to be echoed by the companies' lawyers. Leo Bernheimer was a frequent witness to all sorts of mishaps. Once, while on his way to his uncle's house in South Philadelphia, Bernheimer saw a derailed cable car but noted no injured people. Often in the 1890s, he was delayed because of minor electrical problems with the then-new trolleys, a useful reminder that cutting-edge technology is seldom perfect. More seriously, many passengers sustained minor injuries when they were entering or exiting the cars. Bernheimer ran into friend "with his face all bandaged. Had missed his hold yesterday while boarding a Woodland Trolley. Not seriously hurt, though sufficient as a caution." Injuries to passengers while they tried to board a moving trolley were common; about a year after seeing his bandaged friend, Bernheimer witnessed another accident on the same line: "Had just got in Woodland Av. car, . . . when we were a little past the church, a fellow jumped on the car and fell, looking as though he moved a somersault. The conductor stopped the car. . . . I don't think it was the conductor's fault." The accidents, however, could be far more serious, even deadly. One morning, on his way to Penn, Bernheimer "had a close shave from a trolley collision. Cars at right angles almost crashing together, the tracks being slippery." Other people were not so lucky, deadly accidents were not uncommon on the streets of Philadelphia in the late nineteenth century. Pedestrians were run over when they crossed the often busy streets of the city without being alert for the cars. The same reduction in friction that allowed the horse cars and trolleys to travel quickly also made them difficult to stop. Passengers also died from falls from the open platforms at the ends of the cars.[39]

Accidents also plagued the steam railroads that served the city. Trains derailed, ran into each other, and ran over pedestrians at grade crossings. The high train speeds that allowed middle-class Philadelphians to assert control over their environment contributed to these railroad accidents, as did the lack of effective safety regulation. John L. Smith had his "first Experience in R.R. accidents" on a Philadelphia & Reading train for New York in 1880 when "the Engine Broke the Piston Rod it Broke in Half + tore wood work of Locomotive fearful wonder it did not kill the Engineer." No one was killed and Smith made it to New York only an hour behind schedule. Accidents at grade crossings (where streets met the tracks at level) were also common. On his way to school one morning, Leo Bernheimer noticed a crowd near the Philadelphia & Reading crossing "at 9th and Girard. . . . A man had been struck by a train. I have since learned that his name was Goldman, Jewish. He died." These crossings were dangerous in part because the space between the railroad and the pedestrian was poorly defined (a topic that will be revisited in Chapter 2).[40]

During the late nineteenth century a number of strikes against the railroads and traction companies also disrupted service. Most of the labor actions were short in duration. In 1887, for example, there was a strike against the Philadelphia & Reading that lasted for only a few days and had little impact on passenger service.[41]

On December 17, 1895, however, workers struck the newly formed Union Traction Company (which by then operated most of the trolley and streetcar service in the city) at the peak of the Christmas shopping season and maintained the action for a week. Leo Bernheimer noted by the afternoon of the first day of the strike that "practically none [of the city's transport services] except the Broad St Bus, and the Hestonville, Mantua RR. cars are going. . . . Most of the people have to walk." Although the labor action did not last long, it was a crucial event in the world of middle-class Philadelphia. By 1895, many bourgeois families had used the trolley to separate home from work and shopping. No longer could they easily walk to their daily destinations, and people coped as best they could. The traction company's attempt to operate service with police escorts met with limited success because of the combination of union solidarity, public support for the strike, and violence. Leo Bernheimer rode some of these "scab cars" and his experiences were not positive. Early in the strike he "took a car, a Market Streeter then coming along, police fore x aft and four mounted police as escort to the bridge [over the Schuylkill River]. The conductor said he would not make the next trip, had had enough." Later, Bernheimer rode another trolley "with a 'scab' conductor. He had no uniform on and did not seem to be a conductor. The remarks made about him were not complimentary. He seemed to be a very poor man, and anything but happy. I felt very sorry for him." Bernheimer, like other middle-class Philadelphians, also took the steam trains (all three of the railroads serving the city continued to operate) and "huckster wagons" to work and shopping (see figure 7 for the triumph of practicality over bourgeois respectability during the strike) . Mary Smith's father either walked the two miles to work or took a crowded train on the nearby Pennsylvania Railroad.[42]

Despite the violence, many middle-class Philadelphians supported the strike because of their dislike of the new traction monopoly. Albert Edmunds, a librarian at the Historical Society of Pennsylvania and no friend of organized labor, recorded, "General *strike* of motormen and conductors of the Union Traction Company, which has created popular disapproval of late

Figure 7. The victory of practicality over respectability: passengers on a huckster wagon during trolley strike. Courtesy of the Print and Picture Collection, Free Library of Philadelphia.

by raising fares and reducing wages." Septimus Winner, a small-business owner, expressed his toleration of the violence: "A 'magnificent' day, splendid for pedestrians, we all had to walk on account of the *Great Strike in opposition to the 'Trolley Grab'* of double fare 8 cents. A very exciting day all over the City big rows, cars smashed and lots of fun." Another indication of the anti-monopoly feeling was the "people going along with cards on their hats, saying 'we are walking,' " noted by both Edmunds and Winner.[43]

The strike ended on Christmas Eve with a partial victory for the union. The workers received a small wage increase and a twelve-hour day. Middle-class women and men were happy to have their cars—and their lives—back to normal. Albert Edmunds was not the only Philadelphian who had missed "the roar of the street-cars by day and night" during the strike and found the "thunder of electric cars" on Christmas Eve "music."[44]

The strikes, accidents, and storms disrupted both Philadelphia's transportation system and the rhythm of everyday life for middle-class men and women in the city. By the turn of the century, the women and men of the bourgeoisie were dependent on the trains and the trolleys that had given them the physical mobility to remake their mental images of the city. Many middle-class Philadelphians found themselves wedded to a monopoly institution—the Union Traction Company—that they did not like but needed every day to travel the length and breadth of "their" city.

For the bourgeoisie, the steam trains and the electric trolleys represented modern society's triumph over nature. The middle class used these bourgeois corridors to remake the physical and mental geographies of their Philadelphia. Going from one carefully classified, perceived middle-class space to another within the safety and comfort of the region's trains and cars, late Victorian bourgeois Philadelphians felt confident in the continued progress of their city by the dawn of the twentieth century. This new middle-class world also included the buildings that served as entrances to these corridors. The next chapter will look at the remaking of space and time in and around Victorian Philadelphia's railway passenger terminals. But, as will be developed in Part II, the monopoly traction company and the transit workers' strikes hinted that all was not well in the order created by Philadelphia's subset of the transatlantic middle class. Caught between a rapacious elite and an increasingly demanding proletariat, the early twentieth-century bourgeoisie would have to resort to politics to defend their carefully classified version of the world.

Chapter 2
Such a Well-Behaved Train Station

I checked my bag at Reading Terminal and suddenly felt like false pre-
tenses. I wondered if anybody had ever done anything dishonest before at
Reading Terminal, it always seems like such a well-behaved train station.[1]

During the Victorian era, the downtown railway passenger terminal developed as a distinctive middle-class place in the multi-classed city
throughout the Westernized world. Whether Reading Terminal in Philadelphia, Grand Central in New York, St. Pancras in London, or Central Station
in Glasgow, space and time became more precisely ordered for bourgeois
passengers during the late nineteenth century. The interiors of the newly
constructed stations became more complex and better defined. Both inside
and outside the structures, the railroads more clearly divided space meant
for trains from that for humans. Time also became more precise and increasingly divorced from its natural setting as the railroads adopted standard time
and devised new schedules. Railway timetables—like the depots owned by
the same companies—became more detailed and exact as the century progressed. By the turn of the century, middle-class women and men lived by
railroad time, traveled on carefully scheduled train paths, and arrived and departed from complex, well-planned central depots. The rhythms of bourgeois
life can be found in and around the Victorian trains stations.[2]

Reading Terminal, built in 1893 by the ever ambitious but often bank-
rupt Philadelphia & Reading Railroad, is a wonderful example of a middle-
class portal to and from the bourgeois city. Usually the structure is seen as a
reflection of both the grand dreams and the harsh realities of the Reading's
always unsuccessful attempts to best its crosstown rival, the Pennsylvania
Railroad. Reading Terminal was neither as busy nor as palatial as the Pennsylvania's Broad Street Station three blocks to the west, and the two depots

immediately defined the relative importance of two corporations. But Reading Terminal and the other late nineteenth-century stations in Philadelphia indicated far more than just the relative business acumen of their owners. From the very respectable dining room on the second floor (see figure 8 for a view of this facility when new) to the more hectic farmers' market under the train shed, Reading Terminal mirrored middle-class culture in Victorian Philadelphia. It and the other depots quickly became important parts of everyday life for the bourgeois women and men of the region. For many observers, the buildings themselves took on a middle-class tone. By the early twentieth century, Reading Terminal had become, in the eyes of the novelist (and ex-Philadelphian) Christopher Morley, a "well-behaved train station."[3]

Before we enter Reading Terminal, we should step back and consider the evolving relationship between the railway stations and the main commercial district during the nineteenth century. In Philadelphia, this relationship can be divided into three distinct phases. First, during the 1830s and 1840s the small, independent railroads attempted to locate their passenger facilities on the fringes of downtown. Later, in the 1850s, the railways moved their now larger depots farther from the business district and began to rely on the then new horse-drawn streetcars for the final delivery of their passengers. The last phase began in 1881, when the now consolidated lines started to move their facilities back into Center City. The map in figure 9 shows the placement of the railroad termini in relation to the central business district in 1876. Not one of the stations stood within the commercial core. Few were convenient to each other; note the nearly four mile gap between the Kensington depot in Northeast Philadelphia (marked as 7 on the map in figure 9) and the Prime Street station in South Philadelphia (1). The railroads had located their stations to these outlying points in the 1850s for a number of legal and economic reasons, including the cost of land and municipal ordinances and agreements that effectively banned steam locomotives from most of the streets of the original city (from river to river between South and Vine Streets). Because of the distance between the terminals and downtown, almost every passenger had to begin or end his or her railway journey by omnibus or streetcar.[4]

The streetcars were the key to station location in Philadelphia from mid century on as they allowed the steam railroads to end the expensive and inefficient practice of using horses to propel their trains within the limits of the pre-1854 city. Prior to the introduction of the streetcars, most steam railroads placed their facilities at the fringe of downtown, even though this meant that

Figure 8. The dining room at Reading Terminal when new in 1893. Courtesy of the Print and Picture Collection, Free Library of Philadelphia.

the last few miles of the journey had to be made on rails laid in the city streets and the trains had to be pulled by horses. After the coming of the streetcars in 1858, the steam railroads withdrew to operationally more efficient terminals that ended this switch from steam to horse power. In 1866, for example, the West Chester & Philadelphia Railroad moved its passenger station from Eighteenth and Market Streets to West Philadelphia (shown at 2 on the map in figure 9) to save the time and expense of the transfer. An 1869

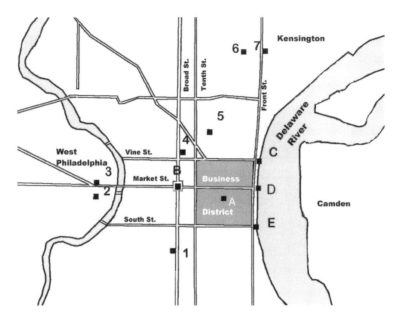

Figure 9. Philadelphia's central railroad passenger terminals in 1876. Based on an 1876 John L. Smith map of Center City in collection of author.

Key:

1   Prime Street depot   Philadelphia, Wilmington & Baltimore
2   West Chester depot   West Chester & Philadelphia
3   West Philadelphia station   Pennsylvania
4   Main Line depot   Philadelphia & Reading
5   Ninth and Green station   Philadelphia & Reading
6   North Pennsylvania depot   Philadelphia & Reading
7   Kensington depot   Pennsylvania

A   Old State House
B   Centre Square
C   Vine Street ferry
D   Market Street ferry
E   South Street ferry

guide to the railroad makes explicit the importance of the street railways in this process when it notes that the "passenger depot, at Thirty-second and Chestnut Streets, [was] accessible every three to five minutes by Chestnut and Walnut Street cars, and within one square [a city block to Victorian Philadelphians] of those on Market Street."[5]

This movement away from the commercial core at mid century had a significant effect on railroad passengers: it shifted the risk of delay on the busy streets of the city from the railroad companies to the travelers. In the 1840s, once an outbound passenger boarded a horse-drawn car in or near Center City, he or she was on their railway journey. By 1876, passengers had to carefully calculate their travel times to the outlying passenger facilities or risk missing their train. Some passengers—John L. Smith was one example—consistently had trouble getting their timing right and often missed their trains.[6]

The travel time between these mid-century railroad passenger facilities and the central business district varied greatly, from under ten minutes for some of the ferry terminals to nearly an hour for the stations located in Northeast Philadelphia. For most passengers bound to or from the old State House (Independence Hall to non-Philadelphians), a ride or walk of twenty to thirty minutes was typical. The old State House, located at Fifth and Chestnut Streets, was in the center of the commercial district and serves as a good surrogate for typical middle-class business and shopping destinations of the period.[7]

The location of these passenger facilities influenced the development of middle-class housing in the region. Although the majority of commuters continued to live within the city limits throughout the nineteenth century, suburbanization began on a small scale for the elite and upper-middle class a little after mid century. Haddonfield, in Camden County, New Jersey, developed as an early bedroom community in part because of the quickness of the commute to Center City via train and ferry. One reason that the progress of Philadelphia's famous "Main Line" suburbs lagged a few decades behind that of Haddonfield was the relative inconvenience to downtown of the Pennsylvania's West Philadelphia station compared to the ferry terminals.[8]

Of the ten railroad passenger facilities in use in the mid-1870s, the busiest by far were these four: Prime Street, West Philadelphia, and Ninth and Green rail terminals, and the Market Street ferry. Prime Street was the northern terminus of the Philadelphia, Wilmington & Baltimore Railroad, an independent line that served the cities in its name and formed part of the jointly operated route between New York and Washington. The Pennsylvania Railroad's West Philadelphia station had trains for New York, Pittsburgh, and Washington (the through trains from New York). The Ninth and Green depot, operated by the Philadelphia and Reading Railroad, was the city's busiest commuter terminal, with trains to Germantown, Chestnut Hill, and Norristown. Ferries from Market Street connected with trains in Camden for many points in southern New Jersey, including the rapidly growing resort of Atlantic City and the elite suburb of Haddonfield. The remaining facilities were not as busy. They either served less important lines (like the small West Chester & Philadelphia) or were the downgraded remnants of once major stations, as the Kensington depot had become following the takeover of the Philadelphia & Trenton by the Pennsylvania Railroad and the subsequent transfer of most of its train service to the West Philadelphia station.[9]

Through the 1870s, the Philadelphia railroads remained committed to their outlying locations. But on December 5, 1881, the Pennsylvania Railroad made travel more convenient for many middle-class Philadelphians and contributed to the radical alteration of the fabric of the city when it opened its Broad Street Station at Centre Square. The new structure replaced not only the railroad's West Philadelphia depot but, because of corporate consolidations, the West Chester & Philadelphia and Prime Street terminals as well. When it opened, the new station was just west of the central business district, about a ten-minute car ride from the old State House.[10]

By the turn of the century, as illustrated in the map in figure 10, the station stood within the expanded downtown. Four separate but related decisions dramatically shifted the focus of the city core to Centre Square from the old State House in the late nineteenth century: the municipality's construction of a new City Hall in the square, John Wanamaker's 1876 conversion of an abandoned railroad freight station into a large retail establishment one block to the east, the opening of Broad Street Station one block to the west, and the establishment of a new Philadelphia & Reading passenger terminal three blocks to the east in 1893.

The complement of modern train stations in Philadelphia was completed by the Baltimore & Ohio's Twenty-fourth and Chestnut Streets depot in 1887 and the Philadelphia & Reading's 1893 Reading Terminal. The B&O facility befitted the railroad's late arrival and minor role in the city: it was smaller and was the only late nineteenth century station not built within or near the central business district. Reading Terminal at Twelfth and Market Streets in Center City, however, was an appropriate competitor for Broad Street Station. When it opened, the Reading closed both the Ninth and

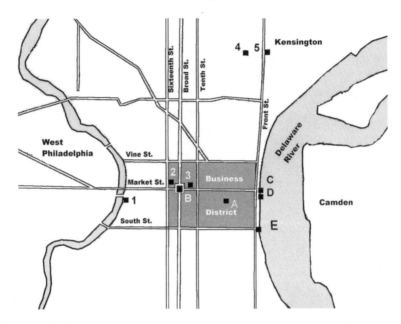

Figure 10. Philadelphia's central railroad passenger terminals in 1901. Based on an 1876 John L. Smith map of Center City in collection of author.
Key:

1	Twenty-fourth and Chestnut Streets station	Baltimore & Ohio
2	Broad Street Station	Pennsylvania
3	Reading Terminal	Philadelphia & Reading
4	Berks Street depot	Philadelphia & Reading
5	Kensington depot	Pennsylvania

A	Old State House
B	Centre Square
C	Market Street ferry
D	Chestnut Street ferry
E	South Street ferry

Green and Broad and Callowhill depots and significantly downgraded the Berks Street station.

By 1901, the two main railroad stations for Philadelphia were in the heart of the commercial district. The only two passenger facilities that were far from downtown were the two in Northeast Philadelphia, both of which survived as distinctly minor terminals serving largely local needs in an industrial section of the city. As one guide to the city put it: "Third and Berks and Kensington depots . . . are but little used, because the major part of the business has been transferred to [the new stations.] They are, moreover, remote from the center of the city, and offer few conveniences for travelers." By the turn of the century, most train riders bound for Center City could walk from either the new Pennsylvania or Reading depot to their final destinations. The travel time to Wanamaker's department store, for example, was reduced from twenty minutes by street car from the Reading's Ninth and Green station to just a two-minute walk from the new Reading Terminal (or a five-minute one from Broad Street Station). In addition, passengers traveling to locations in the city outside the central business district had access to more car lines at the new locations. According to the Pennsylvania Railroad's official history, "the superior location of [Broad Street Station] seemed to create new traffic." By moving their terminals closer to the new offices, stores, and theaters, both the Pennsylvania and the Reading dramatically increased the potential for local passenger traffic. The Center City anchors of the middle-class metropolis were firmly in place.[11]

Broad Street Station and Reading Terminal were not only more convenient to downtown but were also larger and qualitatively different because of the services that they offered to the public. During the late-nineteenth century, the railroads redefined the very nature of space in and around their central terminals. The depots were transformed from simple transportation hubs to civic landmarks. To reach these new terminals the railways separated their trains from road traffic by an increasingly elaborate network of bridges, viaducts, and tunnels. Not only did space become more carefully defined between the railroad and its surrounding community, but it also became more ordered within the stations. Passenger trains were separated from freight trains. Space for trains became more clearly divided from that for people. Incoming and outgoing passengers had separate routes through the buildings. The number of amenities dramatically increased. All in all, the world of the railway traveler became more elaborate and better organized.

The Ninth and Green Streets depot was typical of the enlarged "train barn" stations built throughout the United States in the 1850s. In Philadelphia, both the Philadelphia & Reading's Main Line depot of 1859 and the Philadelphia, Wilmington & Baltimore's Prime Street station were similar. At its base, this style of building consisted of a head house structure, which usually contained waiting rooms and ticketing and baggage facilities on the first floor and company offices on the second, attached to an enclosed train shed (typically with a largely solid, wooden roof). The structures, though palatial compared to the original depots of the 1830s that they replaced, tended to be small; the station at Ninth and Green Streets (figure 11) took up half of a smaller than average city block and its train shed contained but three tracks.[12]

Like most antebellum stations, the interior layout of the Ninth and Green terminal was simple, with few divisions. In part, this was because these depots offered little to the public except those services directly related to train travel. The only people who ventured to these inconveniently placed mid-nineteenth-century railroad facilities were passengers or people accompanying or meeting train riders. The largest portion of the structure consisted of the dark wooden train shed that covered the three tracks and the "platforms" that were little more than walkways between the tracks. Four other interior spaces are shown on the plan in figure 12 as being used by the public: two waiting rooms, a package room, and a baggage room. The larger waiting room likely contained both the ticket office and the newsstand (the only non-railroad service in the building). The smaller waiting room was probably the Ladies' Waiting Room, a feature provided at most major urban terminals by mid century. There was no restaurant; nor did the Reading provide a place within the building for its passengers to smoke, as it officially designated both waiting rooms as non-smoking. All in all, its interior was simple and its amenities spartan.[13]

Simplicity in interior layout, however, did not guarantee safety at stations like Ninth and Green Streets. The location of both the tracks and the platforms at street level meant there was no clear division between the areas meant for trains and those for passengers. People walked across the running lines within the station to reach their trains or the street. Railroads could do little to stop this practice, other than having their employees attempt to discourage it. For example, on a Sunday in 1881, John L. Smith left his mother's house in North Philadelphia to spend the day with friends in Germantown. After dinner, he returned home via the Ninth and Green depot. His day came to a dramatic, and nearly fatal, conclusion when he "made a narrow escape" from a locomotive as it backed into the station while he was crossing the tracks. Smith leapt out of its way, prompted by the shouted warnings of nearly "40 train Hands." Accidents like this were not uncommon in the United States, as a guidebook for English travelers warned: "A special word of caution may be given to the frequent necessity for crossing the tracks, as the rails are frequently flush with the floor of the station and foot-bridges or tunnels are rarely provided" as was then the practice in Europe.[14]

Conditions were particularly bad at this depot. In addition to the many

Figure 11. A classic mid-century depot: the Philadelphia & Reading depot at Ninth and Green Streets circa 1895. Courtesy of the Print and Picture Collection, Free Library of Philadelphia.

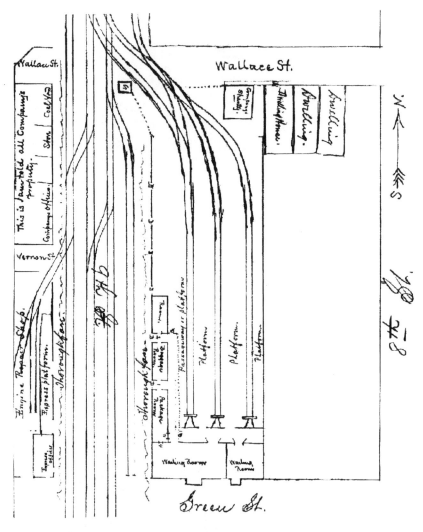

Figure 12. The simple interior layout of the Ninth and Green Streets depot. Courtesy of the Hagley Museum and Library.

passenger switching movements (like the one that nearly felled Smith), the Reading operated a busy freight line down the center of Ninth Street. The ground-level tracks also created numerous grade crossings of streets for trains using the station. This both slowed the trains and disrupted life in the surrounding neighborhoods. This mix of railroad and street traffic also led to many accidents.[15]

In addition to these problems, the lighting was poor both within the train shed and on Ninth Street. By the mid-1880s these issues had become serious enough for Reading operating officials to express concern over passenger safety at the aging depot. One manager proposed locking most of the entrances to the station, posting additional watchmen, and petitioning the city to close Ninth Street as a public thoroughfare in order "to reduce the high number of accidents . . . as locomotives and cars are being constantly moved." In other words, the railroad would begin to define more clearly the boundary between trains and people. Another supervisor was concerned with the "many narrow escapes [the railroad has had] while unloading our passengers at night. . . ." Although the Reading installed additional electric lights in 1883 and did close some entrances, the cramped, dark, and busy station at Ninth and Green remained a relatively unsafe place until its abandonment in 1893.[16]

The movement away from buildings like the one at Ninth and Green began in 1876 when the Pennsylvania Railroad built a new passenger station in West Philadelphia and the Philadelphia, Wilmington & Baltimore substantially reconstructed its facility in South Philadelphia. These two depots were important transitional structures, built largely on the scale of the mid-century terminals but with far more complex interior designs presaging the elaborate facilities of Broad Street Station and Reading Terminal. Because they were essentially the same size as the earlier stations, these Centennial depots affirm that the Victorian redefinition of space was not developed in reaction to physical expansion.

The Prime Street station had been one of Philadelphia's most impressive railroad depots since it was built by the Philadelphia, Wilmington & Baltimore in 1851–52. Although similar in appearance to the Reading facility at Green Street, it was larger and more elaborately decorated. Its train shed held seven tracks and three "platforms." When built, the railroad claimed that the head house contained "every convenience known or believed to be essential to a station of such prominent importance." It was probably the first depot in Philadelphia to contain a dining room in addition to the standard waiting room, ticket office, and baggage facilities supplied at the other stations. But the terminal also had many of the same problems as the Green Street facility. The Prime Street train shed was low and dark. Its tracks and the platforms were placed at street level, allowing passengers to enter the station through the train shed. In addition, until the 1876 renovation, freight trains shared the facility with their passenger counterparts.[17]

If space was not well defined in and around the mid-century Prime Street, the Philadelphia, Wilmington & Baltimore station was a masterpiece of planning when compared to the jumble of tracks and structures that made up the Pennsylvania Railroad's first depot in West Philadelphia. The Pennsylvania had moved its main Philadelphia terminal to a small structure at Thirty-first and Market Streets from an even smaller building at Eleventh and Market in 1864. By the early 1870s, the Pennsylvania's passenger facilities at West Philadelphia had grown to two separate stations with three sets of platforms sprawling over two city blocks, with a group of freight depots and tracks intermixed (see figure 13 for a map showing this conglomeration of tracks and platforms taken from a city atlas). The original 1864 terminal ("A" in figure 13) had two tracks under a train shed and was used by trains to Harrisburg and Pittsburgh. A short distance to the west was the separate "New York" station, built in 1867, with its own two-track train shed for service to Trenton and Jersey City ("B"). Finally, still farther to the west, a wooden walkway led from the New York depot to a platform located on a low-level connecting line that was used by through Washington to Jersey City trains ("C"). With the large number of freight trains running on the tracks adjacent to these passenger facilities, this complex of buildings and platforms was neither safe nor terribly easy for the first-time passenger to navigate. Not only was their little separation between freight and passenger space, there was effectively none between the railroad and the community.[18]

At the Pennsylvania and the Philadelphia, Wilmington & Baltimore depots in 1876 space became noticeably better defined both in and around the facilities. Perhaps the single most important change resulting from these improvements was the clear separation of passenger traffic from freight traffic at the new or renovated termini. In South Philadelphia, the Philadelphia, Wilmington & Baltimore built a new freight facility adjoining its Prime Street station. This allowed the existing structure to be used exclusively for passenger purposes. In West Philadelphia, the Pennsylvania finally built a depot at Thirty-second and Market Streets large enough to house all its passenger services in one building. Like the renovated facility at Prime Street, the new Pennsylvania terminal was for passenger trains only. Also like its counterpart in South Philadelphia, the West Philadelphia depot's head house had a complex interior that consisted of "gentlemen's" and "ladies'" waiting rooms, separate ticketing and baggage offices, a restaurant, and company offices.[19]

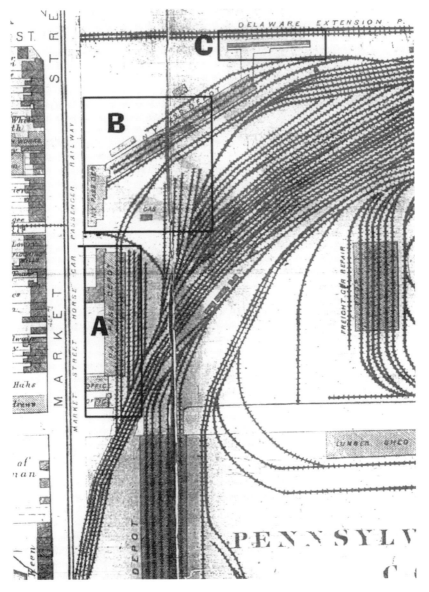

Figure 13. Complex and confusing: the Pennsylvania Railroad's West Philadelphia stations in 1872. Courtesy of the Map Collection, Free Library of Philadelphia.
Key:
A   Original depot for the trains to Pittsburgh
B   Station for trains to New York originating in Philadelphia
C   Platform for through New York to Washington trains

Additional evidence that these changes in interior and exterior layout were related to a new vision of space and not just reactions to increased traffic or growing size can be found at the Pennsylvania Railroad's rather insignificant Kensington depot. Despite its location far from downtown and its infrequent use (because the railroad had transferred most of its major passenger services to the West Philadelphia station), the Pennsylvania board still authorized some "much needed improvements" there in the mid 1870s. The result was a small brick station building attached to a two-track train shed exclusively for passenger services. The track layout around the passenger facility was also revised to more clearly separate people from cargo.[20]

The trends apparent in these mid 1870s improvements became fully articulated in the three main depots built in the 1880s and 1890s. Broad Street Station, the Baltimore & Ohio facility, and Reading Terminal all were exclusively passenger structures with complex, well-defined interiors in which the railways clearly separated human space from train space. This unmistakable division continued outside the buildings, where the railroads spent freely to isolate their trains from road traffic.

The first of these stations to open was Broad Street Station in 1881. Qualitatively different from any previous depot in Philadelphia, its facade was unlike that of any existing railroad structure in the city; it was in the style and on the scale of a great London railway terminus, such as the recently completed St. Pancras. Its first floor was made of large blocks of gleaming granite, its upper floors fabricated of brick. The elaborate gothic style made it look more like a cathedral than a train depot (figure 14). It was a fitting temple to the power of Philadelphia's most influential corporation: the Pennsylvania Railroad. But its grandeur was more than a simple projection of power by its owner, a proclamation that it and its industry had arrived. It was also a manifestation of the wealth and the culture of the Victorian bourgeoisie.[21]

The rational spatial patterns of the Victorian middle class were immediately apparent at the depot. The Pennsylvania built a block-wide brick viaduct from the Schuylkill River to Fifteenth Street, which allowed its trains to reach Broad Street Station totally separated from street traffic. Not only did this elevated approach eliminate grade crossing and allow the railroad to increase train speed and safety, but it also allowed the PRR to gain more control over passenger access to the trains within the station. Unlike at ground-level depots such as Ninth and Green, where passengers could and did enter the structure through the train shed, at Broad Street Station passengers could reach the platforms only through access points designated by the rail-

Figure 14. A temple to transportation: the Pennsylvania Railroad's Broad Street Station in 1881. Courtesy of the Print and Picture Collection, Free Library of Philadelphia.

road. The company used this new form of control to full advantage by separating the platforms from the station concourse by a series of train gates that were guarded by railroad employees. By keeping travelers off the tracks, accidents, like the one John Smith narrowly avoided at Ninth and Green, could be largely eliminated.

Smith was a frequent visitor to Broad Street Station and can serve as our guide to the new facility. He and a friend went there to catch a train for a brief visit to the suburbs not long after the depot opened. Smith met his companion at Market Street in front of the depot a little before ten on a Saturday morning. They likely stopped for a moment to admire the exterior of the new station and would soon find its interior equally striking. To enter the building, they walked north, first passing the exit for arriving passengers, then the pedestrian and carriage passages to Fifteenth Street. Near the north end of the station they went through polished wood and leaded-glass doors into a small lobby and then on to a large booking hall. They noted the separate local and through tickets windows and, while waiting to buy their tickets, also observed the Pullman Company office (for parlor and sleeping car reservations) and outgoing baggage room, all carefully classified spaces targeted at the departing passenger. After completing their transaction, they went up the sixteen-foot-wide grand stairway, which was lined with gleaming enameled bricks. Above them on the stairs was a hand-carved and inlaid wood ceiling befitting a private club. When they reached the second floor, they saw more well-organized and elaborately decorated rooms. This level was the train floor because the railroad entered the station via elevated tracks. They immediately noticed the airy and spacious feeling of the well-lit, two-story general waiting room: eighty feet by fifty-two feet, with large windows, a skylight, polished hardwood wainscoting and details, and painted plaster walls. A large map of the Pennsylvania system dominated the north end. The room had padded benches, and opened onto smaller spaces containing a confectionery store, a newsstand, a package room, and a telegraph office. Although Smith and his friend would have liked to have explored more of the new station, train time was approaching. They went through one of the two arched openings into the train lobby, where they found their departure track clearly indicated above the gate. To reach their train, they showed their tickets to the uniformed attendant at the gate. As they approached their train, they noted how—unlike at Ninth and Green—even the train shed seemed bright, because of the many glass panels in the roof. As a guide to the city observed: "The [four train sheds] of this great station [create] a wide, lofty apartment."[22]

On this visit, Smith did not have time to take in all of the station's amenities, but he would return often and have many opportunities to explore the remainder of the building. A few years later, on a Sunday morning, he boarded the wrong horse-drawn street car and missed his train to the suburbs. With an hour to kill until the next departure, he may have visited some of the areas of Broad Street Station he had rushed by on his first trip. This time, after buying his ticket and ascending the main stairs into the general waiting room, he may have walked to (but not through) the ladies' waiting room. The ladies' waiting room was not quite as large as the main one but was similarly furnished and decorated. A guide to the city noted: "The ladies' waiting-room is a magnificent apartment, having tall, Gothic-arched windows, set with ornamental glass, a hardwood paneled ceiling, and a great, cheery, open fire-place, ornamented with tiles. It is very comfortably furnished with settees, rockers and easy-chairs and rugs." Both rooms were well lit, by natural light during the day and by electric lamps (backed up by gas fixtures) at night. The reason Smith could not go through the ladies' waiting room was that it and the adjoining ladies' retiring room were guarded by a railroad matron. Smith could wander into the restaurant, however. Here he found both a lunch counter and a dining room (which had a small section reserved for women). He walked through them and returned to the general waiting room. If truly bored, he may have explored the separate arriving and departing baggage areas or used the elevators to reach the third floor, where he could find the barber shop and the bathing facilities for male travelers.[23]

As Smith's visits demonstrate, Broad Street was very different from the mid-century stations like Ninth and Green. It was not only larger and more conveniently located but was also better organized and offered more services. Space continued to become better defined and more refined. Arriving and departing passengers had separate passages, stairs, and baggage rooms. For the person leaving the city, ticketing, reservations, and luggage were cared for on the first floor. Wrought iron gates separated people from the trains. The station also offered special services for the traveler: bathtubs, barbers, and breakfast. As the business district moved west to meet the station, the restaurant became a popular dining location for non-passengers, too. John Smith would stop at the station for lunch if he was in the area on business or pleasure. He was not the only middle-class man or women to do so; a guide to the city recommended "the restaurants of both the Broad Street Station and the Reading Terminal [as] excellent, and not extravagant in price." As this entry illustrates, all these changes that took place at Broad Street would also occur at the other new downtown stations constructed in the next decade: the Baltimore & Ohio's Twenty-fourth and Chestnut Streets station and Reading Terminal (the main dining room of Reading Terminal is shown in figure 8). All three stations were featured in an 1890s treatise on railway station construction and operation.[24]

Similar to Broad Street, the interiors of the other two late nineteenth-century termini demonstrate the same complex organization of space. Although the exterior of Reading Terminal was very different from that of Broad Street (it looked more like an office building than a cathedral), the internal layout and the services offered within the structure (and the Baltimore & Ohio's smaller depot) were nearly identical to that of its rival. All contained grand, soaring interiors, meant to both impress and inspire passengers. All also bespoke the wealth and power of their corporate owners and indirectly the city and its middle class. The interiors of these late-Victorian depots were less open than those of the mid-century stations (such as Ninth and Green Streets); their floor plans were divided into a variety of differentiated uses (figure 15 illustrates the first and train floors of Reading Terminal). A disadvantage of this new layout was that passengers frequently got lost in the bewildering array of rooms and passages. What was so logical on the architect's plan could be quite challenging for the neophyte to negotiate in real life. Passengers wandered into railway offices and, over time, directional signs proliferated. The railways divided space by gender: all stations included special areas set aside exclusively for the use of women, carefully guarded by railroad matrons. Space was also divided by class. The Pennsylvania routed its immigrant traffic through an entirely different facility in South Philadelphia, so as to not sully the bourgeois character of Broad Street Station, while the Reading provided a separate waiting room for immigrants. In addition, railroad policemen and others patrolled the stations to maintain the middle-class tenor of the facilities.[25]

All in all, these late Victorian terminals were largely bourgeois spaces in the city that reflected broader middle-class trends in spatial use and design. This elaboration, refinement and specialization of space could also be found in the Victorian home, the new department stores, the office buildings, the pages of middle-class newspapers, and even the streets of the city itself. And as bourgeois space in the city became more rationally defined, so did time.[26]

When Reading Terminal opened in 1893, both the city and Philadelphia & Reading were very proud of their new downtown station. *The Philadelphia Inquirer* called the depot "The first step taken for the New Philadelphia." After lagging behind for a decade, the railroad finally had a structure comparable to that of its arch rival, the Pennsylvania. The Reading issued a press release in which it recounted the multitude of modern devices and conve-

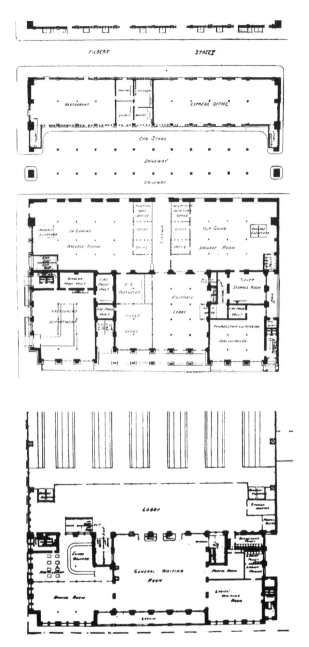

Figure 15. Floor plans of Reading Terminal as built in 1893. Walter G. Berg, *Buildings and Structures of American Railroads: A Reference Book* (New York: John Wiley & Sons, 1893).

niences the new depot contained. A few years later, however, *The Evening Bulletin* noted in a lead editorial one important feature Reading Terminal lacked: an exterior clock. Much to the chagrin of railroad officials, the journal not only reported that their depot did not have one but that "the tower of Broad Street Station" did. Within days the Reading started the process of placing a free-standing clock on Market Street outside the station. Exactly why a newspaper would opine on so seemingly trivial a subject and, equally importantly, why the ever poor and often slow-moving Philadelphia & Reading would respond with such speed highlights the importance of time to the late nineteenth-century bourgeoisie.[27]

Time, like space, gradually became more rationally defined during the Victorian period. For a city like Philadelphia, which depended heavily on railroads, the introduction of standard time on November 18, 1883, was not a significant moment and had very little effect on everyday middle-class life. Its creation went unnoticed in part because the few minutes' change in Philadelphia on the "day of two noons" was so minor. But equally important was that railway employees and passengers had long been used to substituting the railroads' definition of time for nature's. For decades before the creation of standard time, the city's railroads had operated either their entire systems or large parts of them on "Philadelphia Time." It was the Quaker City's noon, not the local one, that mattered to the trains serving outlying communities. At best, a major city like Baltimore and New York would have its local time noted in addition to that of Philadelphia in timetables serving that destination. For middle-class Philadelphians, standard time was not the sudden triumph of science over nature but instead simply part of the gradual redefinition of time in Victorian culture.[28]

Throughout the nineteenth century, the railways slowly increased the precision of their train arrival and departure times. When railroads first came to Philadelphia in the 1830s, trains almost always departed or arrived on the hour. Time was usually measured at intermediate stations in fifteen-minute increments: "quarter after," "half past," and "quarter of." This rough time division remained adequate through the early 1840s. By mid century, however, railroad timetables began to measure time to the minute; the train now left Philadelphia at "10:00 A.M." not "ten o'clock in the morning." This wave of increased accuracy not only affected the busy lines like the Philadelphia, Germantown and Norristown, which operated dozens of daily trains, but also smaller companies with few passenger services. Because the minor railroads adopted this change at about the same time as their busier counterparts, this new precision in time was motivated by both operating considerations (the need to fit more trains on the intensely worked lines) and cultural ones (the modernity of accurate time).[29]

As the nineteenth century came to a close, time on the major railroads became even more detailed and specific. Trains began to leave their main terminals at "odd" times: 10:49 rather than 10:45 or 10:50. The Philadelphia & Reading operated trains on its busiest commuter lines in the metropolis to the minute according to its schedules. That the Reading's actual timekeeping was often abysmal during this period seemed to have little effect on its employees who created the well-ordered world of the railway timetable. On the logical, precisely controlled pages of the timetable, trains were never late and they really did stop at Germantown at exactly 6:14 A.M.

The railroad timetable is one of the few places where the usually ephemeral nature of time is reduced to print, and it was there that the changing definition of time for middle-class Philadelphians becomes clear. The public timetable, that small booklet of schedules printed by the railroad for the use of its passengers, seems to have been a mid-century creation. Prior to the 1850s, travelers learned train times from posted notices, privately printed guides, and daily newspaper advertisements. These early sources gave very little information: usually only the departure time from Philadelphia and the train's estimated arrival at its final destination. Seldom were all intermediate stations listed, and often, when they were, no exact times were printed for the train. The Philadelphia & Trenton Railroad advertisement from 1834 shown in figure 16 is typical of these early announcements. The railroad-issued timetables at first only supplemented these other sources of information, but by the turn of the century most passengers relied on the timetables and made special trips to the downtown stations to acquire new ones when they were planning vacations. Leo Bernheimer was a timetable afficionado; one Friday he used a few to puzzle out when a group of visitors would be likely to arrive at his local station. The result: "After considerable study of the timetables, we decided to go to Oak Lane station to meet the 8.22 from Jenkintown" (which, in the best tradition of the Reading, "was a little late").[30]

Throughout the late nineteenth century, railroad timetables became more detailed and complex. In the 1870s they seldom gave more information than the arrival and departure times of trains at all stations along certain lines. In general, trains either made all stops and were labeled "accommodation" or only made the most important ones and were called "express." By the 1890s, however, the world of the railway traveler was much more complicated, and the timetables reflected this in their increased complexity. Not all "expresses" or "accommodations" stopped at the same stations or for the

PHILADELPHIA AND TRENTON RAIL ROAD.

THE Directors have the pleasure to announce to the public, that the Philadelphia and Trenton Rail Road is so far completed, as to admit of cars being run throughout the Line of the Road.

On and after Monday next, the 3d of November, two Lines of Cars will run daily between Philadelphia and Trenton, starting as follows:

From Philadelphia.

At 8 o'clock, A. M. with Locomotive.

Do. 2, P. M. with horses.

From Morrisville.

At 8 o'clock, A. M. with horses.

Do. 2 do. P. M. locomotive.

Arrangements have been made with Ann's Line of Omnibusses, to leave the Exchange in time to arrive at the Depot in Kensington at the hours of starting, passing up Walnut to 3d, up 3d to Chesnut, up Chesnut to the United States Hotel, down Chesnut to 3d, and up 3d to Kenshaw's Hotel, near Willow st. and from thence to the Depot, calling at all the principal public houses on the route.

Also, the Line from the Navy Yard to Kensington, passing up 2d st. Will call for passengers at the principal public houses on the route.

Fare to Bristol, 50 cents.

Do. to Trenton, 75 do.

The Omnibusses will take the passengers to and from the Depot free of charge.

For passages, for the present, apply at Heiskill's City Hotel, 3d st. above Market, and at Yoget's, in 3d near Arch st.   C. LOMBAERT, Agent.

re 30 d

Figure 16. Railroad time in the 1830s. Courtesy of the Newspaper Collection, Free Library of Philadelphia.

same reasons. Some trains called "only on signal or notice to Conductor" and others only to receive or to discharge passengers. Still other trains accepted special low-fare tickets or ran only on certain days of the week. The railroads explained all these details in increasingly long lists of footnotes and messages in their timetables. Many of these notes reflected the railways' early attempts at yield management, to better match the supply of seats with the demand. By century's end, timetables had become so detailed and difficult to read, that railroads produced "pocket schedules" for their busiest lines that left out most of the minutiae and listed only a handful of stops and the express trains on the route. The Pennsylvania, Philadelphia & Reading, and Baltimore & Ohio all had these abbreviated versions for their Philadelphia to New York services, for example, as did the Pennsylvania and the Reading for their frequent Atlantic City trains.[31]

Some railroad passengers never internalized this new precision in time. Poor John L. Smith kept missing trains because he never fully adapted to this new exactitude that began to develop when he was in his forties. Throughout the late nineteenth century, Smith continued to think of time in quarter-hour increments. For example, he recorded the following trip to a friend's house in the country one Sunday: "took 10 ½ train for his Farm at Upton Station it is a Beautiful Place . . . took 12 ¼ train Home." Smith was also not very good at keeping track of timetable changes. For both reasons, he often missed his intended train. Smith's temporal problems are particularly surprising because he was a mapmaker and was used to precision in space.[32]

Edwin Jellett did not have the same difficulties with railway time as did Smith. Jellett was nearly twenty years younger than Smith and had been raised in the Philadelphia of exact time. Jellett kept his watch in careful repair and noted train schedules to the minute. His diary was as precise (and often as dry) as a railroad timetable. A typical weekend entry read: "I went to town in the morning on the 6.24 train, to go to Schwenks for a week. Left Callowhill St. at 7.40, and got to Schwenksville at 9." If Jellett missed a train, it was seldom his fault.[33]

Between the extremes of Smith and Jellett lay the typical middle-class acquiescence to this late-Victorian redefinition of time. Men and women took trains and planned their daily lives around railroad schedules. Timetables effectively recorded the rhythms of bourgeois life. Middle-class Philadelphians accepted these changes with few complaints. In fact, railroad time became so important to middle-class Philadelphia that the lack of a clock at Reading Terminal in the mid-1890s could cause a minor crisis.[34]

Time and space changed in and around the major railroad terminals in downtown Philadelphia during the late nineteenth century. Both interior and exterior space increasingly became divided and classified. Time took on a new precision. Such transformations were not unique to the world of the railway traveler but reflected broader trends in middle-class society. The rhythms and rituals of bourgeois society became more rational—"scientific" to the Victorians—as the nineteenth century drew to a close. Within a few blocks of these central passenger depots could be found another middle-class commercial institution that manifested similar changes: the dry goods stores. The buildings of John Wanamaker and Strawbridge & Clothier became landmarks much like the train depots. The selling floors of these merchants were as rationally categorized as were interiors of the railroad stations. Like the railroads, the retailers also remade time in the form of the retail calendar. The dry goods stores offer yet more examples of bourgeois Philadelphia's love of rationality that permeated everyday life during the Victorian era.

Chapter 3
A Pretty Friendly Sort of Place

Just where it is—but filling only part of the space it now occupies—was the old Wanamaker building. Quite a curiosity, really. . . . It was a circular building, with the aisles and counters, coming like the spokes of a wheel toward the hub, or Rotunda. . . . It is my impression that following one or more of the aisles upstairs, one came to the Tea Room, a pretty friendly sort of place, where you could easily find your luncheon date, without beforehand designating a particular spot for her to stand or sit.[1]

The always observant Eugenia Barnitz was right; the John Wanamaker Grand Depot was certainly a curious-looking store in the late nineteenth century. Outside, wooden towers and false fronts gave it a carpenter's gothic look (figure 17), while inside, the arrangement of the counters in concentric circles surely made it distinctive (figure 18). Even the company's official historian, who managed never to admit that the firm made a mistake in its first fifty years of existence, described the interior as "bizarre to look upon" (although he quickly recovered his far more typical enthusiasm, concluding that "the old store had its undeniable *cachet* [and] there was nothing monotonous about the place"). Whether one liked its looks or not, it was an important structure. When John Wanamaker began offering dry goods in 1877 and effectively converted his clothing store into Philadelphia's first department store (in all but name, the term would not come into common use in the city until the early twentieth century), he led a commercial revolution that transformed everyday life in the city and the region. By 1901, as other retailers followed Wanamaker's lead, the expanded dry goods stores established themselves as important middle-class destinations in Center City.[2]

As with the transformations that affected the city's railroads and newspapers, these changes in retailing were not confined to Philadelphia. Throughout the United States and the Europeanized world, dry goods stores, clothing

Figure 17. Centennial annex: the exterior of John Wanamaker's Grand Depot in 1876. Courtesy of the Print and Picture Collection, Free Library of Philadelphia.

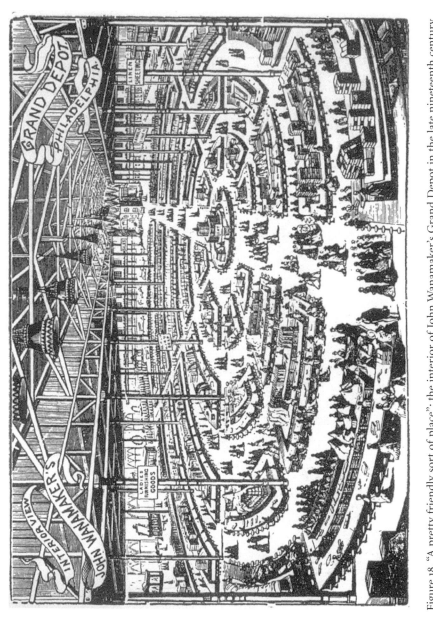

Figure 18. "A pretty friendly sort of place": the interior of John Wanamaker's Grand Depot in the late nineteenth century. Courtesy of the Print and Picture Collection, Free Library of Philadelphia.

shops, milliners, and drapers added lines of merchandise and enlarged their premises in the last few decades of the nineteenth century. These new "department stores" not only affected how and where goods were sold but they also reflected the Victorians' use of "science" as a trope to understand their world. The retailers were a central part of the new bourgeois definitions of space and time in the city. On a grand scale, the location of these large emporiums downtown helped to establish the central business district as the leading commercial zone in the metropolis. Equally important was what transpired inside the buildings, where the merchants quickly developed a detailed taxonomy of interior space for shoppers to buy their way through. Perhaps even more impressive than the retailers' mastery of exterior and interior geography was their control over time: they not only extended the selling day by using technology but they also created new buying rhythms for the year. By 1900, Philadelphia—in common with other large cities—no longer had just nature's four seasons but also Wanamaker's January White Sale, June Shoe Sale, and dozens of other annual retail "events."[3]

The creation of the modern department store in Victorian Philadelphia is a fascinating story, in part simply because it happened so quickly. In 1876 there was nothing like it in the city and all the retail dry goods houses were small (the larger dry goods concerns—like Hood, Bonbright & Company on Market Street—devoted most of their floor space to wholesale operations). Within a decade, the department store existed in fact, if not in name. In 1887, Strawbridge & Clothier, although still insisting it was a dry goods store, compared itself favorably with the already legendary Bon Marché of Paris. By the turn of the century, there were at least nine major department stores in Center City, and these establishments dominated retail sales in the metropolis. At that time, middle-class Philadelphians could look back with nostalgia to the dry goods stores of mid century. One man recalled that the old time shops were "located, like the Drug Stores + Groceries, chiefly at the corners [and] had a comfortable, home like look." He lamented that "The colossal establishments, now in full blast, with their heavy capital, extensive appliances + profuse advertising, have almost annihilated them." But despite these concerns, he and tens of thousands of other bourgeois men and women shopped at Wanamaker's and the other retailing leviathans on a regular basis. By the late nineteenth century, such visits helped to define the department stores as key nodes in the geography of the middle-class city.[4]

Philadelphia's great Victorian retailers—John Wanamaker, Justus Strawbridge, Isaac Clothier, Nathan Snellenburg, Isaac Gimbel, and their competitors throughout Center City—used a variety of means to lure customers to their sales floors in the late nineteenth century. On a truly monumental level they constructed buildings that altered the fabric of the city; structures that were an integral part of a new urban landscape that was being increasingly divided by class, gender, ethnicity, and race as the century progressed. On a far smaller—but as important—scale, they carefully designed the interiors, using technology and science to control both the environment and human behavior. The department stores were in the forefront of the creation of a largely bourgeois consumer market. The merchants had to convince middle-class Philadelphians that "cheap" meant "inexpensive" and not "poorly made". That they succeeded can be seen in the patterns of middle-class shopping during the late Victorian era. By far the most popular retail location for bourgeois men and women was the John Wanamaker store; at century's end its only serious rivals were the sales floors of Gimbel Brothers and Strawbridge & Clothier.[5]

Department stores used low, fixed prices on returnable, quality goods to attract middle-class shoppers. The firms could lower prices for a variety of reasons: initially they sold for cash not credit, they stressed volume sales, and they usually purchased in large quantities directly from the manufacturers. John L. Smith shopped at department stores because of the low prices; for example, he went to Wanamaker's one day in 1877 but failed to buy anything because he saw "nothing Cheap I wanted." The liberal return policy helped convince more than one reluctant member of the bourgeoisie to part with his or her money. Susan R. MacManus of West Philadelphia, for example, could purchase a shirt for her husband, confident that she could return it for a full refund if he did not like it. Part of the rhythm of middle-class shopping in the late nineteenth century was buying a few items, examining them at home, and returning the less-pleasing ones. Sometimes this cadence was formally recognized by the stores; Leo Bernheimer and his father once had a selection of suits sent home "on approval." At other times, customers effectively created their own approval policy. MacManus recorded this not atypical series of transactions at Wanamaker's in 1880: "Bot three more pair drawers for May returning the too large apron, + got a large brown straw hat, returning the small felt."[6]

Besides low prices on returnable goods, the major retailers offered a variety of services to entice middle-class men and women into their department stores. As early as 1876, when the Grand Depot was still only a men's and boy's clothing store (albeit the largest retail establishment in the city), Wanamaker supplied both a waiting room with "newspapers and magazines" for the "convenience of ladies and gentlemen accompanying persons making purchases" and an office where customers could "get information about railroad trains, places of interest, etc., and can leave any packages for safekeeping." By the 1880s, the largest Philadelphia dry goods stores offered a vast array of services to the public: package delivery, elaborate waiting and toilet rooms, telephone and telegraph facilities, and bureaus of information. Customers could shop all day and have their purchases sent from each department to a central office for either later pickup or free home delivery. In 1883, Wanamaker added a restaurant to the Grand Depot. His competitors soon followed; Gimbel Brothers, for example, urged their middle-class patrons who were in the city for pleasure or business during the summer to "breakfast here when your home is closed." Leo Bernheimer and his mother regularly met for lunch at Wanamaker's in the 1890s. By 1900, both Wanamaker's and Gimbels' stores contained branch post offices. Shoppers could spend an entire day within a single dry goods store.[7]

Beyond these services that the retailers offered on a daily basis, they created many special events that featured music, art, history, science, public service, and other staples of bourgeois existence to lure middle-class women and men to the stores. One retired businessman recalled spending part of an enjoyable afternoon at Wanamaker's in 1887 in "a small room surrounded with [a] looking glass [that] multiplies people ad infinitum—8 persons were in and it looked like a vast room crowded with people. . . . It is a most amusing and deceptive place." In 1891, Leo Bernheimer went to Wanamaker's with some friends to see an industrial display. May and Helen Smith from West Philadelphia went to the store in 1894 to enjoy a flower show. Other early examples from Wanamaker's include a celebration of the centennial of the adoption of the Constitution, an elaborate parade in honor of a Pan-American Congress meeting in Philadelphia, and a display of art from Paris.[8]

The merchants also constructed attractive and interesting buildings in order to lure shoppers to the selling space within. In 1876, Wanamaker remade the bland exterior of an old freight depot by adding towers, turrets, and false fronts. The store was gaudy and exciting, much like the structures of the Centennial Exposition a few miles to the west in Fairmount Park. The firm's official historian made this link explicit when he wrote that "during the summer [the Grand Depot] was a sort of Centennial 'annex.' " Although none of the Philadelphia department stores of this period achieved the grandeur of A. T. Stewart's "marble palace" in antebellum New York, Strawbridge & Clothier probably came the closest. By the 1890s, all the major merchants had built substantial structures in Center City.[9]

The buildings were not only middle-class areas in the city but they were also largely female spaces. Although bourgeois men shopped at the department stores, most of the customers were women. The exact sex ratio probably varied greatly among the stores. Wanamaker's, for example, had a large men's clothing selection (this is not surprising as it was the only major dry goods house in Philadelphia that had begun as a men's store), and many middle-class males shopped at the store. A very common experience would be for a bourgeois father to take his teenage son to the store for a suit. Marks Brothers, on the other hand, may have been more typical; it was founded as a millinery shop and had become a full-service department store by 1900. In that year, the firm estimated that "85 per cent. of the business of a department store is done by women" and declared that its "new store [then under construction] will be above all a 'women's store.' " Marks Brothers' competitors in Philadelphia all attempted to capture this large female market and helped make their stores female, middle-class space in the metropolis.[10]

Finally, the religious and racial composition of the clientele varied among the department stores. Although there is insufficient evidence to come to firm conclusions, some broad trends are evident. First, John Wanamaker and Strawbridge & Clothier attracted customers from across the middle-class spectrum in Philadelphia. Their patrons, although overwhelmingly Protestant and white (as were the members of Philadelphia's bourgeoisie), included Catholics, Jews, and African Americans. None of the other retailers had so diverse a clientele. Many of the customers of Lit Brothers and N. Snellenburg, for example, were Jewish in this period.[11]

The merchants divided this largely female, mainly middle-class terrain into well-defined areas from the beginning. First with selling counters and later with formal departments, the stores developed an increasingly precise taxonomy of space as the nineteenth century progressed. As with the design of the railroad stations, this detailed, logical interior layout preceded the physical expansion of the stores in the 1880s and 1890s. A good example is the small ground floor plan of Strawbridge & Clothier shown in figure 19. Occupying just three shop fronts (801, 803, and 805 Market Street), the establishment was only slightly larger than a typical store in the city, but its interior consisted of a series of carefully defined counters. Unlike the often jumbled layout of the general retailers of the antebellum period, Strawbridge & Clothier left little to chance in the design of selling counters of the store.[12]

Most of the department stores built or acquired structures with open floor plans that allowed the merchants a great deal of latitude in interior

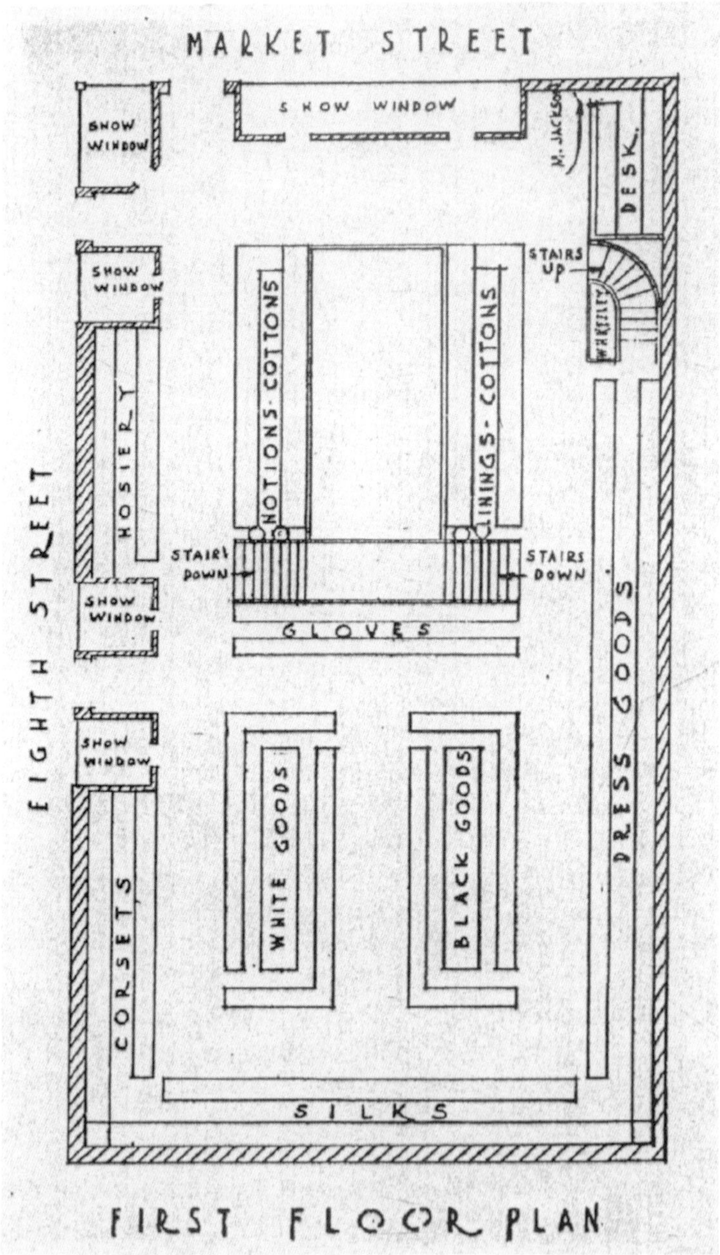

Figure 19. Main selling floor of Strawbridge & Clothier in 1876. Courtesy of the Hagley Museum and Library.

design (and redesign, for the merchants were constantly rearranging their sales space). John Wanamaker's purchase of an old freight station from the Pennsylvania Railroad in 1875 gave him a massive (for the time) empty stage that he could fill with various retail sets. As Strawbridge & Clothier slowly expanded throughout the 1880s and 1890s by purchasing adjoining shops, they usually broke through the walls to produce large, unobstructed spaces. One of the most striking examples of this "blank slate" approach to interior design can be found on the architectural drawings for the store that Gimbel Brothers bought in 1894 but was built in 1890 for another firm. Although the structure occupied the place of six shops on Market Street (828 to 838), the sales floors contained no interior partitions.[13]

The department stores employed new technologies to dramatically expand the size of their buildings. At Wanamaker's, for example, the selling space expanded from less than three acres in 1877 to five acres in 1880 to eight in 1883 to fifteen in 1889 to eighteen in 1899. The merchants used electric lights (first arc and later incandescent) to add additional sales space and to lengthen the retail day. They also added elevators to their stores, permitting customers equal access to more floors and pneumatic tubes to speed money from the sales floor to the cashiers. Force-air ventilation not only allowed the stores to grow in size (by making the basement a selling floor) but also helped make them more tolerable in the heat of a Philadelphia summer.[14]

Equally important, the department stores used these same technologies as spectacles of sophistication and modernity to attract middle-class customers. The store guidebooks during the late nineteenth century emphasized the modernity of the physical plant in both text and illustrations. Innovations, such as electric lights and pneumatic tubes, were part of the excitement of the department store. Like many great merchandisers, John Wanamaker was a showman in the mold of P. T. Barnum. One striking example occurred following Wanamaker's acquisition of the remaining stores on the block, when he held a "grand illumination" on November 11, 1878. That night, he lit the interior and exterior of the building with "myriads of gas-lamps and numerous reflectors" and allowed Philadelphians to walk through the store until ten in the evening. With a band playing and the staff available to answer questions, potential customers could look at the new merchandise for Christmas but could not purchase any items. Thousands of women and men took advantage of the free entertainment that night and visited the store.[15]

The Philadelphia merchants used a variety of techniques to encourage people to walk through their stores. Wanamaker, for example, designed the main floor of the Grand Depot in a circular pattern and always placed something of interest in the center. In the 1880s and 1890s, the elaborate network of pneumatic tubes all converged there to form a quite impressive show of technology. This circular layout also reflected the difficult problem of bringing shoppers into a space that had entrances on all four sides. Strawbridge & Clothier and Gimbel Brothers, on the other hand, occupied corner sites with entrances on but two sides. Both drew customers through the main floor selling departments by placing the elevators and stairs in the rear of the store, away from the main doors. Merchants also placed impulse and gift items on the main floor and reserved the upper floors and the basement for departments (like furniture) and services (such as the restaurant) that were likely to be a shopper's destination.[16]

Philadelphia stores not only expanded in size during this period but also regularly refined their interior layout. The number of departments at Wanamaker's, for example, increased from sixteen in 1877 to forty-six in 1883 to fifty-three in 1889 to fifty-five in 1899. The departments multiplied not just because the stores added new lines of merchandise but also because the retailers often revised and reconfigured their floor plans based on sales. As the department stores generated increasingly precise sales statistics during the late nineteenth century, merchants used this information to reallocate resources, including floor space. At the heart of what John Wanamaker called the "science of merchandising" were the accurate statistics. Thus, this growth in the number and type of departments can be seen as both a reflection and reinforcement of the Victorian cultural belief in order. Inspired by increasingly detailed statistics and rational sales strategies, retailers refined their taxonomy of space to make it more precise and hence more "scientific." To use the great dichotomy of the Victorian middle class, merchandising had ceased to be an art and became a science.[17]

By following a typical customer through a store, we can better understand the shopping rituals of middle-class Philadelphians. On December 22, 1887, Edwin Jellett of Germantown took the train into Center City after work to do some last-minute Christmas shopping at Wanamaker's. He walked from Broad Street Station and entered the store on Juniper Street a little after six o'clock. His first stop was the book department, located directly across the floor from where he entered. To arrive there, he had to weave his way through the crowds in the intervening departments, passing counters that sold stationery, underwear, women's accessories, soaps, perfumes, trimmings, and notions (many of which qualified as impulse items). After completing his purchases in the book department (at the time the largest in

America), he walked upstairs to buy a vase for his mother. Arriving on the second floor in the furniture department, he walked through silverware to china and glass (all departments that a shopper would seek out). There he found his gift, purchased it, and then took the grand staircase in the center of the store back down to the ground floor. Walking toward the Juniper Street exit, he stopped in the stationery department to purchase a few cards. It was now eight o'clock, and Jellett decided to catch the 8:16 train home.[18]

Jellett was a regular shopper at Wanamaker's, so he likely found all three departments he stopped in that day with relative ease. But the sheer number of store guides and the frequent signs announcing the locations of various departments indicate that the rational interior layouts created by the merchants may not have always been easy for the occasional customer to navigate. At Wanamaker's in 1891, for example, in the same room on the second floor with baby clothing was (logically) children's clothing and (perhaps not so logically) women's jackets. At the same time, Wanamaker placed baby carriages in the basement with toys. Sometimes the store divided space by gender: most men's clothing was located in the northeast corner of the main floor. At other times, Wanamaker arranged the departments by product type: all shoes—men's, women's, and children's—could be found together on the same floor.[19]

On one level, the dry goods merchants arranged and rearranged their interior layouts to maximize sales. They were in business to make money by selling merchandise to mostly middle-class shoppers and they worked very hard to develop effective selling machines. At the same time, the floor plans can also be seen as detailed taxonomies of space that were an important part of bourgeois Philadelphia's cityscape. In part what drove the merchants to define space with increasing precision was the same cultural source for order that motivated their counterparts at the railroads and the newspapers. The interiors were clear reflections of bourgeois values and the popularity of the department stores among middle-class women and men helps to locate this cultural impetus for order firmly within that group.

Retailers not only remade space in Victorian Philadelphia, they also created a more rationalized, organized system of time. Electric lights allowed the merchants to rearrange the interior layouts of their buildings and also permitted Wanamaker and others to extend the retail day. Philadelphia retailers changed not only daily shopping rhythms but annual ones as well. Once, merchants had reacted to the seasons: they offered heavier clothes in the fall and winter, lighter in the spring and summer. Starting in the late nineteenth century, the large dry goods stores began to redefine the seasons by creating annual sales events. The January White Sale quickly became a yearly tradition; as much a part of middle-class life in the city as spring walks in Fairmount Park. As the electric light allowed Philadelphians to wrest control of the day from nature, so too did these special sales permit retailers to gain some control over the calendar.

First with gas lights, and then with brighter and safer electric ones, Wanamaker transformed the retail day in Philadelphia, and eventually most (but never all) of his main department store competitors extended their selling hours until late into the night during the busy holiday season. Quickly middle-class men and women took for granted these extended hours. By 1900, every major department store in the city (except Strawbridge & Clothier) stayed open until ten in the evening during the weeks before Christmas. That year, John Wanamaker began the evening hours by keeping just the jewelry and clock departments open late beginning Monday, December 10. Starting Saturday of the same week, the entire store remained open until ten, and Gimbels and Lits both extended their hours the same day. Partridge & Richardson joined the rush of late-night retail sales the following week.[20]

Strawbridge & Clothier's refusal to extend the retail day—although it possessed all the technology to do so—is an intriguing anomaly that helps to highlight the cultural drive behind these changes. The store had both a large generating plant and an impressive array of electric lights and featured both as examples of modernity in its store guides. But Strawbridge & Clothier was also proud of its paternalistic relationship with its employees. When all its main competitors announced their extended hours, Strawbridge & Clothier advertised that "No matter how great the pressure on business, these stores will remain open no later than 6.30 P.M." So neither technology nor economics could sway this firm's often conservative and always paternal policies then.[21]

Although this use of technology by the department stores to change the day was impressive, it paled in comparison to the same firms' mastery over the calendar. By the 1870s, retailers found themselves with an annual sales peak in December. (It was, of course, a spike that they had helped to create.) They spent the remainder of the nineteenth century trying to nurture other selling seasons to help balance out this peak so that the firms could better use their space and their employees. At first, stores advertised seasonal items and special purchases: "one hundred and fifty styles of new spring dress goods" in late March and "a remarkable offering" of "French printed Organdy lawns at half the original price" are typical examples from the 1880s and mid 1890s. But by the late 1890s the large dry goods stores began to create major events that took place on a regular basis. Initially these special sales had some relationship to nature's calendar (for example, Wanamaker began holding spring and fall French fashion shows in 1893), but eventually these events developed an annual rhythm all their own. By 1898, Gimbel Brothers began the new year with a series of otherwise unconnected sales that it called "Gimbels' January Sales." From underwear and furniture to carpets and silks, Gimbels declared that "January is a season of great opportunities here. All over the store there is a general movement of merchandise—either new goods, that have their opening sales during this month, or a sweeping clearance of tardy sellers or broken lines to make room for new spring stock."[22]

This new retail calendar was largely in place by 1900 at most major department stores, which makes it a particularly good one to examine in depth. The after-Christmas linens sale came to Philadelphia on Thursday, December 28, 1899, when John Wanamaker started "selling a million dollars' worth of White Goods at third to half less than usual prices." It continued through January and in its advertising Wanamaker made it clear that this was a special event. The store claimed that it had "spent almost a year . . . getting . . . ready" for the sale and it had "put extra selling places almost everywhere." Material abundance was a selling point in itself.[23]

The other stores quickly reacted to Wanamaker's white sale. By early January, Strawbridge & Clothier, Partridge & Richardson, and Gimbel Brothers all had their own linen sales. By 1900, January in Philadelphia was the month of after-Christmas clearances and white sales at all the dry goods emporia. For the retailers, these sales served two business purposes, to clear out old stock so that it did not have to be inventoried and to keep the sales force fully employed after the Christmas rush.[24]

Spring clothing, hopelessly early for Philadelphia's climate, came in February along with a more creative "tradition": the February furniture sale. Clothing specials probably represented something of a necessity, as the merchandise was beginning to arrive from the manufacturers and there would be little demand for winter fashions by then, but the attempt to institutionalize scheduled furniture events clearly demonstrates the creation of a retail calendar based on the desire for more regularized sales patterns. After all, very few items of furniture are seasonal in nature. More likely, the merchants placed a furniture sale in a slow sales month in order to allow the stores to focus on a capital intensive area when they had little investment tied up in clothing and seasonal gifts.[25]

The summer was the slowest selling season for Philadelphia stores because the city's hot and humid weather inspired members of the middle class to emulate the elite's habit of escaping the metropolis for as long as possible. Although middle-class Philadelphians could not spend the entire season in Maine or Canada, they could afford a few weeks in the cooler portions of the region, such as the mountains or the shore. Retailers responded to this downturn in business in a variety of ways, from keeping fewer employees to early closings. They also created several summer sales events, such as summer shoe sales. So that the public would not mistake their sale for an everyday clearance, Gimbel Brothers boldly announced its "First Annual Shoe Sale" in June while Wanamaker's reminded its customers of the simple equation "June = Shoe Sales." Partridge & Richardson held its first annual shoe sale the next month and conservative Strawbridge & Clothier, showing a little less willingness to create traditions, simply advertised shoes on sale throughout the summer.[26]

Although there was no consensus on the other summer sale items, John Wanamaker and Gimbel Brothers, the two largest stores in the city, followed similar programs. Gimbels, for example, decided that July was a good month for another white sale as well as a notions sale. Wanamaker declared a "Half-Yearly Carpet Sale" during the same month. Both stores then countered the other's programs, and both determined that August, like that other quiet month of February, was a good time for a furniture sale.[27]

Elite and middle-class Philadelphians returned to the city slowly throughout September and found a variety of events to entice them back to the dry goods stores. Other than a barrage of fall clothing openings at most of the major retailers, however, there was no consensus among them on what items to promote in September. Joseph G. Darlington ran clearance sales. Gimbels felt that September was a good month to move china and school supplies. Strawbridge & Clothier focused on school supplies and children's clothing. The ever-creative John Wanamaker sold "everything for the house and family" in its "Autumn Replenishing Sale." Although it was unlikely that most of Wanamaker's largely middle-class clientele had been away from their homes for so long that the structures needed "replenishing," the sale's title was a clear link with elite habits that the bourgeoisie could appreciate.[28]

Retailers tried very hard to convince middle-class women and men to start shopping for Christmas early in order to lessen the inevitable (by 1900) crush in late December. The holiday season began in 1900 on November 3 when Wanamaker opened its toy department, "a fairy land of joy and delight." A little over a week later, the store opened its "Swiss Village" display to further increase traffic. Gimbel Brothers was a few weeks behind when they opened their toy land the Saturday before Thanksgiving.[29]

Christmas sales began in earnest around Thanksgiving when all the stores began to advertise gift ideas and special events with more frequency. Merchants also began to instruct their customers on ways to avoid the seasonal rush. Not surprisingly, their main advice was to shop as soon as possible. In the polite words of Joseph Darlington (a store that the ever-observant Eugenia Barnitz once described as "elite and exclusive"), buy early "as the assortments and stocks are now complete and crowds and disappointments, sure to be met with later, will be avoided." John Wanamaker—befitting its more plebeian position in the retailing pantheon—was a bit more direct: "*Early in the season,* and *early or quite late in the day*—that's the time to do Christmas shopping."[30]

By the second week in December, every department store had opened its Christmas displays and toy lands. A "real live Santa Claus" had arrived at Wanamaker's (replacing a chocolate one that had been there for a few weeks). It was now too late to shop early and the retailers' advertisements highlighted their abilities to handle large crowds. Gimbel Brothers—"The Christmas Store"—reminded reticent shoppers that it had spent four months of planning to create an "orderly, convenient, roomy" store. Finally, all the major firms (except, of course, Strawbridge & Clothier) extended their hours at the start of the following week. Christmas shopping was officially in full swing.[31]

By the week before Christmas, the merchants had given up their attempts to control the calendar. The stores could not make the day any longer, and their advertisements simply warned of crowds and urged patience. John Wanamaker went so far as to request a "favor" of its customers: "*carry small packages*" home to lessen "the strain upon our much-increased delivery force." Shoppers confirm this last-minute crush. In 1888, one potential customer wrote to a friend that she had visited Wanamaker's just before the holiday "to see all the wonderful things they have for Christmas but it was so crowded I could hardly see any thing." A few years later, a woman from the city's hinterland commented, "The city streets and stores were crowded with people, making it quite difficult at times getting around." Even with the most rational retail calendar and the most organized stores, retailers could not stem the chaos of the Christmas season at its peak.[32]

In 1900, the Philadelphia department stores all closed by seven on Christmas Eve, but there was little time to rest, as the retail year quickly began anew. Two days after Christmas, John Wanamaker announced in an artistic advertisement its "Annual Sale of White." Gimbel Brothers responded the next day with the "Biggest Showing of White Goods Any Store Ever

Made." After the Christmas rush, the merchants were probably glad to be able to exercise some control over the calendar again.[33]

During the late nineteenth century, the department stores used technology and planning to extend the day and to remake the calendar. And while they created some creatures that they could not fully control, such as the Christmas season, merchants invented other events, such as the White Sale, that became successful institutions that helped them more evenly distribute the sales volume throughout the year. Other attempts at "annual" events disappeared after a try or two. All such attempts at controlling retail time and space point toward a concerted effort on the behalf of merchants to create an ordered and orderly shopping experience, and all became part of the daily and annual rituals of middle-class Philadelphia.

Along with trains and streetcars, department stores were at the heart of bourgeois commercial culture in the city. To reach their customers, department stores increasingly relied upon another middle-class institution—the daily newspaper. And like the department stores, Philadelphia's newspapers also became more ordered and rational in the late nineteenth century. To discover this order and rationality, we must go beyond the words of the journalists and consider the newspaper as a material artifact that sheds light on the broader cultural impulses of the time.

Chapter 4
A Sober Paper

June 9, 1894: The following cuttings are from the Daily Evening Telegraph *of Philadelphia, a sober paper which I have been in the habit of occasionally reading for years.*[1]

Many Philadelphians would have agreed with Albert J. Edmunds, the librarian at the Historical Society of Pennsylvania, that *The Evening Telegraph* was a very sober paper. It, the *Public Ledger*, *The Press*, and *The Times* were all examples of the genteel metropolitan press, yet another urban, largely middle-class institution then developing. The story of the newspaper industry in Victorian Philadelphia is a complex one. Like the department stores, no journal was ever exclusively patronized by the middle class. With the days of the "penny press" long gone, however, high prices largely restricted daily newspaper readership to the bourgeoisie and above until the late 1880s. Then prices fell and readership soared. In this booming market, certain journals—such as *The Evening Telegraph*—actively courted middle-class women and men through both increasingly rational layout and more sober content. In this way, the newspapers that comprised the genteel metropolitan press became, in effect, a distinctively middle-class space in the city.[2]

Like railroads and dry goods stores, newspapers in Philadelphia changed dramatically in the late nineteenth century. Publishers built structures to house their publications that became civic landmarks and helped redefine Center City (see figure 20 for a wonderful advertisement for *The Times* that highlights its building). Editors created and then refined a taxonomy of news on the pages of their journals. The newspaper as a physical space became as organized and classified as the bourgeois city. But before we can explore the daily newspaper as an artifact—the layout of its pages as a significant

Figure 20. The newspaper as urban space: a *Philadelphia Times* advertisement. Courtesy of the Print and Picture Collection, Free Library of Philadelphia.

component of urban geography—we must explore the complex relationships between Philadelphia's middle class and the city's daily press.

During the late nineteenth century, the daily newspaper developed into a quintessentially urban and largely middle-class institution. The press entered into the rituals of everyday bourgeois life in Philadelphia in a myriad of ways. Men and women, of course, obtained their news and entertainment from its pages. The legion of news boys (and girls) helped make street life a noisy and exciting part of the urban experience. The newsstands at train stations added to the importance of these already busy nodes. By announcing breaking news at their offices, the press made the newspaper district a vibrant part of the city's fabric. And by building increasingly large and impressive structures to house their enterprises, publishers added to the civic grandeur of Center City.

Naturally enough, most studies of Victorian newspapers have focused on words and pictures: the content of the articles. The words did matter; they contributed to Edmunds' perception that *The Evening Telegraph* was "a sober paper." But like railroad timetables, newspapers are also material artifacts that shed light on larger cultural patterns. By studying the design and layout of the pages of Philadelphia's journals, we can discover an often overlooked element of urban geography. Between 1876 and 1901, editors divided the pages of the *Public Ledger* and those of its competitors into clearly demarcated departments, in much the same manner (and for the same reasons) as John Wanamaker and other merchants divided their stores (and their advertisements in the very same papers). The press was yet another example of the application of rationality to the urban environment by the Victorian middle class. Much like the internet today, the Victorian newspaper was an exemplar of a communications revolution in which man and technology shrank the world both physically and temporally. Thanks to the electric telegraph and the steam printing press, news from Europe could appear on the streets of Philadelphia within hours of when the event took place. And thanks to the design conventions first adopted by Victorian editors, readers could quickly find the relevant news on the pages of their journal.[3]

Both contemporary observers and subsequent scholars looking at Victorian newspapers in the United States have subdivided the universe into two types: yellow journalism or "journalism as entertainment" and the serious press or "journalism as information." This division—although well established in the history of American journalism—is of little use when studying Philadelphia's newspapers, as few editors fully adopted the yellow journalism of Joseph Pulitzer and William Randolph Hearst. Instead of a clear dichotomy as evidently existed in New York, Philadelphia newspapers can be more easily placed in a spectrum that tended toward "journalism as information."[4]

More importantly, in late nineteenth-century Philadelphia certain newspapers developed a special relationship with the middle class. As in other social aspects of late nineteenth-century America, such as department stores and residential neighborhoods, social class became an increasingly important determinate of spatial use. These daily papers that became, effectively, bourgeois space in the city can be termed the "genteel metropolitan press." When looking at these journals, however, one must remember that all newspapers in Philadelphia had a substantial middle-class readership. Particularly prior to the price decreases of the 1880s and 1890s, most papers were simply too expensive to be purchased by many working-class Philadelphians on a regular basis. Some newspapers, however, were more bourgeois than others. In the late nineteenth century, middle-class Philadelphians began to develop particular affinities for certain newspapers. At its peak, these bourgeois journals consisted of but four titles: *The Times*, the *Public Ledger*, *The Press*, and Edmunds' "sober" *Evening Telegraph*.[5]

The editors of all four of these journals not only placed their offerings squarely at the "journalism as information" end of the spectrum but also actively marketed the respectability of their papers. George W. Childs, editor of the *Public Ledger*, by far the most bourgeois and "genteel" of the genteel metropolitan press, described his aim for the paper as "to make it fit for the purest home and welcome to all honest society—a journal that, while furnishing the intelligence of the world, excludes what is demoralizing and useless. . . ." The other three examples of the genteel metropolitan press adopted similar standards—not just accuracy but also respectability—and succeeded in creating special bonds with the men and women of the middle class.[6]

What of the remaining newspapers in Victorian Philadelphia? They can be termed the "general circulation press" as they less actively—and less successfully—courted middle-class readers. Most combined "entertainment" with "information" (although with few exceptions—such as the *Item*—were much closer to the information end of the spectrum than their New York contemporaries) and were much less self-consciously conservative and respectable than the *Public Ledger*.[7]

Reading a specific newspaper can be both a habit and a statement. Most middle-class Philadelphians consistently purchased the same titles over long periods of time. For some people, the act of dropping one paper for another was so important an event that they noted it in their diary. For example, Chalkley Matlack, a teacher-turned-farmer, recorded one day that "I also subscribed for the 'Public Ledger' daily for a year, having rather tired of 'The Press' which we have had for two years." A number of factors could motivate the initial choice; the genteel metropolitan press, for example, had a middle-class cache. Part of this was tone, as was noted by Albert J. Edmunds, the librarian at the Historical Society of Pennsylvania. The style of the headline could change the presentation of the news; general circulation papers like the *Philadelphia Evening Item* often had much more emphatic front pages than bourgeois ones like the *Press* for essentially the same story. The *Public Ledger* in the late nineteenth century was deliberately conservative in news presentation. The political affiliation of the reader also made a difference; *The Philadelphia Record* was the only major Democratic journal published in the city throughout most of this period and most middle-class Democrats bought it (not all *Record* readers, however, were Democrats). Convenience was another factor in the decision; William Hemsing bought *The Sunday Press* because it was the first paper to reach Souderton in the morning. The first two reasons for choosing a specific journal also illustrate why reading a particular title could also be a statement: choosing a genteel metropolitan newspaper over *The Philadelphia Evening Item* identified one as middle class and selecting *The Philadelphia Record* over the pre-1899 *North American* told the world that you were not a machine Republican in a city notorious for its political corruption.[8]

Like the railroad stations and the department stores, the buildings that housed Philadelphia's newspapers became important civic landmarks in the late nineteenth century. The major journals built structures that were among the city's first skyscrapers. Both Philadelphians and visitors marveled at the size and complexity of these buildings and the equipment they contained. The newspapers—like the department stores—used technology as a draw; electricity (for the telegraph, the telephone, and lighting) and steam (for the printing presses) made the buildings into technological marvels in the heart of the thoroughly modern city.

The Philadelphia Record gave a complete "tour" of its building every year in its almanac that highlighted its modernity in much the same way as department store guides focused on the retailers' abundance of technology. Readers discovered that the press room contained "four of Hoe's latest perfecting presses, the most magnificent printing machines in use anywhere." This quartet of presses could print, fold, and collate two thousand copies of the eight-page paper per minute. The Record building was lit throughout by "three hundred and seventy-two Edison electric incandescent lamps" that created a "flood of light" (although interior views show that many fixtures were also fitted for gas, to protect against failures in the new technology). *The Record* was not the only journalistic showpiece in the city; a few blocks away stood "the splendid brown-stone building of the *Public Ledger*," which one guidebook to the city described as "one of the most perfectly appointed newspaper offices in the world."[9]

After lauding the *Ledger*, the guidebook goes on to note that *The Day*, *The Evening Bulletin*, *The Press*, and *The Times* had their offices nearby. By the late nineteenth century, all of Philadelphia's newspapers could be found clustered in a relatively small area of Center City. *The Evening Bulletin*, *The Evening Telegraph*, *The North American*, *The Philadelphia Record*, *The Press*, *Public Ledger*, and *The Times* had their offices on Chestnut Street between Sixth and Ninth. Even the exceptions did not stray far from Philadelphia's version of Fleet Street: *The Philadelphia Inquirer*'s building was on Market Street between Eleventh and Twelfth and *The Call*, *The Daily News* and *The Philadelphia Evening Item* all had offices on Seventh Street between Market and Chestnut. There were both technological and social reasons for this cluster: the papers wanted to be near the telegraph company (for wire service news), the business and legal district (for local news), and the railroad stations (for distribution).[10]

Newspaper publishers were not the only Victorian Philadelphians to place their businesses in close proximity. The development of a recognizable newspaper district in the city paralleled similar groupings in other industries and represents a new way in conceptualizing the urban environment. Before Philadelphia formally adopted planning or zoning, the city was moving to a rational land use plan in which specialized spaces became increasingly common. Like the department store zone, the newspaper district was so much a part of the Victorian middle-class city that its nickname ("Chestnut Street") regularly appeared on the pages of diaries kept by the women and the men of the bourgeoisie.[11]

Middle-class Philadelphians often came to "Chestnut Street" to obtain the latest news, and the major papers realized the value of giving away some of their stories in order to increase circulation. Initially, the journals would post breaking news on boards outside their offices. In late July 1877, John L. Smith regularly purchased multiple newspapers to keep up with a major railroad strike, but he also noted "crowds of People Scanning the Bulletin Boards for the latest news." As the violence subsided, Smith recorded "Not So

Much Excitement today, but Great many people on the Street, at news Boards—+ Papers sell brisk." Before radio and television, people frequented the area whenever they wanted the latest news. First with election results and later with sports scores, most journals developed ways to "broadcast" news to crowds outside their buildings. In 1881, Robert Hinch, a huckster, went to Chestnut Street to learn the latest vote count. In 1888, Edwin Jellett "went down [to] Chestnut St. to . . . watch the [Republican presidential] convention Bulletins." Later that same year, Howard Edwards described the mob scene on the day of the general election: "The excitement was unbounded. Chestnut St. near the newspaper offices was densely crowded, making travel almost impossible. . . . At the south west corner of Eight + Chestnut the '*Times*' had the day before suspended a large sheet across the street on which were thrown the various votes as announced by telegraph."[12]

The passion shown by male bourgeois Philadelphians toward elections in the 1880s within a decade had largely shifted toward sports, both professional baseball and college football, and the newspapers became more sophisticated in disseminating their teasers. In addition to the bulletin boards, the journals mounted scoreboards on the facades of Center City buildings that updated not just the scores but even the plays in "real time" thanks to the telegraph. Leo Bernheimer, then a law student at the University of Pennsylvania, regularly joined the crowds to watch the Quakers defeat gridiron rivals in the late 1890s. For one game, he followed the scores outside the "Press, Ledger and Inquirer offices" and judged "the latter . . . the quickest." By giving away part of the news, the papers not only increased sales (after all, you had to buy the newspaper to savor all the details) but also cemented their reputations for speed and accuracy.[13]

This newspaper zone, like other public spaces in the late nineteenth-century city, was never exclusively middle class. In the hustle and bustle of the crowds, there were surely members of the numerically superior working classes. The newspaper district may have been multi-classed in fact but was a part of middle-class city for many members of the bourgeoisie. Smith, Jellett, Bernheimer, and the others could come and go along the bourgeois corridors and never leave their imagined middle-class city.

But not everyone came to Chestnut Street to get their news, as most bourgeois women and men relied on the dependable and elaborate distribution systems developed by Philadelphia's newspapers in the Victorian period. More people were involved in the distribution of a journal than in its production. In 1885 *The Record* employed 271 men and women in production and 344 in distribution, "exclusive of newsboys." This exclusion probably accounted for at least another hundred people. A middle-class Philadelphian could get his or her paper delivered directly to their home or buy them as needed from a number of sources, the two most significant of which were "newsboys" (who, despite the title, could also be female) and newsstands.[14]

Many bourgeois Philadelphians subscribed to their favorite papers. John Cecil Holm's father did so in West Philadelphia, as did Chalkley Matlack in suburban New Jersey, the Hemsings in outlying Pennsylvania, and Edwin Lehman in West Philadelphia. The *Public Ledger* was particularly proud that a vast majority of its circulation came through subscriptions. It reprinted (without comment) a claim made by *The New York Times* that "nearly the entire circulation of the *Ledger*—amounting to ninety thousand copies daily—is delivered by carriers at the houses of regular subscribers." Home delivery was a reliable way to get your daily dose of news and many middle-class Philadelphians received at least some of their journals in this manner.[15]

Perhaps the most evocative way to buy a newspaper in this period, however, was from a news boy or girl; it was a distinctive part of the urban experience. A guidebook to the city in 1887 gives an idea of their quantity and function: "The army of newsboys numbers about 600, who may be said to give their entire time to the sale of papers, but the number varies very much. Several morning papers sell 5000 to 8000 each, daily by the boys." But this brief description misses the sights and sounds that the news boys and girls added to the city. They tended to congregate at certain key locations so, for example, when John L. Smith was making his way through Reading Terminal he might run into a dozen of them between the front door and the train gates. On the streets of Center City and in the neighborhoods the cries of the news boys and girls selling their papers were part of the urban symphony. The curmudgeon Howard Edwards remembered "when there was not a *Sunday Newspaper* issued in Philadelphia + when they eventually made their appearance, for a long time they were not cried by the news boys in the Streets. At last, this innovation commenced. . . . At the present time, the streets resound with the cries of 'Philadelphia + New York Sunday Papers.' " Their oft exaggerated claims of major news, in order to sell more papers on a slow day, was, quite literally, the stuff of fiction. And although they had a reputation for dishonesty, the news boys and girls could also be cheated by purchasers in the often quick transactions. For example, Leo Bernheimer, then a student living in North Philadelphia, felt guilty about "giving the boy one cent instead of two, by mistake" for *The Press* and he declared that night to his diary that "I am still his debtor by the other cent."[16]

While the news boys and girls offered convenience—they brought the news and entertainment to you—the newsstands offered selection. A news boy or girl usually only sold one title at a time while the major newsstands carried a vast number of city and out-of-town journals. Newsstands tended to be in key locations, like the railroad stations. The stands added to both the traffic and the importance of the depots. In fact, some people went to the stations just to buy their newspaper.[17]

Even if they purchased only morning newspapers, middle-class Philadelphians read those journals throughout the day. Many commuters read the papers on their train and trolley rides to Center City. Small-businessmen and clerks could often read their morning news at their place of work. An early twentieth-century postcard issued by *The Philadelphia Record* (a morning journal) shows the act of reading the paper as a gendered, social event: here a middle-class family gathered together (most likely in the evening) with the father and eldest son reading the paper as other family members went about their activities (see figure 21). Leo Bernheimer read his "morning" papers, *The Philadelphia Record* and the *Public Ledger*, all day long; depending on his schedule, he quickly scanned them at breakfast, dawdled over them on slow mornings, or read them as he prepared for bed at night. Robert Hinch, a huckster, also read his newspaper in the evening, in order to help him wind down after a difficult day.[18]

Hinch, one of the poorer members of the middle class, gives us an interesting clue as to why the bourgeois press consisted overwhelmingly of morning papers in this period: time, like space, can be divided by social class. Not only were three of the four members of the genteel metropolitan press morning papers, but throughout the Victorian era the genteel metropolitan press represented at least half of the morning titles published in the city and, until the mid-1890s, the papers of the genteel metropolitan press dominated the morning circulation. What this suggests is that middle-class Philadelphians were more likely to have free time in the morning than their working-class counterparts. Few factory workers could afford public transport during this period, so they could not read the journals on trains or trolleys. They were also less likely to be able to dawdle over breakfast or read the news at work. An evening paper, however, could be read as they relaxed at home or elsewhere.[19]

Hinch, Bernheimer, and the others retained a broad range of choice in reading matter; there were never less than twelve English-language dailies published in city in the late nineteenth century. In 1880, the three most widely read papers were the *Public Ledger* (circulation 65,000), *The Philadelphia*

Figure 21. The favorite newspaper in the home: *Philadelphia Record* postcard. Courtesy of the Print and Picture Collection, Free Library of Philadelphia.

Record (50,000), and *The Times* (32,500). Together the sales of these three morning newspapers made up three-quarters of the total for the city; none of the remaining eleven journals claimed a weekday circulation in excess of 15,000. In addition to these major papers, almost all the outlying communities and many of the city neighborhoods had daily or weekly journals. William Hemsing in nearby Souderton stayed abreast of local developments by reading *The Souderton Independent* every Saturday. In the city, local news was covered by journals such as *The West Philadelphia Telephone* and *The Germantown Telegraph.* Their names are suggestive of how even local late nineteenth-century newspapers placed themselves within the broader communications revolution and how they used technology as a draw. Edwin Jellett, the florist-turned-draughtsman, followed all the happenings at the Germantown Horticultural Society in *The Telegraph* and its competitors (middle-class Germantown was a very active market for local news). And for those for whom this was not choice enough, out-of-town, particularly New York, papers were also available in the city. John L. Smith regularly supplemented his Sunday morning diet of the *Record, Times,* and *Inquirer* with the entertaining *New York World.*[20]

The last twenty-five years of the nineteenth century saw a massive expansion in daily newspaper circulation and with it the creation of a segmented newspaper market. In 1876 reading the paper was an expensive habit: John L. Smith paid two or three cents each for his daily journals. High newsprint prices during the Civil War had effectively ended the era of the "penny press" in the city and *The Philadelphia Record* was the only major journal in the Centennial city that sold for a penny. During the 1880s prices fell and Smith could choose between five papers (four morning and one afternoon) priced at one cent. The cost continued to decline and by 1900 the *Public Ledger* at two cents was the only daily charging more than a penny a copy. Newspapers, like the contemporary middle-class mass-circulation magazines, became an integral link in the growing culture of consumption. By dropping their prices, circulation skyrocketed and publishers could "deliver" more readers to their advertisers and charge those advertisers higher rates. The increase in newspaper sales was far greater than the rise in population. As figure 22 illustrates, one newspaper was sold for approximately every four people in the city in 1880 but by 1900 that ratio was nearly five papers for every six Philadelphians. As prices fell and circulation grew, the market became more segmented. The pages of the daily press that had once—because of price—been a largely middle-class space in the city became increasingly diverse during the late-Victorian period. Some newspapers—in

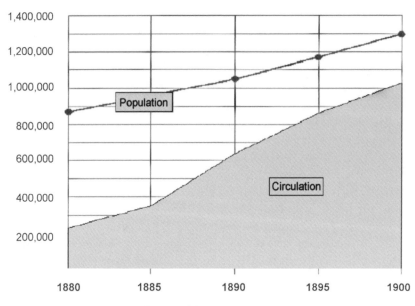

Figure 22. Newspapers triumphant: circulation compared to city population, 1880–1900.

Philadelphia the *Evening Item* is a good example—actively courted working-class readers through low prices, contests, and emphatic headlines. Others, such as *The Philadelphia Inquirer* and *The Philadelphia Record*, aimed at a more general circulation, hoping to catch a broad array of readers with a variety of articles and features. While still others, the genteel metropolitan press, targeted the middle class.[21]

The final general change in the newspaper industry in Philadelphia during this period was the increase in the circulation and importance of Sunday editions. In 1880 there were eleven English-language newspapers published in Philadelphia on Sunday, but only three of them had companion weekday editions. Only one Sunday paper, *The Times*, had a circulation over 15,000. The Sunday newspaper simply was not an important part of middle-class life in the city in the early 1880s. By 1900 this had changed dramatically; five of the thirteen dailies had Sunday editions and their total circulation was nearly 700,000 copies.[22]

The reaction to this increase in the Sunday press by middle-class Philadelphians varied greatly. Some were enthusiastic readers: William Hemsing, for instance, rushed to the Souderton railroad station to meet the "milk train" (usually the first train of the day, so called because it stopped at every station picking up milk for urban markets) in order to secure his copy of *The Sunday Press*, which, as he noted in his diary, was "the earliest of the Sunday papers" to arrive in town. Others had mixed emotions. John L. Smith had been a dedicated reader of the Sunday press from the early 1880s. Although he considered himself an Episcopalian, he seldom went to church on Sunday mornings; instead, he read various Philadelphia and New York newspapers. By 1898, however, Smith thought the papers had become too bulky. It now took him two hours "to wade through the Sunday Papers" as there was "so much trash in them." Still others, like Howard Edwards, disliked this commercial invasion of their day of rest. Edwards felt that " '*Sunday Papers*' are the most vicious, shameless and disgraceful [of all newspapers and t]hey spread more scandal, smut, gossip, lies + filth than the Daily Papers."[23]

The rapid growth of the Sunday newspaper parallels other changes in Victorian society and perhaps indicates a shift in the meaning of middle-class time. John L. Smith was not the only Philadelphian to substitute (or at least supplement) the secular ritual of reading the newspaper for the religious one of going to church. Newspapers, like public transport and the amusement parks, helped to make Sunday increasingly a day for amusement rather than one of contemplation. In 1876, few Philadelphians read Sunday newspapers and, despite requests from members of the working classes, the gates to the great Centennial remained locked on Sundays. By 1900, over 700,000 papers were sold on Sundays and the trolleys and trains allowed Philadelphians by the tens of thousands to go to the amusement parks and the Jersey shore.[24]

These changes took place not just throughout the country but throughout the Europeanized world; they were not unique to Philadelphia but simply local reflections of larger trends. For example, a circulation war broke out in New York City in 1884 after Joseph Pulitzer purchased *The New York World*. The rapidly falling prices of the New York papers even may have forced their Philadelphia counterparts (just ninety miles to the south) to lower their prices. But there were also two major technological advances by the 1880s that allowed newspapers to print more copies at lower costs. The first was the high-speed web press and the other was the linotype machine (which permitted type to be set much more quickly). Combined with a number of other innovations, the technological basis for the modern, multi-edition newspaper was in place by the mid-1880s.[25]

Publishers used this new technology to remake their industry into a vital part of the rising middle-class culture of consumption. Delivering readers to advertisers became the goal and to do this cost effectively, the papers dropped their prices to increase circulation. By the end of the nineteenth century, *The Philadelphia Record* claimed in its advertisements that "[t]o advertisers, the circulation of THE RECORD offers the assurance of the largest publicity. It sells publicity like the farmer sells wheat or the grocer sugar—by the measured quantity. No other journal within the area of its field of every delivery offers equal inducements."[26]

In the last few decades of the nineteenth century the layout and design—or the "geography"—of the daily newspaper in Philadelphia underwent a dramatic transformation. Not only did the journals grow in size but the editors also chose new ways to present the news: bigger headlines, photographs, more drawings, explicitly organized departments, and new page layouts. Like the floor plans of the new railroad stations and department stores, the new layouts of the daily newspapers were extremely well ordered. And like the floor plans of the railroad stations and dry goods stores, these layout changes preceded the growth in size of the journals. This shift to a more rational organization of the news was led by the very bourgeois genteel metropolitan press.

As with much of Victorian social geography, few contemporaries noted the changes in newspaper layout. Editors regularly commented on the accuracy and respectability of their journals but seldom the design. It was not until the end of the Victorian period that journalists seem to be aware of the late nineteenth century design revolution. In 1899, for example, the *Philadelphia Record Almanac* recognized the departmentalization of the daily papers when it stated in an advertisement "No department of The Record is more scrupulously edited than its financial and trade news." The first reference to design in the most consistently departmentalized newspaper in the city—the *Public Ledger*—does not come until 1900. This silence on layout is not unique to Philadelphia; on both the pages of the journals and in the reflections of the journalists, newspaper layout changed throughout the Victorian world with virtually no comment. It was not until the early twentieth century that scholars (often ex-journalists) began to reflect on newspaper design and layout. A journalism professor writing in the 1920s about this period stated that "the press both reflected and contributed to the standardization of American life [and that newspapers] found it advantageous to present news so that it could be read at a glance." By the 1930s, the same scholar concluded that "[w]ell-edited newspapers in their make-up aim: (1) to give prominence to news in proportion to its importance, (2) to make the different parts of the content easy to find and easy to read, (3) to give pages an attractive appearance, (4) to create a desire to purchase the paper by displaying interesting news on the front page." By the early twentieth century, newspaper design was an accepted part of the discipline of journalism.[27]

During the last two decades of the nineteenth century the layout of Philadelphia's newspapers changed dramatically. If we study the pages of the newspaper as an artifact, its layout becomes another form of urban geography. We can find forms and functions on individual pages and in entire papers, much the same way as we find them on the floor plans of buildings and maps of cities. Like the city, its railroads, and its department stores, the layout of Philadelphia's newspapers became more rational and structured during the Victorian period.[28]

The starting point for almost any exploration of newspaper geography should be the front page as this was (and is) the most public face of the press. During the final two decades of the nineteenth century, Philadelphia editors redesigned page one to include livelier headlines, to contain more graphics, and to be less vertically oriented. We know very little about what compelled virtually all of the city's editors to make similar changes, as few records from the period survive and almost none address issues of design, but individual motivation seems unimportant as all but the most minor journals adopted similar layouts by 1900. Journalists looking back upon the period—and historians following their lead—have usually argued that these design changes were attempts to cope with the increased number of pages in daily newspapers, but for the members of the genteel metropolitan press and some of their general circulation counterparts this switch to a more rational layout preceded their expanded girth.[29]

It should not trouble us that Philadelphia's editors (or New York's or London's, for that matter) fail to tell us why they made these changes; in fact their collective silence speaks volumes. Because virtually every major newspaper nearly simultaneously adopted similar design conventions, these conventions reflected broader cultural values. This is further reinforced by the fact that transformations in the geography of the late nineteenth-century newspaper parallel so many other changes throughout Victorian middle-class society. Neither the bourgeois editors nor their middle-class readers needed to articulate the advantages of the taxonomy of news.

The front page of a Philadelphia newspaper in 1880 looked a great deal like its predecessors from the 1850s and 1860s. Long-time readers like Susan MacManus and John L. Smith would have noticed little difference. None of the city's journals had, to use the words of a modern editor, broken "the tyranny of column rules." All still used a vertical layout with single-column headlines on page one. *The Philadelphia Inquirer* (figure 23) illustrates these conventions; it consists of six columns of nothing but text and small headlines. The columns are all carefully separated by thin lines: these are the column rules. As recently as mid-century, these rules had been a technological requirement, as each column had been set by hand within them. This was no longer true because of changes in typesetting, but they remained part of the "traditional" look of a serious newspaper. Confining text and headlines to a single column gave the paper a very vertical format in which layout options were limited. Another aspect of this traditional design was for a column on page one not to be topped by a headline; the editor simply carried over the text from the previous column (this is illustrated in column two in figure 23). All told, this layout did little to signal the relative importance of the different articles. In fact, the *Inquirer* did a better job than many of its contemporaries; in the issue shown in figure 23 the lead stories are clearly those that top columns one, three, and five. To take two further examples, on a typical day in 1880 it was impossible to determine the lead stories in *The Evening Telegraph* (as all articles were set under two similar types of headlines) or in the *Public Ledger* (because of the lack of distinct headlines).[30]

By 1900, newspaper editors did a much better job of indicating to their readers the significance of news stories. Bigger headlines and photographs made for a more eye-catching page one. Column rules became less important as text and graphics flowed across the paper. The front page of *The Press* shown in figure 24 is an excellent example of these new design conventions. The layout immediately tells the reader that the article on the White murder is the paper's lead story, its graphics and headlines take up parts of five of the eight columns. The editor placed two other stories over multiple columns to indicate their relative importance. There is also a news summary in column one, guiding the busy reader through the day's top stories quickly. Like *The Press*, the other major newspapers also used photographs on the front page and generally followed similar layouts. The ever-conservative *Public Ledger* still did not use multi-column headlines and seldom broke column rules for anything other than graphics, but even it adopted bigger headlines and had moved from a nine- to a seven-column front page, making it visually far less dense.[31]

During the late nineteenth century, Philadelphia's editors not only changed page one but also reordered the presentation of the news throughout their papers into subject matter departments. Although this shift was nearly universal in Philadelphia, affecting all but the most minor general cir-

Figure 23. Traditional nineteenth-century newspaper design: *The Philadelphia Inquirer*. Courtesy of the Newspaper Collection, Free Library of Philadelphia.

culation newspapers, it had its origins in the bourgeois journals of the genteel metropolitan press.

Figure 24. Turn-of-the-century newspaper design: *The Press.* Courtesy of the Newspaper Collection, Free Library of Philadelphia.

In 1880 the *Public Ledger* was the most consistently well ordered of the Philadelphia press, and it used a mixture of subject matter, source, and time labels to signal its four pages of content. Typical divisions by subject included "Local Affairs" and "Congress" on page one and financial news and "New Jersey Matters" on page four. It also used indications of source to group diverse news articles together: "By Atlantic Telegraph" and "By the Cuban Cable" are two usual front page examples. In addition, the *Ledger* placed a number of recent but otherwise unrelated articles on page one under the heading "The Latest News," and this division of news by time was not unusual in 1880. The high degree of organization in the four-page *Ledger* suggests that the late nineteenth century changes in presentation were efforts to organize knowledge and not simple reactions to increased girth. And the *Public Ledger's* key location in the bourgeois firmament helps to place that quest firmly within the ranks of the middle class.[32]

None of the other Philadelphia newspapers in 1880 defined their news content as well (or as consistently) as did the bourgeois *Public Ledger,* but all used some of the same techniques in varying degrees. All the newspapers examined had some of their business news grouped together on a single page under a heading like "Financial & Commercial." Other than business news, there was little subject matter order in the press in 1880. Both of the afternoon titles (*The Evening Bulletin* and *The Evening Telegraph*), however, explicitly used time to divide their news. Their editors placed otherwise unrelated news articles under the headings "First Edition," "Second Edition," and so forth, with each "edition" being a collection of more recent news. This had the odd effect of putting later news on the inside pages instead of highlighting the stories on page one. These "editions" at times also represented sources of the news (such as the Atlantic cable) but this was not always the case.

By 1900 every newspaper in the city (except for the minor *Daily News*) had moved further with the subject-matter classification of the news. No paper consistently used either time or source to order its content. The members of the genteel metropolitan press had fully adopted these new conventions. The now twenty-page *Public Ledger* continued to be the most well-organized journal in the city. It had a news summary on page one and explicit subject-matter groupings throughout, including sports, financial, and women's news. Some general circulation papers, such as *The Philadelphia Inquirer,* were nearly as well demarcated by subject headings.[33]

Even the afternoon papers shifted toward this new layout by 1900. All of them (again, except for *The Daily News*) had some subject grouping of articles; business and sports were the two most common. *The Call* and *The Evening Bulletin* even had explicitly headed sections like their morning rivals. Other than a page one "stop press" column in *The Evening Bulletin*, the afternoon journals had all abandoned their use of time as an ordering technique by 1900. This is a bit surprising, as some of these papers produced multiple editions throughout the afternoon, and timeliness should have been an important selling point, indicating again the importance of subject order to editors and readers during this period.[34]

In part, this transformation in the presentation of news indicated a different mode of reading the newspaper. In 1880, a reader approached a paper like a book: he or she read it from beginning to end. To find an article on a specific person or event, a reader had to look through the entire journal. The key indications of this are the small headlines, the lack of consistent order in news presentation, and the tendency for text to run from the bottom of one column to the top of the next. By 1900, readers could digest the newspaper in parts, skipping from section to section. Bolder headlines and a subject-oriented approach to content made this process possible. This new design also allowed newspapers to serve broader audiences with varying interests. But these changes also paralleled other late nineteenth-century attempts to organize (or reorganize) knowledge along more rational lines.

Although this new layout meant that turn-of-the-century editors imposed their hierarchies more clearly on the readers, many middle-class customers probably welcomed the change. Many members of the bourgeoisie consistently focused on a small number of subjects, and the new layout allowed them to find the articles that interested them and to avoid more easily those which did not. A few examples should suffice. Recall that Edwin Jellett, the florist turned draughtsman, continued throughout his life to follow the happenings at the Germantown Horticultural Society. Sidney Smith, an eighteen-year-old from Chester (a small city firmly in Philadelphia's orbit), loved to follow the exploits of his uncle, a prominent lawyer, in the press. Anna Broomall, a doctor, was fascinated by local history and for decades clipped any article she could find on Delaware County in the Philadelphia papers. Finally, consider two examples from opposite ends of the middle-class spectrum on race relations during this period: William Armstrong, a white Democrat, scanned the journals to find evidence of African-American inferiority, while a few years later, James Stemons, a black Republican, regularly looked through the papers for indications of progress in civil rights.[35]

What accounts for these dramatic shifts in the layout of all newspapers in so short a period? Traditionally, scholars have focused on one of two types of factors to explain this: the idiosyncrasies of individual newspaper editors or the demands of the competitive marketplace. More recently historians have linked changes in the rise of a culture of consumption. Support for all three of these positions can be found within the pages and the newsrooms of the Philadelphia papers. The ownership (and with it, the editorial policy) of a number of the journals changed during this period. Both contemporaries and subsequent scholars, for example, have ascribed the conservative tone of the *Public Ledger* to the personality of its owner, George W. Childs. The division of the market into "informational" and "entertaining" is borne out by the various page layouts. But none of these interpretations explain why subject matter organization became the only model for newspapers by 1900. Other methods—ranging from the "organic" page layout of *The Daily News* (and the mid-nineteenth-century journals) to page organization by time or by source—had been tried and rejected. This shift to a subject matter typography also occurred in the spatial divisions within department stores and middle-class homes during the late nineteenth century. When we place this transformation in its broader cultural context, changing newspaper layout becomes a further example of the new bourgeois vision of the Victorian city. The carefully classified pages of the newspaper were just one more component in the rational, scientific urban geography.[36]

From the layout of the news in these journals, we can turn to what made that space possible: advertising. Changes in advertising content paralleled those in news presentation during this period. Divisions by social class and subject matter also defined the placement and design of ads as they did for the news. These shifts in advertising content are important because they help to link the layout changes to the broader cultural matrix because they happened throughout the newspaper industry and thus cannot be tied to the idiosyncrasies of one journal or editor.

The advertising content of Philadelphia's dailies varied greatly throughout this period. This examination of advertising begins with an interesting paradox: as advertising revenue became more important to newspapers during the late nineteenth century, the percentage of space allocated to ads actually fell. However, because the size of the major newspapers grew over this time, the actual column inches devoted to advertising increased. The result was that the average reader saw more advertisements in his or her paper in 1900 than in 1880, but the commercial material took up less of the total space, so he or she also found more space dedicated to news and features.[37]

In 1880 a reader would find many small advertisements aimed at both businesses and consumers. Most ads consisted only of densely packed text. Figure 25 shows a page from *The Philadelphia Inquirer* in 1880. The majority of the page consists of advertising for a variety of goods and services. Among this commercial melange are ads from John Wanamaker in columns two and three. Dry goods stores (which had then just begun their expansion that would lead to the modern department store) were starting to develop more elaborate display advertising. Most commercial announcements aimed at

Figure 25. Advertising in 1880. Courtesy of the Newspaper Collection, Free Library of Philadelphia.

consumers tended to be small and textual in 1880. Like the news itself, the advertisements were designed to be read, not to be scanned. The balance between advertisements aimed at businesses and at homes varied greatly among the newspapers. For example, most of the announcements in *The*

Evening Bulletin were targeted at the home while those in *The North American* were directed toward the office.[38]

By 1890 department store display advertising had become far more important to the genteel metropolitan press. For example, all four of these largely middle-class papers in Philadelphia had an ad from Wanamaker's and at least one other dry goods house every day. At that time, Wanamaker was the only department store to include line drawings in its announcements, but other consumer ads featured illustrations at this point. Wanamaker and its competitors continued to use the general circulation press but not as often as the bourgeois papers. In 1890 *The Philadelphia Record* had the largest morning circulation in the city but did not have as many department store advertisements as did the three morning examples of the genteel metropolitan press. The only dry goods ads to appear consistently in *The Call, The Evening Bulletin,* and *The North American* were from Wanamaker (by far the city's largest store at that time).[39]

Also by 1890, in a reflection of the growing national culture of consumption, consumer-oriented advertising had become more important to all the Philadelphia newspapers. In addition to the department stores, illustrated and text-only announcements for a variety of brand-name products (such as Hood's Sarsaparilla and Royal Baking Powder), retail establishments (from the Model Coffee House to the jewelers J. E. Caldwell to small, local firms like John L. Smith's map store), and providers of services (the Quaker City Carpet Company, "Carpet Cleaning Exclusively," and dozens of Atlantic City hotels) appeared in the Philadelphia papers. By then, the emphasis of newspaper advertising was largely on the home and the individual; announcements to businesses became increasingly relegated to the financial page and the classified sections.[40]

Both of these trends, the correlation between certain advertisers and the genteel metropolitan press and the consumer-oriented nature of the ads, became more clearly defined at the turn of the century. Department stores still advertised in almost all the newspapers in the city but their announcements in the bourgeois papers were larger and more numerous. The journal most read by middle-class men and women, the *Public Ledger*, had the most department store display advertising of any newspaper in the city in 1900. The other two members of the genteel metropolitan press had large announcements from three of the largest middle-class retailers in the city: John Wanamaker, Strawbridge & Clothier, and Gimbel Brothers. Most of the general circulation papers in the city (the exceptions were *The Call* and *The Daily News*) had some department store advertising but none had examples from all three bourgeois stores as did the *Ledger, Press,* and *Times.* Wanamaker, for example, did not advertise in the morning newspaper with the largest circulation, *The Philadelphia Record.* The shift to consumer-oriented advertising continued and with it came more national brands. Examples include Anheuser-Busch in the *Public Ledger,* Hires Rootbeer and Missisquoi Mineral Water ("Flushes the System") in *The Press,* and Srosset Collars in *The Times.* By 1900, the movement of business ads to the classified and financial pages was nearly complete.[41]

The large department store display advertisements that dominated the press during this period reproduced the subject matter divisions present in both the newspapers and the stores themselves. Figure 26 shows a Gimbel Brothers ad in 1900; although not as artistic as a contemporary Wanamaker's layout, it is more typical of the period because it lacked illustrations. Gimbels used "headlines" to clearly call out the main offerings of the day. The store placed under each title related items: underwear at top, white goods in the middle, and other smaller groupings throughout. In one sense these clusters are similar to the actual departments in the stores. But they did not precisely replicate the internal structure of Gimbel's emporium; Men's and Women's underwear and hosiery, for example, which are placed together at the top of the ad, would be in separate departments in the store.[42]

The advertising content of the papers changed as greatly as did their news presentation in the late nineteenth century. First, the connections among the major department stores and the *Ledger, Press,* and *Times* confirm the definition of the genteel metropolitan press. By 1900, middle-class space in the city consisted not only of homes in West Philadelphia and dry goods stores in Center City but also the pages of these journals. The shift toward a more consumer-oriented advertising base illustrates that by 1900 both the genteel metropolitan newspapers and their general circulation counterparts were firmly entrenched in the new culture of consumption. In addition, subject-matter order was important to advertising as well as to news. Two otherwise unrelated changes demonstrate this; by 1900 newspapers consistently placed business advertisements on their financial page or within clearly denominated classified sections, and department stores had better organized the layout of their ads. The growth of display advertising reinforces the conclusion that the mode of reading newspapers had changed; the ads' bold headings and illustrations were designed to stop the quickly scanning eye.

The press in Philadelphia changed dramatically between 1876 and 1901. The papers grew in both circulation and physical size. During this period the

Figure 26. Department store advertising in 1900. Courtesy of the Newspaper Collection, Free Library of Philadelphia.

genteel metropolitan press—journals aimed at the middle-class market—came into existence. Beginning with the genteel metropolitan press and later encompassing most newspapers, layout became more hierarchical and nearly universally ordered by subject matter. This taxonomy of space on the pages of Philadelphia's dailies parallels those developed in urban geography, the railroad stations, and the department stores. The daily newspaper emerged as another key component in the middle-class city. Like much of bourgeois Philadelphia, the pages of the city's genteel metropolitan press were well-ordered, rational spaces.

As the nineteenth century drew to a close, middle-class Philadelphians found themselves living in a rational, scientific city. Every day, in well-ordered rituals, they rode streetcars and trains, read newspapers, and shopped at department stores. These daily rhythms reflected the meter of their culture. The bourgeois city became more organized not from fear of change or of the working classes but from a middle-class faith in science and rationality and progress. Responding to their increased power and wealth, the market allowed the bourgeoisie to revisualize their world. In the late nineteenth century, this well-ordered world was not imposed on others but was largely specific to the middle-class experience of the city. The newspapers *they* read, the dry goods stores *they* shopped in, the neighborhoods *they* lived in, not surprisingly, reflected *their* culture. In the twentieth century, the same market forces that had created this bourgeois vision of the metropolis would transform middle-class Philadelphia yet again.

Interlude: Went to Willow Grove

> *Saturday, July 20, 1901: After getting lunch, I at 1.45 took a car on 13th St, +
> went to Willow Grove. There about 4 oclock, I met Anne, Bessie, + Mrs.
> Bard. I heard the afternoon concert, + the first half of the evening concert.
> We met Mr. Harobin about 5 oclock, and we took a walk through the
> Grove. We saw Mrs. Bard to the train at 9 oclock, + we took a trolley on
> York Road, + reached home at 10.15.*[1]

Edwin Jellett, forty-one years old when he recorded this entry in
his diary, lived in the bourgeois Germantown section of Philadelphia. An old
farming settlement, Germantown had become a bedroom community by
mid-century thanks to the arrival of the Philadelphia, Germantown & Norristown Railroad, the city's first commuter line. Although not as sylvan as
Chestnut Hill, its tonier neighbor to the northwest, Germantown had much
more of a suburban feel—with its irregular streets, stone detached houses,
and numerous trees—than did the blocks and blocks of brick row houses
that made up West and North Philadelphia. Every weekday morning, Jellett
went to his job as a draughtsman at 245 North Broad Street, on the northern
fringe of Center City. He had recently switched to commuting by trolley with
Bessie Harobin, a friend from church. It must have been true love, for the
trolley took far longer than Jellett's old route via the Reading Railroad and
whenever Bessie did not go to Center City, he returned to the quicker but
more expensive steam train.

Saturday, July 20, 1901, was a sultry summer day in the city. The temperature was in the upper-eighties as Jellett finished his work for the morning (like most white-collar Philadelphians at the time he worked a half day
on Saturdays). There was little breeze and no chance of relief from the heat
and humidity in the city, so he was glad he had planned to spend the afternoon and evening at Willow Grove Park. Willow Grove, just outside the city

limits in eastern Montgomery County, was by far the most popular of the many amusement parks in the Philadelphia region. It was owned by the same Union Traction Company whose trolleys would transport Jellett directly from Center City to its gates. The park served as a cool respite from the long, hot, humid Philadelphia summer for the women and men of the city's middle class. Jellett went there regularly with friends to escape some of the less pleasant aspects of summer in the metropolis.

After buying lunch at one of the many inexpensive restaurants that lined the minor streets of Center City, Jellett made his way through the crowds to join the queue on Thirteenth Street to catch a northbound car on Union Traction's line to Willow Grove Park. He did not have long to wait, for on busy summer days the trolleys ran every few minutes on this very lucrative route. He paid his ten-cent fare (twice the typical charge as the trolley company cunningly had located the park outside the city limits and in the "suburban" fare zone) and looked in vain for a seat. The car was crowded and his ride was a slow one: it took him over two hours to go the thirteen miles. On a more typical day, according to the trolley guide books that Jellett regularly consulted in planning his jaunts into the countryside, the trip could be made in just an hour and a quarter. Most likely the trolley was an open one (figure 27), and the gentle breezes created by the motion of the car kept him cool on the long trip. A crowded, closed trolley on a hot day would not have made for an enjoyable start to his afternoon and evening of merriment with friends.

Once he arrived at the park, he met Bessie, her sister Anna, and an older acquaintance, Mrs. Bard. They then did what thousands of other middle-class Philadelphians did that day (and every day and night in the summer): they attended a free concert (figure 28). Arriving a bit late (the program had begun at three), Jellett and his friends heard an exciting mix that included Rossini and Wagner, ending with the "Ride of the Valkyries." Saturday was the penultimate day that season for the very popular Walter Damrosch Symphony Orchestra. Damrosch, son of a Metropolitan Opera conductor, was one of New York's leading conductors, and many middle-class Philadelphians considered his visits to Willow Grove Park the high point of the summer season.

Jellett and the entourage later met Bessie's father and the enlarged group took a walk around the grounds and ate dinner at the park. They caught most of the first half of the evening concert, leaving during yet another work by Wagner. After sending Mrs. Bard home via the train (as the Reading also served Willow Grove Park, although with less frequent trains

Figure 27. A summer idyll: a Union Traction Company open trolley on the Willow Grove route. Courtesy of the Print and Picture Collection, Free Library of Philadelphia.

Figure 28. Bourgeois respectability: an early twentieth-century postcard showing a crowd outside the concert pavilion at Willow Grove Park. Courtesy of the Pennsylvania State Archives, Pennsylvania Historical and Museum Commission.

and at a higher cost than Union Traction), the remainder of the party took the trolley back into the city. About half way to Center City, in North Philadelphia, they transferred to the Germantown line of Union Traction (for free, using what Philadelphians called "passes"). The entire trip home took a little over an hour. In nine hours, Jellett had met with friends, heard parts of two concerts, taken a walk in a sylvan grove, ate dinner, escaped the summer heat, and traversed miles of Philadelphia landscape in three transit vehicles.[2]

PART II

Early Twentieth-Century Philadelphia

The New Century: The Magnificent Metropolis of Today

With demonstrations that are destined to become memorable the twentieth century was ushered in at midnight by the city of Philadelphia. . . . If at the stroke of 12 the spirit of William Penn could have animated the colossal figure crowning the tall tower at Broad and Market streets, he must have marveled [at] the wondrous spectacle that broke loose in the court yard and the streets around the huge marble pile where the municipal affairs are administered for the present City of Brotherly Love. The changes, the progress of two centuries, seemed emphasized by his solemn, peaceful image, and to make more vivid the unimagined contrast between his little town of settlers on the banks of the Delaware and the magnificent metropolis of to-day.[1]

At the dawn of the new century, Philadelphians were convinced that their city had undergone a dramatic transformation over the previous decades. Central to this new image was the spectacular shift from William Penn's town to the modern metropolis. An ex-patriot artist claimed that Penn "might have recognized his peaceful green country town in the Philadelphia of our earlier years, though probably not without dismay at its already amazing growth" but "after almost thirty years' absence, we returned in 1912 to visit our old Philadelphia, it had transformed itself into a new Philadelphia, changed beyond belief." A small part of this massive transformation was the creation of the late nineteenth-century middle-class city. Progress did not suddenly come to a halt with the dawn of the new century. The story of middle-class Philadelphia in the early twentieth century was one of continuity and change with the patterns of the Victorian past. Continuity in the sense that the faith in science and rationality that had so shaped the late nineteenth-century bourgeois vision of the city continued to mold the newer version. Equally important, however, was the change wrought by the expansion of the market beyond the middle class to encompass an increasing portion of the working classes.[2]

Two things had shaped the geography of the bourgeois Victorian city: money and rationality. During the last quarter of the nineteenth century, the city's middle class grew in numbers, wealth, and power. They, and the entrepreneurs responding to their new wealth, created a vision of the city that reflected bourgeois values, including a faith in science and rationality. This new metropolis stretched from the western suburbs to the Jersey shore, carefully and regularly connected by the bourgeois corridors—the trains and trolleys. In this middle-class city, logic and order reigned triumphant. From the residential streets of Germantown to the various districts of Center City to the pages of the *Public Ledger* to the floors of the John Wanamaker store, there was a place for everything and everything was in its place. This Victorian middle-class urban vision was never the only one present in late nineteenth-century Philadelphia; separate elite and working class versions also existed, but the middle-class metropolis seemed particularly coherent to its inhabitants. It also seemed timeless, although it was largely the creation of post–Civil War economic changes. To many bourgeois men and women, middle-class West Philadelphia would always be.

This middle-class metropolis, however, turned out to be far more fragile and fleeting than many of its inhabitants had assumed. For the very market economy that had allowed J. Harper Smith and his neighbors to create the 4400 block of Pine Street in West Philadelphia began to shift and undermine this order around the turn of the century. There was no magic moment, no bright line dividing the largely middle-class Victorian city from its more multi-classed early twentieth-century counterpart. Instead, change came slowly as working-class wages rose and with them a new, broader mass market. With this new mass market, the Victorian middle-class city slowly became the early twentieth-century multi-classed metropolis.

During the first few decades of the twentieth century, working-class incomes began to rise both nationally and in Philadelphia after a long period of stagnation and decline. Nationally, the annual income of the average factory worker rose from $420.48 in 1899 to $511.82 in 1909 to $1,141.64 in 1919 to $1,267.95 in 1925. These increases were real; not only did they outpace inflation, but throughout much of this period, grew at a faster rate than did middle-class salaries (see figure 29). Philadelphia—the "workshop of the world" according to its boosters—largely followed these national trends. During the key decade between 1899 and 1909, the average factory worker's

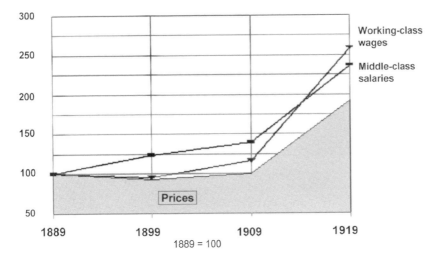

Figure 29. Wages, salaries, and prices, 1889–1919.

wage increased 13.77% (from $441.10 to $501.82). Not only was this significantly greater than the rate of inflation for the period (8.00%), but it also outstripped middle-class salary gains (8.99%).[3]

With this rise in working-class disposable income came an expansion in the consumer market. Increasingly, the culture of consumption—a largely middle-class phenomenon in the late nineteenth-century—extended to the women and men of the working classes. Interestingly, the same rationality and order that had helped to create the middle-class Victorian city now allowed its commercial institutions to respond to the new mass market. The layout of the early twentieth-century newspaper was as logical as its Victorian predecessor, but the middle-class *Public Ledger* declined as the multi-classed *Evening Bulletin* became the paper that "nearly everybody in Philadelphia read." Early twentieth-century merchants organized their department stores just as exactingly as did their Victorian predecessors but added "bargain basements" to reach these new customers. Amusement parks and the Jersey shore also began to cater to an expanded clientele.[4]

This transformation was not a sudden, wrenching one. Slowly, the once largely middle-class locations in the nineteenth-century Victorian city became the increasingly multi-classed ones of early twentieth-century Philadelphia. Even though the trains and trolleys still ran, Wanamaker's was still open for business, and thousands of middle-class homes still covered much of the metropolis, by 1926 the Victorian city was largely gone. For the most part, bourgeois Philadelphians accepted these changes and adapted to the new metropolis. Sometimes, however, the women and men of the middle class were less comfortable sharing parts of their city. And in this discomfort are the roots of the Progressive Era's political search for order.

Chapter 5
If Dad Could Not Get . . . the Evening Bulletin It Was Practically the End of the World

If Dad could not get his morning paper and the Evening Bulletin *it was practically the end of the world. If the papers were late he was in a nervous state and paced the floor until he saw the boy.*[1]

It is significant that decades later, when John Cecil Holm thought back to his childhood, he remembered *The Evening Bulletin* by name while forgetting the title of its morning counterpart. *The Evening Bulletin* was not important just to Headley Holm (Cecil's electrician father) but to tens of thousands of other middle-class Philadelphians in the early decades of the twentieth century. It quickly became a civic institution: as much a part of the bourgeois metropolis as the John Wanamaker store or the trains of the Pennsylvania Railroad. Cecil Holm was not the only person to link *The Evening Bulletin* with early twentieth-century Philadelphia. In his novel *Kitty Foyle*, Christopher Morley referred to the journal as "the paper that never forgets" and a journalist would later call it "the paper that was tailored to a city." Daily the publisher claimed—on page one and in the masthead—that "in Philadelphia, nearly everybody reads the Bulletin." By 1920 this boast was largely true, as the paper truly dominated—and defined—the Philadelphia market.[2]

The rise of *The Evening Bulletin* was an important part of the evolving relationships among the members of the bourgeoisie and the press around the turn of the century and illustrates both the continuities and changes in middle-class culture between the late nineteenth and early twentieth centuries. At the center of this complex web of relationships was the same irony present in Philadelphia's department stores and elsewhere in the city. The nineteenth-century bourgeois concern for order—page layout in newspapers, floor design for the retailers, and terminal design in the major train depots—allowed once largely middle-class institutions to extend to serve a multi-class market in the twentieth century. This combination of an expanding market and a detailed taxonomy of space slowly eroded the world of the Victorian bourgeoisie.

The first quarter of the twentieth century was a period of sharp contrasts. In many ways it represented the full articulation of the trends present in the late nineteenth-century newspaper industry: the affinity between the middle class and the genteel metropolitan press became even more pronounced, space on the pages of all newspapers became better defined by subject, the journals grew larger still, and consumer advertising gained more importance. But in other equally important ways the world of late-Victorian journalism began to unravel between 1895 and 1925: the number of titles shrank, per capita circulation declined, the genteel metropolitan press was increasingly irrelevant to the market as a whole, and most of the new papers launched during this period were tabloids very different in tone from that of the very sober genteel metropolitan press.

It was the general circulation newspaper, a well-organized journal that targeted its articles and features at the mass market, that came to dominate the early twentieth century. General circulation newspapers had working-class, bourgeois, and elite readers and delivered this mixed customer base to their advertisers—both local and national—in large numbers. The genteel metropolitan press—a largely middle-class institution in the city—declined in the face of an ever-broadening culture of consumption and was replaced by multi-class journals for which the bourgeoisie was only part of the targeted audience. But the general circulation newspaper could not have succeeded without the layout and design conventions developed in the Victorian period.

Before examining the relationships among the middle class and the press in greater detail, a brief look at the structural changes in the newspaper industry in Philadelphia should help set the stage. The shift from the largely middle-class market of the Victorian city to the multi-class, mass market of the early twentieth-century metropolis was not an easy one for Philadelphia's journals. The dramatic rise in per-capita circulation in the late nineteenth century ended abruptly about 1905, and sales of all journals stagnated until the 1920s (figure 30) despite continued population growth. Although a number of factors contributed to this, including the decline in titles and (by the teens) rising prices, perhaps the most important was the increase in alternative sources of inexpensive entertainment in the city. Starting in the 1890s,

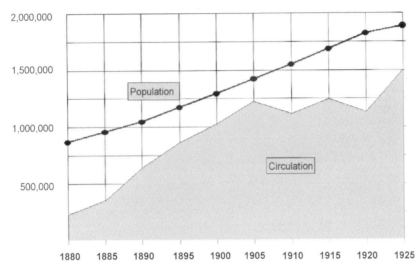

Figure 30. Twentieth-century stagnation: circulation compared to city population, 1880–1925.

amusement parks, movies, vaudeville, and other forms of mass entertainment competed with newspapers for the discretionary dollar. For example, in 1915, Clair Wilcox, a student at the University of Pennsylvania, observed " 'crowds' watching [the] baseball scoreboard" provided by *The Evening Bulletin,* but unlike fellow Pennsylvanian Leo Bernheimer two decades before, Wilcox did not join in; instead he and his friends went to the Stanley Theatre to see a show. As the twentieth century progressed, middle-class (and other) Philadelphians would have more and more entertainment choices, and newspapers reacted to this by adding more features.[3]

Without a doubt, another major component in this stagnation in overall circulation was the dramatic decline in the number of titles during this period. Many readers bought multiple papers daily (recall that Headley Holm took an unnamed morning journal in addition to *The Evening Bulletin*), and the demise of one might not lead to its replacement by another. In 1902 Adolph S. Ochs (better known as the publisher of *The New York Times*) thinned the ranks of the genteel metropolitan press when he purchased the *Public Ledger* and merged his Philadelphia *Times* into it. The *Times* and the *Public Ledger* had been fierce—and equal—competitors throughout the late-Victorian era, and both claimed a daily circulation of 70,000 in 1900. Following the merger, the surviving *Public Ledger* sold 75,000 copies a day, and none of the other morning papers sustained significant circulation gains.[4]

This trend continued when Cyrus H. K. Curtis (owner of the *Ladies Home Journal* and the *Saturday Evening Post*) acquired the *Public Ledger* from Ochs in 1913 and, within a few years, bought and terminated three papers as part of his rather expensive (and ultimately unsuccessful) attempt to make the *Public Ledger* Philadelphia's dominant journal. From thirteen titles in 1900, newspaper selection hit its nadir in 1920 with but seven options. In the mid-twenties, two tabloids were launched in the city, but the closure in 1925 of *The North American* meant readers still only had eight choices. By 1926, the once highly competitive Philadelphia newspaper market had changed dramatically: three morning broadsheets remained (down from seven in 1900), three afternoon broadsheets (down from six), and the two new tabloids.[5]

Some things did not change; the genteel metropolitan press continued to present the news in a sober tone. The *Public Ledger* remained extremely conservative in its design and presentation; it avoided bold graphics and unconfirmed reports. In fact, the *Public Ledger* became more conservative in layout and tone throughout this period, further illustrating that its design was a social—and not a technological—construct. In 1900, the *Public Ledger* regularly used photographs on the front page and, although it did not use multi-column headlines, its general design was only slightly more restrained than its competitors. By 1910, the *Public Ledger* still did not use multi-column headlines, and photographs had vanished from page one. Photographs were still often absent from the front page in 1920 and few stories in the *Public Ledger* received even two-column headlines. The far more popular and less genteel *Evening Public Ledger*, first published by Curtis in 1914, used photographs and multi-column headlines to present a breezier and more entertaining version of the news. The layout and news presentation of the *Public Ledger* in the teens and twenties was self-consciously restrained, in much the same way as that of the front pages of the *New York Times* and *Wall Street Journal* are today.

The morning *Public Ledger*'s conservatism appealed to many middle-class readers who often questioned the accuracy of the press. William Hemsing noted his trust in the *Public Ledger* when he recorded in 1905 that "The strikers in St. Petersburg in their effort to reach the Winter Palace to petition the Czar were stopped by bullets. . . . Some papers think as high as 2100 were killed and 5000 wounded. The Ledger had only 250 killed." In cases of doubt, Hemsing implicitly believed the bourgeois *Ledger* was correct. Chalkley Matlack confirmed this view when he recorded his general views of the industry in the same month that he switched his subscription to the *Public Ledger* from *The Press;* he felt that "[n]ewspapers might be of much greater service than they really are if they were more truthful and reliable institutions."6

The affinity between middle-class Philadelphians and the *Public Ledger* and the other members of the genteel metropolitan press intensified in the early twentieth century, even though the genteel metropolitan press declined in importance to the market as a whole. During this period the men and women in my sampling consistently purchased two newspapers, *The Press* and the *Public Ledger*, in far greater numbers than did the general population. The scrapbooks of Dr. Charles K. Mills, a neurologist at the University of Pennsylvania, are largely filled with clippings from these two papers. The *Public Ledger* in particular was a well-defined part of the bourgeois city; regardless of sex, race, religion, occupation, or residential location, middle-class Philadelphians read it regularly. One testament to the centrality of the *Public Ledger* to bourgeois life is that it was often the paper of record for important personal milestones; the only newspaper clipping about her marriage that Henrietta Ulman Newmayer saved was from it. But the genteel metropolitan press as a whole was of increasingly less relevance to the city; the *Public Ledger*'s circulation remained stagnant between 1900 and 1920, while that of *The Press* shrank by half. In 1890 one-third of the journals sold in the city were copies of the genteel metropolitan press; by 1920 that fraction had declined to about one-twelfth. On October 2, 1920, the date Curtis closed *The Press*, the genteel metropolitan press in Philadelphia consisted solely of the *Public Ledger*.7

The decline of the genteel metropolitan press, however, did not mean an end to the presence of middle-class rationality in the organization of space in Philadelphia's newspapers. As the examination of the rise of *The Evening Bulletin* below will illustrate in greater detail, the general circulation dailies adopted the design conventions of the genteel metropolitan press and, like the large Center City department stores in the twentieth century, were multi-class institutions. *The Evening Bulletin* and *The Evening Public Ledger* and their morning counterparts, *The Philadelphia Inquirer* and *The Philadelphia Record*, presented a wide range of news and features in discreet departments designed to draw as large as possible an audience. For the elite and the upwardly mobile bourgeoisie the "society" pages offered expanded coverage of the comings and goings of the city's upper crust (and their middle-class pretenders). For bourgeois readers there were columns on dealing with household servants (and increasingly in the 1920s, running a home without help) and the stock market listings beloved by Headley Holm (who, according to his son, read them every day, although he owned no shares).[8]

What made these multi-class newspapers possible was the trend toward clearer content signaling and more rigid page layout that began in the late nineteenth century and accelerated in the early twentieth. The press offered a large variety of news and features in clearly demarcated space under bold headings to assist the scanning eye to find items of interest. And this brings us back to the central irony of the period: these conventions had initially been adopted by the genteel metropolitan press as a part of the middle-class Victorian faith in science and rationality. By the early twentieth century, however, this same well-ordered layout permitted the general circulation press to reach the expanding mass market and effectively compete with the genteel metropolitan press for middle-class readers.

The story of newspaper advertising is also one of continuity and change. The most important shift was the steady increase in the amount of space devoted to advertising throughout the first two decades of the twentieth century, reflecting the expanding consumer culture. In 1900, a little over one-third of the average paper was advertising; by 1920, that figure had nearly reversed and stood at sixty percent. Some journals, notably *The Philadelphia Inquirer* and *The Evening Bulletin*, had large classified advertising sections that appealed to consumers and businesses alike. Stray animals seemed to have been a preoccupation with middle-class Philadelphians, both the Holms and the librarian Albert Edmunds advertised lost dogs in *The Evening Bulletin*. National consumer advertising continued to increase in importance. By 1920, ads for automobiles and other consumer goods (including Coca-Cola and breakfast cereals) were found in all the major Philadelphia papers. At approximately the same time, the listings in the *N. W. Ayer & Son's Newspaper Annual and Directory* included whether the journal accepted "mats" (pre-packaged advertising that allowed the Packard announcement in Philadelphia to be identical to the one in Peoria).[9]

Department stores remained the most important advertisers throughout the early twentieth century and, like selling space on their floors (see the next chapter), their advertisements were no longer targeted at the readers of middle-class newspapers. Every major Philadelphia journal had large, prominently placed department store announcements daily. Although the column inches purchased by these retailers increased during this period, its proportion of total advertising fell because of even greater rises in national and classified advertising. At no time, however, did department store display advertising occupy less than thirty percent of the space devoted to ads in the

major dailies. Department stores maintained the visibility of their advertisements in two ways: size and placement. In a time when full-page ads were
rare, the stores took full- and seven-eighths-page ads on a regular basis. Location was as important as size in catching a reader's eye. By the 1910s, the
stores consistently took the same pages day after day in journals; a regular
reader of *The Philadelphia Record*, for example, knew that the Gimbels' ad
was on page three. As editors defined newspaper space by placing editorials,
sports, and financial news in consistent locations, advertisers did the same
with their announcements. In addition to regular placement, to aid the
would-be consumers searching for the stores' announcements, the ads were
placed prominently on either the final page of a section or on the upper-
right of an odd-numbered page (which is so noticeable because it appears to
the reader first when a newspaper is opened).

The first two decades of the twentieth century saw the newspaper in
Philadelphia become a crucial part of the expanding culture of consumption. Not only did the journals devote more space to advertising but the ads
became more artistic and inviting. Newspapers brought announcements
of new products and lower prices on established items into the home and
enticed readers-turned-customers out to the shops. The Holms only went
downtown in response to an "advertised sale," and Lou Holm (Cecil's
mother) probably was not the only shopper who took the ad with her "just
in case 'anybody tried to pull anything over on' " her. The relationship between the newspaper industry and consumer advertising began to develop
in the late nineteenth century but was not fully articulated until the early
twentieth.[10]

"In Philadelphia, nearly everybody reads The Bulletin" appeared on the
masthead and in the advertising of *The Evening Bulletin* for most of the
twentieth century. There was a great deal of truth in this statement, for
The Evening Bulletin overshadowed the early twentieth-century Philadelphia
market like no newspaper had ever done before. By 1911, when the paper issued the advertising card shown in figure 31, it was well on its way to becoming a Philadelphia institution. The illustration seeks to reinforce this with a
variety of visual cues. It starts by showing the statue of William Penn atop
City Hall perusing the journal. It then highlights the proximity of the Bulletin Building (in the right background) to City Hall. Centre Square was
truly the institutional hub of Philadelphia during this period. Within the
square was City Hall; to its east, the John Wanamaker department store; to its
north, the Bulletin Building and a masonic temple; to the west, the station

Figure 31. The newspaper as an institution: an *Evening Bulletin* advertising card circa 1911. Courtesy of the Print and Picture Collection, Free Library of Philadelphia.

and headquarters of the Pennsylvania Railroad; and to the south, the city's skyscraper zone.

The *Evening Bulletin*, however, had not always been an icon of Philadelphia's commercial culture. Its rise from obscurity in 1895 to circulation leadership in 1905 to dominance by 1920 is an oft-told story in both Philadelphia and journalism histories. Usually the tale focuses on the paper's publisher, William L. McLean; this examination, however, will center on how the journal successfully reacted to the expanding consumer market. This shift of focus in no way diminishes the importance of McLean; he chose the right format at the right time. By comparing McLean's decisions involving *The Evening Bulletin* with his cross-town rival Cyrus Curtis' at the *Public Ledger*, we can better understand the transition from the largely middle-class consumer culture of the late nineteenth century to the increasingly multi-classed consumer culture of the early twentieth.

Without a doubt, the rapid rise of *The Evening Bulletin* was the most noticeable trend in the Philadelphia newspaper industry during the period. In 1895, when William L. McLean purchased *The Bulletin* for $70,000 (largely borrowed), it had a daily circulation of approximately 6,000, making it the smallest of the thirteen English-language dailies serving the city. By 1926, *The Evening Bulletin* had a daily readership of over 500,000, which was by far the largest in the city. At that point, the paper accounted for nearly 40% of the total audited circulation for Philadelphia's eight dailies.

As one would expect, with the growth in circulation came increases in both size and advertising content. In 1900, *The Evening Bulletin* was twelve pages long, typical for an afternoon paper but smaller than all its major morning rivals. By 1910, it consisted of sixteen pages, about average for the city's journals. *The Evening Bulletin* became the largest paper by 1920 (tied in size with *The Evening Public Ledger*), printing twenty-eight pages daily. During this period, the advertising content of *The Evening Bulletin* increased dramatically (from approximately one-third of the paper in 1900 to nearly three-quarters in 1920), while the total space devoted to news and features remained relatively constant until it increased slightly in absolute terms in the 1920s. The amount of news and features in *The Evening Bulletin* on an average day in the 1920s would fill a small book; in fact, it did—in 1929 the paper printed a typical day's editorial content in book form and the volume was over three hundred pages long. By the 1920s, the *Bulletin* was a fat and efficient purveyor of news, advertisements, and features to its readers.[11]

The traditional explanation for the stunning rise to prominence of *The Evening Bulletin* is a once common journalistic trope: experienced newspaperman buys new presses, avoids sensationalism and produces an accurate, wildly successful journal. McLean and his paper fit this explanation almost perfectly. Born into a middle-class family in 1852, he received an early start on his journalism career when, as a schoolboy, he delivered a Pittsburgh paper to his small, western Pennsylvania town. He later worked in variety of positions at the Pittsburgh *Leader* and came to Philadelphia in 1878 to be secretary and treasurer of *The Philadelphia Press.* After a very fruitful career at *The Press,* he purchased the nearly moribund *Evening Bulletin* in 1895. By investing heavily in modern presses, committing the paper to the new journalistic norm of objectivity, and covering all the local and national news that fit, *The Evening Bulletin* under McLean quickly established itself in the Philadelphia market.[12]

This version (first institutionalized at the time of McLean's death in 1931) accurately recounts what happened but does not really offer a satisfactory explanation of why it happened. If simply buying high-speed presses and covering the news accurately was enough, the *Public Ledger* and *The Evening Public Ledger* also should have dominated the Philadelphia market, as their owner did both with a passion (and with a great deal more money than was available to McLean). Instead, the circulation of the morning *Public Ledger* stagnated and the afternoon edition remained a poor second to *The Evening Bulletin.*

If William L. McLean's *Bulletin* was the great success story of early twentieth-century journalism in Philadelphia, surely the industry's most unmitigated tale of woe belonged to Cyrus H. K. Curtis and his stable of papers. Curtis had made his fortune publishing a variety of middle-class national magazines in the city, of which the two most famous were the *Ladies' Home Journal* and *The Saturday Evening Post.* In the late nineteenth and early twentieth centuries, the circulations of and the profits from Curtis' magazines boomed. In 1913, he decided to turn his business acumen to the newspaper industry in his adopted hometown when he purchased the very bourgeois *Public Ledger* from Adolph S. Ochs for $2,000,000.

Curtis spared no expense in expanding the morning *Public Ledger* and soon launched an afternoon edition to counter the rise of *The Evening Bulletin.* His tactics were both brutal and extravagant; to quote one standard history, Curtis "bought and killed the *Press* to get its newsprint contracts; bought and killed the *Evening Telegraph* to get its Associated Press membership; bought and killed the *North American* to get its library." Spending money freely, Curtis built the morning *Public Ledger* into one of the finest newspapers in the United States, rivaling Ochs' *New York Times.* Befitting largely Anglophilic middle-class Philadelphia, Curtis thought in English metaphors. He advertised his paper as the "Manchester Guardian of America." Not only was the *Guardian* an excellent journal but significantly it was also the only British national paper not based in London. Clearly, Curtis hoped his journal would serve a market beyond the city's hinterland and compete with the New York press on the fledgling national market. He positioned *The Evening Public Ledger* as a more entertaining supplement to its morning counterpart and a better-written alternative to *The Evening Bulletin.* In 1925 he launched his final paper, *The Illustrated Sun,* a breezy photo-oriented tabloid, similar to its contemporaries in New York, the *Daily News* and *Daily Mirror.* All of Curtis' spending, however, was for naught. The circulation of the *Public Ledger* never reached its nineteenth-century peak and by the late teens, perhaps ashamed of the failure, Curtis refused to report it separately from its more widely read afternoon edition. *The Evening Public Ledger,* although more popular than its morning counterpart, never had a circulation of more than half that of *The Evening Bulletin.* Curtis' *Sun* was the most abject failure; it folded three years after its launch. By the time of his death in 1933, Curtis had lost $30,000,000 in his foray into the newspaper industry with little to show for it: his *Sun* predeceased him, the *Public Ledger* barely survived him (folding in 1934), and *The Evening Public Ledger* continued as a minor nuisance to *The Bulletin* until 1942.[13]

Curtis' debacle seriously undermines the standard explanation of McLean's success. For Curtis bought new presses and "objectively" covered the news, just like McLean, but the *Public Ledger* and its progeny failed, unlike *The Evening Bulletin.* By almost all journalistic criteria (except for perhaps the two most important, profitability and circulation), the *Public Ledger* in 1920 was a far better newspaper than was *The Evening Bulletin.* Many bourgeois Philadelphians loved the *Public Ledger* and helped firmly establish it as a key part of the middle-class geography of the city. In the words of one contemporary author: "The *Ledger* is a journal without which no Philadelphia family is complete. It is as important an adjunct to the breakfast-table as stewed kidney and scrapple." In the novel *Kitty Foyle,* Christopher Morley, Haverford born and bred, reflected back upon this special role of the *Public Ledger* in the lives of middle-class Philadelphians: "Sunday mornings, [father] used to sit under the arbor and read the *Public Ledger.* . . . Maybe it's a good thing that he died when he did, he'd be pretty sore at the old town now. There's no steam engines at Broad Street Station, and no morning *Ledger,* and I guess they've almost forgotten how to play cricket." Morley, having the benefit of hindsight, hints at the *Public Ledger's* weakness even as he writes of its centrality; like cricket and steam-powered trains, the paper reflected a middle-class Victorian vision of Philadelphia.[14]

The failure of Curtis and his *Public Ledger,* however, helps to explain the success of McLean and his *Evening Bulletin.* *The Evening Bulletin* was a phenomenal success because it reflected the new mass consumer market of the early twentieth century while the *Public Ledger* failed because it continued to target the bourgeois market of Victorian Philadelphia. Morley's *Kitty Foyle* captured this; the title character was thoroughly modern—and found the *Public Ledger* dull—but her father, who loved the *Public Ledger*, steam trains on the Pennsylvania Railroad, and cricket, was as Victorian as his paper of choice. As the twentieth century progressed, the *Public Ledger* became increasingly tied to the bourgeoisie. This intensifying identification with the middle class was both a product of Curtis' plan and a cause of the paper's decline. As working-class discretionary incomes rose in the early twentieth century, the culture of consumption slowly expanded from a largely bourgeois focus to an increasingly mass market one. To succeed, a newspaper had to reach as broad a readership as possible. McLean did this with *The Evening Bulletin* while Curtis did not with his conservative and restrained *Public Ledger*. Ironically, Curtis' tactics succeeded brilliantly—arguably he made the *Public Ledger* into the finest middle-class daily in America—although his strategy failed miserably: this excellent paper never made money.[15]

The Evening Bulletin (and the other general circulation dailies) captured this new mass market by offering a little something to all its potential readers in a format that made finding those items of interest relatively easy. The highly departmentalized, completely indexed layout was the same as used by the genteel metropolitan press, but the content was more inclusive. *The Evening Bulletin* (and its general circulation rivals) literally offered something for everybody. The paper's local news coverage was exhaustive: if an event happened anywhere in the region, an article—albeit often small—could be found on the pages of *The Evening Bulletin*. David Stern, later publisher of *The Philadelphia Record* and *The New York Post* but then a young reporter working in Philadelphia, described the early twentieth-century *Bulletin* as "a smoothly efficient machine geared to gather neighborhood items and news. Every fire, accident, and street fight, however trivial, was covered by an army of legmen who kept in constant touch with the office. The saying was that Bulletin reporters arrived at the fire before the firemen and in greater numbers." Reflecting on the paper's success, Stern claimed that "more names the better was the formula devised by [the] publisher, William L. McLean" and that this "formula worked" for "The Bulletin was dull but profitable." Adding to this "dullness" noted by Stern, in an effort not to offend readers, *The Evening Bulletin* under McLean seldom took controversial editorial positions. And like its local news coverage, the paper's national and international articles were competent and complete but usually from wire service sources and often uninspired. McLean defended the flat nature of the news coverage and the editorial voice of his paper by analogizing *The Evening Bulletin* to a guest in a reader's home and noting that "[p]roper guests neither shouted nor screamed."[16]

The front page layout of *The Evening Bulletin* in the twenties reflected this exhaustive but flat approach to news coverage. A typical front page had few graphics or multi-column headlines but many articles. For example, on May 17, 1920, page one contained twenty-seven articles on a very busy page along with seven sports pieces in the "stop press" column. *The Evening Public Ledger* that day had about the same number of articles on page one but did a better job of indicating news value through placement and varying the weight of headlines. The *Public Ledger* managed only to fit about half as many articles on its more restrained and more hierarchical front page (fifteen that morning). It is not that *The Evening Bulletin* during this period never assigned news value through the use of headlines, but that it was less likely to do so on a daily basis. Although *The Evening Bulletin* did not signal news value as clearly as did most of its competitors, there was a market-driven logic to the layout. McLean did not reject all the design conventions of the early twentieth century; for example, the 1920 *Evening Bulletin* was as well indexed and as well departmentalized as most large newspapers in the city, but he did forswear assigning a clear hierarchy to the news on page one. By failing to assign "value" to the news, the front page of *The Evening Bulletin* was less likely to offend a reader than those of its competitors. Throughout this period, *The Evening Bulletin* provided an even balance of local, regional, national, and international stories on page one (along with the very important "Lost Pets" section of the classified) and allowed its diverse readership to assign their own news values.

The Evening Bulletin and its morning general circulation counterparts, *The Philadelphia Inquirer* and *The Philadelphia Record,* could build their mass audiences because of the design conventions first adopted by the genteel metropolitan press in the late nineteenth century. The clear content signaling and the departmentalization of the news were manifestations of the Victorian middle class' faith in science and logic. In the early twentieth century, these same conventions allowed editors and publishers to create the multi-class general circulation newspaper.

Before I leave the pages of Philadelphia's press, a look at the use of gender as a spatial category should help to illustrate this evolving taxonomy of news. Starting in the late nineteenth century, newspaper editors began explicitly to divide the pages of their journals by gender though the creation of women's columns and pages. At the same time, gender was also used to define space in the railroad stations and the department stores. This use of gender was largely a reflection of the developing taxonomy of news, but its rise can also be linked to two broader societal trends: the decline of the early Victorian notion of separate spheres and the development of the general circulation newspaper as part of the mass consumer culture.[17]

At the center of this development is an irony: male editors defined female newspaper space as largely news about home, shopping, clubs, and family, but women readers clearly were as interested in "traditional" news as were men. In other words, the editors tried to continue the concept of separate spheres, but their female readers often rejected it. Early twentieth-century women's diaries, memoirs, and scrapbooks contain largely the same panoply of news as do those of their male counterparts. Sarah P. Sellers' scrapbooks were full of general news in addition to clippings from the women's pages. Anna E. Broomall focused her collection on local Delaware County history. Decades later, Eugenia Barnitz recalled the news of McKinley's death in the *Public Ledger* (and that the paper had "a deep mourning border around it for three days").[18]

In 1870, space in the daily newspaper was not divided by gender because the paper itself was largely a masculine institution in the middle-class Victorian world of separate spheres. At its base, this conceptualization of society placed the roles of women in a "private" sphere (the home and church, for example) and men in a "public" one of politics and business. Although there were limits to how separate these worlds were even at the height of early Victorian bourgeois culture (after all, middle-class men lived in the homes and went to the churches and women ventured at times into the world of business and politics), this concept is useful to help understand the broad outlines of a society in which women could not vote or serve on juries, and married women had limited contractual abilities, and few middle-class married women worked for pay outside the home. In 1870, virtually all the articles in the Philadelphia press fit into one of four categories: political, business, sports, and crime. To the male editors, all four types of news involved "masculine" activities. Women simply did not appear on the pages of the 1870 newspaper on a consistent basis. This reflected national trends; in the words of a 1907 textbook on journalism, "The old-style newspaper was a publication intended to appeal to grown men only [and] [i]t ignored one-half of the adult population entirely—women—in bidding for readers." Although women read newspapers, editors did not target them as readers and implicitly assumed that men chose the family's journals.[19]

A regularly reoccurring, explicitly defined female space first appeared on the pages of Philadelphia's morning newspapers in 1880. Prior to that time, particularly in Saturday editions, there would be articles clearly aimed at women or about the household, but never steadily or in a special location. Not surprisingly, it was the well-defined, very bourgeois *Public Ledger* that had the first regular column devoted to women: "In and Out of the House-hold" ran every Saturday on the top of page five. During the 1880s, other journals developed daily features aimed at women. In *The North American,* this gendered definition of space was implicit: there were no headings but articles about women were grouped together on a single page (which was filled out with other news). By 1890, *The Philadelphia Inquirer* developed an explicitly female space: a regular column entitled "Gossip for Women." The editors placed under this heading a variety of short articles that they thought would be of interest to female readers. Its very name indicates that the male editors thought the women's news was different from (and less important than) "men's" news; the 1890 *Philadelphia Inquirer* headed its financial page "The Business World" not "Gossip for Stockbrokers."[20]

During the 1890s, Philadelphia dailies increased their use of gender to define space on their pages. In 1900, five of the eleven papers examined had explicitly denominated columns for women and all but one of the remainder regularly grouped articles about or targeted toward women on the same page. This trend is confirmed by contemporary texts. In 1907, a former editor at *The New York Evening Sun* claimed that at "new-style" papers "particular effort is made to please the women." He claimed that this change was part of a shift in focus from just "news" (read politics, business, and crime) to "offering something for everyone." This increased attention paid to female readers also reflected the expanding cultural opportunities open to middle-class women at the turn of the century. More and more magazines—such as the Philadelphia-based *Ladies' Home Journal*—targeted female readers explicitly during the late nineteenth century and the newspapers' columns can be seen as competitive responses to this development. In addition, the safety of the largely bourgeois trains and trolleys allowed middle-class women to explore more of the region unaccompanied by male escorts, from the suburban amusement parks to the Center City stores and theaters to the Jersey shore. Well before the "new woman" of the 1920s, Victorian editors groped with how to reach this new, turn-of-the-century woman.[21]

Throughout the first quarter of the twentieth century, Philadelphia editors continued to place together what they defined as women's news and advertisers began to focus on this specialized market. In 1910, nine of the eleven dailies had women's pages. This use of gendered space increased further until, by 1920, all seven of the remaining journals had an implicit or explicit women's section. By the early twentieth century, advertisements on these pages also began to be targeted at women. The women's page or column in the press had become a part of the mass-market culture of consumption.[22]

Although perhaps the most obvious because of its title, the women's page was not the only gendered use of space on the pages of Philadelphia's newspapers during the early twentieth century. Reflecting society's sexual division of labor, classified employment advertising had been divided between male and female listings since the 1880s. More enlightening, however, was the development of a distinct yet implicit male space in the turn-of-the-century journals: the sports pages and their advertisements. Sports news had been an integral part of the Philadelphia press throughout the late nineteenth century and, given the overwhelming male attendance at period athletic events, had probably always been more avidly read by men than by women. In the late 1890s, advertisers began to place announcements targeted at a male audience on the sports pages. These advertisements ranged from alcoholic beverages (Anheuser-Busch beers and rye whiskey) to custom tailoring to home cures for "Contagious Blood Poison" (venereal disease). This occurred at the same time female-targeted advertising first appeared on some of the women's pages in the same papers. By 1900, advertisers recognized—and used—both gendered spaces in the press.[23]

Gendered space first appeared on the pages of the Victorian genteel metropolitan press. Although it reflected a number of shifts in society, it is significant that the change began in journals largely targeted at the middle class. Without a doubt, the rise of specialized women's pages can be linked to the same commercial factors that led to the creation of mass-circulation women's magazines like the *Ladies' Home Journal*. Advertisers—and hence publishers—wanted to reach this important segment of the middle-class culture of consumption. But this use of gender also reflected the taxonomy of news that first developed in the bourgeois press of the late nineteenth century. Like sports, international, local, business, and society, women's news became fodder for the carefully ordered pages of the journals. Even if the editors and publishers failed to fully understand what their female readers wanted, their efforts illustrate a new way of understanding the news. Newspaper pages, like any other urban space, could be divided and classified. To use the words of contemporary observers, this was "new-style" or "modern" design. Another way to look at it was that these design changes were the application of rationality—or science—to the news.

*   *   *

The decline of the *Public Ledger* and the growth of *The Evening Bulletin* reflected the shift from a middle-class market to a mass one in the early twentieth century. This transformation parallels that in the interior layouts and customer segmentation of Philadelphia's department stores. In both cases, once largely middle-class urban spaces—the pages of the genteel metropolitan press and the floors of the grand dry goods stores—changed to include areas for members of other classes. As will become evident, though, never did these commercial institutions become classless but instead became multi-classed. During the early twentieth century, the middle-class taxonomy of space found on the floors of the department stores and on the pages of the newspapers began to influence other Philadelphians in complex ways.

In the case of the newspapers and department stores, these influences were largely unintended. Philadelphia's editors and merchants and its bourgeois women and men did not expand the market to the working class in order to extend this middle-class sense of order. Instead, the burgeoning market caused once bourgeois institutions to develop a larger clientele—like the John Wanamaker store—or to decline—like the *Public Ledger*. The ultimate effect, however, was to introduce the middle-class scientific worldview to others.

Chapter 6
We Never Realized That Department Stores Had an Upstairs

*Until my brother and I were in our teens we never realized that depart-
ment stores had an upstairs. We knew there were windows up there, but we
supposed they were there to make the place look large and that nobody
went above the basement. Mother and Dad always took us to the basement. We stepped off the subway and there we were. When we went downtown it was always because there was an advertised sale and Mother went
along with the newspaper page containing the ad just in case "anybody
tried to pull anything over on you."[1]*

The new "bargain basements" where John Cecil Holm and his
family shopped were just one of many twentieth-century innovations at
Philadelphia's department stores. Some changes were simply extensions of
trends apparent in the late nineteenth century: the retailers built still larger
structures, added even more lines and services, and created increasingly detailed and elaborate interiors. Others seemed like more radical departures:
the retailers applied the "science of merchandising" (to use the words of John
Wanamaker) to transform these once largely middle-class havens into multi-
class institutions.

The city's department stores reached the pinnacle of their prestige and
power during the first quarter of the twentieth century. By 1920, annual sales
at John Wanamaker, Philadelphia's leading retailer, had reached nearly $45
million. Middle-class men and women continued to make the department
stores and the Center City shopping area the leading retail destination in the
region. "Shopping and lunch at Wanamaker's" remained an archetypical
bourgeois experience in the metropolis. The bonds were strong. As they did
with friends, middle-class Philadelphians gave the popular stores nicknames;
Holm recalled that "Women [went] shopping not only in Lit's, but Snelly's
[N. Snellenburg] and Wanny's [John Wanamaker]."[2]

As Holm suggests, although both men and women shopped in Center City, the department stores remained a largely female space in the heart of the metropolis. Shopping had a rhythm for many middle-class women in the region. It often began the night before by scanning the pages of advertisements in the evening newspapers; continued the next morning by taking the train, trolley, or subway downtown to visit a favorite store (perhaps like Lou Holm with ad in hand); later returning home unburdened, as the retailers delivered the purchases at no charge; finally ending a few days later when the firm's truck drew up outside the house. It was this cadence that allowed the central retail zone—and its flagship department stores—to thrive.

In the first decade of the twentieth century, each retailer completed a major expansion that usually allowed it, albeit briefly, to be "the largest department store in Philadelphia" (if not "the world"). John Wanamaker finally won this contest in 1911. (Figure 32 shows the new Wanamaker building looming over all its neighbors—except for the tower of nearby City Hall.) Although the successful merchants grew in size, the number of department stores fell, and by 1926, only five major establishments remained: Wanamaker, Gimbel Brothers, Strawbridge & Clothier, Nathan Snellenburg, and Lit Brothers. Even more telling, the long-term future of mass merchandising could be found in the much smaller suburban branches opened by Strawbridge & Clothier in the early 1930s, not their large Center City store.[3]

What is in a name? Although Shakespeare likely would disagree, in the case of the department store, a great deal. The term highlights the importance of classification to the business. The merchants physically divided their buildings into departments and also organized their buying and selling staffs along the same lines. When Philadelphia's dry goods stores expanded in size in the late nineteenth century, they, along with their counterparts across the nation and around the world, created an entirely new, scientific way of selling merchandise to consumers. It took some time, however, for Philadelphians—both within the industry and without—to adopt this new title for these retailers.

Although the term "department store" was coined in the United States in the late 1880s, it took many years to reach Philadelphia. John Wanamaker evidently disliked the appellation and, according to his biographer, avoided using it to describe his firm, preferring instead the awkward label "a new kind of store." Throughout the late nineteenth century, Philadelphia's nascent department stores referred to themselves simply as "dry good stores." This self-description is not surprising, all of the major retailers of the period

Figure 32. The new John Wanamaker department store and City Hall in 1911. *Golden Book of the Wanamaker Stores* (Philadelphia: John Wanamaker, 1911).

had either started as traditional dry goods merchants (Strawbridge & Clothier is an example) or explicitly added dry goods to their existing lines (men's clothing in the case of John Wanamaker or millinery for Lit Brothers). This conservatism was also in keeping with national trends; the trade paper for the industry did not change its title from the *Dry Goods Economist* to the *Department Store Economist* until 1938.[4]

When the term "department store" came into use in Philadelphia at around the turn of the century, it was, perhaps significantly, first applied by outsiders, not the merchants themselves. For example, when Gimbel Brothers expanded their store in 1902 they described the facility as the "largest retail store in the world" and reminded customers in bold type that "this is a dry goods store." Nowhere in their newspaper advertisements or store guides did Gimbels use the term department store. The *Public Ledger*, however, began its article on the opening: "A new standard was set for department stores . . . when Gimbel Brothers' new establishment . . . was formally opened to the public."[5]

Shortly thereafter, Strawbridge & Clothier issued a store guide entitled "The Great Department Store of Strawbridge & Clothier." The first few pages of the brochure highlight the importance of "departments" to the store. The firm ends this discussion by terming itself "the ideal Department Store." This, however, was an isolated example and Strawbridge's continued to describe itself in both newspaper advertisements and city directories as a dry goods store.[6]

The term was finally adopted by the merchants around 1912. Until then, all the major retailers used the term dry goods to identify their businesses in the store guides, newspaper advertisements, and city directory listings. The more enterprising among them used some variation on the theme to help differentiate their grand emporia from smaller, run-of-the-mill stores. Two common labels they adopted were "dry goods, etc." and "dry goods and general merchandise." Suddenly, in the 1912 city directory, the Wanamaker store switched its listing to "dept store." Gimbel Brothers followed this lead the next year and within a few years all of Philadelphia's major dry goods houses were describing themselves as department stores.[7]

Why did this transition happen so quickly? One possible explanation is that Wanamaker wanted a grander term to describe its new retail palace opened in 1911 and, because it was the largest store in the city, once it adopted the label, the others quickly fell into line. Such a simple interpretation, however, belies the influence of rationality and science on Wanamaker's business philosophy. Indeed, just as Frederick Taylor's scientific management depended upon classification, so did John Wanamaker's view of retailing. As early as the 1860s, he had divided his men's clothing store into explicit departments, and he regularly termed how his store operated as the "science of merchandising." At the turn of the century, he addressed the American

Academy of Political and Social Science at their 1900 annual meeting regarding "The Evolution of Mercantile Business." The speech, though primarily a defense of department stores against charges of monopolist practices, is a fascinating melange of Victorian social science rhetoric. It is no accident that John Wanamaker combined the terms "science" and "evolution" with the concept of efficiency through classification; it is instead a reflection of the Victorian bourgeoisie's understanding of the nature of science. At the heart of this long-gone Victorian "popular science" was scientific classification. Wanamaker's specific use of both "science" and "evolution" is also significant as the basis for Darwin's hugely influential study of evolution was taxonomy. Though largely self-educated, Wanamaker nicely represents the worldview of many intelligent, educated middle-class women and men in his use of these terms. But as important as Wanamaker's words were, his actions—and those of his competitors—were far more important. Their rational classification of both space (their sales floors) and time (the retail calendar) was Victorian science at work in everyday bourgeois life.[8]

During the first decade of the twentieth century, all of the major Philadelphia department stores continued to enlarge their buildings and fill these structures with the latest technology. Size and modernity remained important selling (and bragging) points: the bigger and the newer, the better. Both concepts were in keeping with the abundance that helped to define turn-of-the-century bourgeois society. Such grand structures fit into what historians have termed the "culture of abundance" for a number of reasons: not only could the stores stock items in larger quantities and also in more varieties, but the sheer size of buildings was further evidence of Philadelphia's (and the urban bourgeoisie's) wealth. The department stores' spectacles of technology demonstrated both abundance and modernity. Not only did Philadelphia (and the middle class) have material wealth (a lot of things) but this abundance encompassed "cutting-edge" technology (a lot of new, better things). The retailers reflected this core middle-class value by having the latest gadgets both for sale and in use. John Wanamaker suggested that this abundance and spectacle were direct results of the Centennial Exposition. He further argued that abundance and spectacle were good unto themselves. In a 1900 speech he stated: "The rising tide of popular desire to assemble under one roof articles used in every home and with freedom to purchase was a constant suggestion in 1876, not alone because of its convenience, but because to some degree it would form a permanent and useful exhibition." In other words, seeing the world's goods for sale at his store was an educational experience equal to attending an international exposition. By invoking the Centennial, Wanamaker made explicit the link between the selling departments of his stores and the carefully classified exhibits of world's fairs. Such a link further highlights the connections between the well-studied rationality of Victorian exhibitions, museums, and libraries and their less-well-studied commercial counterparts.[9]

The physical expansion of the department stores was a continuation of a trend begun in the 1890s, but the twentieth-century buildings attained sizes that were unthinkable just a few years before. Prior to 1890, most of the stores had been combinations of smaller three- and four-story structures. The built-to-suit eight-story Cooper & Conrad store (Philadelphia's first building designed from the outset to be a complete department store) and the five-story additions made to Strawbridge & Clothier during the 1890s began the push skyward. By the turn of the century, the Snellenburg firm at Twelfth and Market Streets (figure 33) was a typical department store structure in Philadelphia; it was not so much a grand palace of consumption as a terribly efficient selling machine. It occupied approximately one-quarter of a city block, was six stories tall, and was designed to be a unified whole with an open floor plan that allowed the merchant easily to arrange—and to rearrange—the departments based on selling needs. The individual floors were massive blank stages upon which different "sets" could be placed. The trend toward larger edifices continued and by 1902, Gimbel Brothers proudly announced that "the Gimbel Block, Philadelphia" with "nearly 23 acres of floor space" was "the largest exclusively retail store in the world." The firm claimed that "Philadelphia has two [department stores] larger than the biggest in Europe (the Bon Marche of Paris, which has 16 acres of floor space). . . . New York's largest Store is much smaller than Gimbels." Having a store that occupied a full city block front became very important to Gimbels and its counterparts, as it helped to highlight size and, with it, abundance. Like Gimbels, Snellenburg continued to expand and soon advertised that its building took up the "entire block—Market, 11th to 12th Streets." In fact, for most retailers this claim was a bit of a cheat: Center City Philadelphia had unusually large blocks and most of these structures, including Gimbels' and Snellenburg's, only occupied one complete side (or front) of a block and part of two of the other sides. Gimbels, despite its almost constant expansion, never occupied the entire block from Eighth to Ninth, Market to Chestnut Streets. The only merchant who could honestly make this claim was John Wanamaker, as the store took up an entire (albeit a smaller than average) city block (Thirteenth to Juniper, Market

Figure 33. Main building of the Nathan Snellenburg store circa 1900. Courtesy of the Print and Picture Collection, Free Library of Philadelphia.

to Chestnut), and, by its fiftieth anniversary in 1911, was, in the ever modest words of the firm, "the largest and most beautiful building in the world devoted to retail merchandising."[10]

The firms explicitly linked size with modernity in their literature by reminding shoppers how much larger the early twentieth-century buildings were than their late nineteenth-century predecessors. A Gimbel Brothers brochure told customers that its 1902 building dwarfed "the original 'big store' [which was the Cooper & Conrad structure of the 1890s] that seemed so large and fine not many years ago." At the same time, a Strawbridge & Clothier guidebook proclaimed that "few years have passed, in the record of nearly four decades, which have not been signalized by some added room or new department." Later, Wanamaker pamphlets regularly remarked that the Grand Depot had been "a notable building in its day [three decades before], but in time proved too small for the mercantile activity that developed within it." Wanamaker further capitalized on the new building as a tourist attraction by offering daily guided tours at no charge.[11]

Beyond sheer size, the department stores continued their late nineteenth-century practice of using technology to attract customers to their selling floors. All the guidebooks issued by the firms touted the multitude of modern features found throughout the buildings. But note again that the stores linked technology with abundance: not only did the retailers have the latest inventions but they had many of each such marvel. Gimbels in 1905 focused on its one thousand telephones, its thirty-eight elevators, its passenger escalator (which had been the Otis exhibit at the 1900 Paris Exposition), its on-site ice plant (that could produce forty tons a day), its "diffused hot air" heating, its ventilation system that cost $100,000, and its electric plant that was "equivalent to 25,000 16-candle-power lamps." Well before e-commerce, Philadelphians could use an earlier network to purchase goods in real time from home when Strawbridge & Clothier claimed to be "the first large Store in the world to install a complete shopping-by-'phone system." It was both "The Telephone Store" and "The Comfortable Store." It offered telephone order service twenty-four hours a day (as did Gimbels and Wanamaker) and, in summer, pumped "in pure air from the highest point in the building—millions of cubic feet, a constant inflow. . . . Pure air in constant gentle motion—that is far more healthful than churning up a foul atmosphere with many fans." Of course, the 1911 Wanamaker building had the most marvels of them all. It had fifty-two passenger elevators and sixteen freight ones (all "direct hydraulic . . . and hence cannot fall"), ten electric dumbwaiters, the "gigantic Wanamaker power plant" (capable of powering the equivalent to 55,000 18 candlepower lights), a refrigerating plant (with two 75–ton ice machines), and an advanced heating and ventilation system. In 1911 Wanamaker added the "Wanamaker Wireless" to its long list of wonders; this was the first public Marconi station in a department store and it could send messages to "any steamer one hundred and fifty or more miles away." Later, the store and some of its competitors started commercial radio stations.[12]

Massive size and cutting-edge technology not only maintained Philadelphia's department stores' status as civic landmarks but also tied the retailers into the Europeanized world's growing material and technological abundance. The long lists of features, which now seem so quaint, proclaimed not just modernity (the telephone) but also abundance (one thousand telephones). Like the city itself, the department stores expanded greatly in size. The old Wanamaker Grand Depot, all one floor of it, was by far the largest store in the Centennial city. Its successor, the 1911 Wanamaker store, may have occupied only a slightly larger footprint but stretched high into the sky. The merchants used these larger structures to offer not just more and different goods but also more services. The department stores became landmarks not just in the physical geography of the city but also in the mental geography of middle-class Philadelphians.

Within these larger, modern structures the department stores crowded an array of services, comforts, and conveniences to lure potential customers to their selling floors. One reason the firms needed such imposing buildings was the increased demand for non-selling space. Although the merchants had begun to offer most of these services during the late nineteenth century, the stores all expanded their conveniences on a vast scale during the early twentieth century. These facilities at the department stores allowed customers to stay in the stores longer and thus have more time to buy more goods. Like the modern shopping mall with its food court and array of other services, the early twentieth-century department store was an enclosed, climate-controlled world where people could pass an entire day escaping from the outside world (while, the merchants hoped, spending money).

The largest (and most obvious) of these non-selling amenities offered to the public by the department stores was the restaurant. Initially provided by a few firms on a small scale in the 1880s, the eating establishments increased in both number and size in the early twentieth century. By 1902, Gimbel Brothers had a large, full-service restaurant (see figure 34) and a separate delicatessen on the seventh floor as well as a soda fountain and "quick lunch service" in the basement. The same year, Strawbridge & Clothier provided a soda fountain and a "well-patronized and cozy" lunchroom in the basement of its store. Evidently, Strawbridge and its customers found these insufficient, for a little over a decade later, the firm built a much larger "Restaurant . . . on the sixth floor . . . which," according to the store, "in many respects [was] the finest in the city."[13]

Nevertheless, it was the 1911 Wanamaker building that supplied the ultimate in department store dining in Philadelphia. All told, customers had four eating options. In the basement was the Soda Fountain lunchroom, as large as most of its competitors' main restaurants. On the gallery between the ground floor and the basement was the Dairy, continuing the name of the original dining establishment in the Grand Depot. On the north end of the eighth floor was the Buffet for a quick lunch. Occupying the southern third of the same floor was the "Grand Crystal Tea Room," Wanamaker's premier dining facility. It could seat 1,400 people at a time and served three

Figure 34. Postcard view of Gimbel Brother's main restaurant circa 1905. Courtesy of the Pennsylvania State Archives, Pennsylvania Historical and Museum Commission.

thousand patrons on an average day. The Grand Crystal Tea Room was the largest single dining room in Philadelphia and one of the largest in the world. The firm declared that the tearoom was "a feature of the Store that should not be missed," and many middle-class Philadelphians and tourists took this advice and visited it quite regularly.[14]

The Wanamaker facility was much more elaborately furnished than the one provided at Gimbel Brothers, but they both represented well-ordered, middle-class space in the city. To operate these massive venues, the merchants had to impose order not just on the space but also on their employees and customers. It took a legion of workers to seat, to serve, to collect payment from, and to clean up after each patron. Service had to be efficient yet comforting: for many customers, eating at the department store would be their first experience of regularly dining out. The patrons, too, had to conform to this new experience. Not only might they have to wait in line to be seated, but they had to be encouraged to eat quickly. At lunchtime not only was the table needed for another diner but the merchants would clearly prefer to have the customers on a sales floor shopping rather than at a restaurant table eating. The result was the creation of another daily rhythm to middle-class life: standing in a long but rapidly moving line, being marched to one's seat by just one of many hosts, scanning the menu, one of dozens of servers taking the order, quickly being served, standing in line to pay, and resuming shopping. This was a tempo that would become part of life for thousands of Philadelphia women and hundreds of men every day for most of the twentieth century.

The Grand Crystal Tea Room held an important place for women in the middle-class geography of Philadelphia during the 1910s and 1920s. They went to Wanamaker's for lunch regardless of whether they shopped at the store that day. For example, Bess Smith (one of Mary's older sisters) met two friends for lunch at the tearoom before going with them to a matinee of *Snow White* at the nearby Stanley Theater. Most patrons, however, combined dining with shopping, as Wanamaker surely had wished. Margaret Moffat, then a college student, spent an entire Friday during a winter break in Center City with her mother making "many purchases" and they "took lunch" with a friend in the "Tea Room." She arrived "home real late and [was] tired to death."[15]

Bourgeois men also dined at the department stores, although far less frequently than their female counterparts. If he was patronizing the store around lunchtime, John L. Smith, for example, would eat at Gimbel Brothers, a few blocks from his own map shop. Most male diners, however, seemed to eat at the department store restaurants only when meeting women. Cyril Harvey of Haddonfield was more typical; he did not usually eat lunch at a department store but met his wife and daughter at Wanamaker's for Christmas shopping and the family dined there.[16]

The overwhelmingly female clientele of the department stores helped to create at their restaurants a distinctively female space in Center City. John L. Smith once described Gimbel Brothers as a "mass of women in their shopping." Data collected by the John Wanamaker store in the 1920s support Smith's observation, indicating "that of dry goods, women purchased 90 per cent of all that is sold; of food, 87 per cent; of hardware, 49 per cent; of automobiles, 41 per cent; of drugs, 51 per cent; and of phonographs, 60 per cent." This largely female customer base carried over into the restaurants. At the Grand Crystal Tea Room, similar to most of its competitors, this gendering was implicit: the department store dining rooms were open to both sexes but were mostly used by women. Near the tearoom in the 1911 store, however, Wanamaker also explicitly divided space by gender. Three smaller rooms adjoining the main restaurant "comprised," in the words of Wanamaker guidebooks, "the Men's Section." The store allowed smoking in these areas but not in the larger tearoom. One was "a delightful reading or smoking room," another served "luncheon to men, or to men accompanied by women," and the final was a banquet area for private parties. An interesting comparison of gendered space can be made between the dining facilities at the Wanamaker store and those at the Pennsylvania Railroad's Broad Street Station just across Centre Square. At the railway terminal, the main dining room was officially undesignated but served mostly male patrons while a small area was set apart for women. One block to the east, at the department store, the main dining room, also officially not segregated by gender, was used primarily by women and a smaller space was reserved for men. Both illustrate the importance of gender as a classification to early twentieth-century bourgeois Philadelphians. At the largely "male" depot, the railroad made special arrangements for female riders. At the mostly "female" department store, management offered similar encouragement to male shoppers. Regardless, both the department stores and the railway termini illustrate the role of gender in the taxonomy of space.[17]

In addition to dining facilities, the department stores in the early twentieth century devoted more and more floor space to other non-selling services. By 1905, Strawbridge & Clothier joined Wanamaker and Gimbel Brothers in placing a branch post office in its building. This was clearly a competitive move and not a necessity, as the main post office was within a few blocks of all the stores at Tenth and Market Streets. In addition, Strawbridge & Clothier located throughout its structure "Women's Parlors" where the harried female shopper (or "visitor" in the always polite words of this conservative firm) could find "comfortable chairs, roomy tables, stationery for writing, [and] selected magazines and newspapers." Strawbridge's also provided its "visitors" with a parcel check facility, a Bureau of Information, and public pay telephones. Across Market Street, Gimbel Brothers offered customers the same services plus a "Hospital, with [a] trained nurse in constant attendance" and a Recital Hall that could accommodate twelve hundred people. Wanamaker, of course, offered the same broad array of amenities. Some innovations were short-lived; Wanamaker, for example, twice between 1909 and 1921 experimented with attended playgrounds for children in the store (to allow mothers of small children to shop without being distracted) but found that, according to the firm's official historian, "it did not pay and the privilege was abused. Mothers would leave their children here while they shopped in other stores or went to the theatre." More broadly, this failure demonstrates that the merchants carefully studied their services in an attempt to link the added conveniences with sales. Despite Strawbridge's use of the term "visitor," the merchants clearly viewed the women and men who came to the stores first and foremost as customers, and the stores constantly fine-tuned their offerings in order to maximize sales and minimize costs.[18]

Middle-class Philadelphians actively used (and, in the minds of the retailers, at times abused) all these facilities. One college student, for example, spent part of her summer break reading books in Wanamaker's waiting room and seldom purchased anything from the store. She probably chose the store over her home for reading because Wanamaker's, with its tall ceilings and forced air ventilation, was cooler. A young suburban woman regularly contacted her relatives and friends from the public pay telephones at Strawbridge & Clothier (and, fortunately for the store, also shopped there). Tired out-of-town visitors often rested in the lounges between shopping forays.[19]

Besides the services that customers could see and use while at the department stores, the retailers also increased the space in the structures dedicated to "back room" operations, such as credit and delivery. By the turn-of-the-century, all the major stores offered some form of credit to encourage sales. Most were simple charge accounts that the stores required to be paid in full at the end of each month. Some merchants, however, financed larger sales, such as pianos, for longer terms. By the 1920s, Strawbridge and

Wanamaker offered budget accounts that allowed people to purchase house-hold furnishings on extended payments.[20]

Delivery services also expanded rapidly in the late nineteenth and early twentieth centuries. In the 1870s, Strawbridge & Clothier's delivery department consisted of one wagon and two horses that served only Center City and the adjoining neighborhoods. By 1912, it comprised, according to the store, "about three hundred horses, one hundred and fifty wagons and trucks, and twenty-one automobile delivery trucks" and extended "to hundreds of towns throughout Philadelphia County, the counties adjoining, and to scores of towns in New Jersey." The delivery operation at Strawbridge's, however, paled in comparison to that of Wanamaker's. To serve the city in the 1910s, Wanamaker's operated a Center City garage and warehouse, stables in Germantown and West Philadelphia, and a warehouse and stables in North Philadelphia. Not only did John Wanamaker offer free delivery by its own vehicles throughout both the Philadelphia and New York metropolitan areas in 1912 but it also did not charge for mail or express delivery for many items worldwide.[21]

Credit and delivery added to the selling expenses of the department stores. Charge accounts, unlike cash sales, carried the risk of nonpayment for the merchandise. In addition, credit required many additional employees to keep the records. In the days before computers, this all had to be done manually. A legion of clerks collected the sales slips, matched them with the proper accounts, entered the information, and tabulated monthly statements. Delivery services required many employees, horses, vans, and trucks, along with stables and garages. The larger stores, such as Wanamaker's and Strawbridge's, had multiple delivery depots in the city by the early twentieth century. In addition, all the stores required a bevy of employees to coordinate the movement of both the paperwork and the merchandise from the selling floor to the customer's home. Although these services increased the convenience of shopping for the stores' patrons, they also increased the chance for mistakes by sales clerks and delivery people, which could create unhappy customers. One middle-class woman, for example, made a special trip on a Saturday to Strawbridge & Clothier from her home in New Jersey "to see about . . . a couple of coats" that the store had failed to deliver. A few years later, the same merchant delivered to the same woman goods she had not ordered, resulting in another trip to the city "chiefly" to return them. Given the number of exhortations aimed at their employees and the experiments with pre-printed delivery slips and charge tokens, misdirected deliveries and mistaken charges were not uncommon problems for the department stores and their clientele.[22]

In addition to their direct costs, all these new and expanded services—from the restaurants to delivery—also added to the expense of doing business for the department stores simply because they took up valuable space. This meant that the retailers needed bigger buildings and had less room proportionately for the selling departments in the structures. The early twentieth-century department stores attempted to attract a wider range of shoppers in order to help spread out these higher costs over more customers. To bring in some people, the merchants, ironically, offered even more services. To appeal to others, the firms introduced cheaper goods. The result was the gradual replacement of the middle-class Victorian dry goods store by the multi-class twentieth-century department store.[23]

During the early twentieth century, the retailers not only continued to add departments but also changed their division, or taxonomy, of space. The John Wanamaker store went from 99 selling departments in 1908 (when its new building was partially open) to 140 in 1913 (two years after it was complete). During the late nineteenth century, the firms had divided their floors by type (shoes, for example) or type and gender (men's shoes). A little after the turn of the century, the stores added a new factor to this mix: class. Retailers created new divisions within their buildings—the "bargain basement"—and added more exclusive departments "upstairs," such as the "London Shop for Men."[24]

In terms of size, by far the largest space defined by class in the early twentieth-century department stores was the area known as the "Bargain Basement" (at Gimbel Brothers, initially), the "Down Stairs Store" (at John Wanamaker), the "Economy Basement" (at N. Snellenburg) or the "Subway Store" (at Lit Brothers and later at Gimbel Brothers). In 1901, not one Philadelphia merchant had a bargain basement. The first appeared the next year, when Gimbel Brothers opened its new wing and declared "all stocks are duplicated in the basement" with "goods of less expensive sorts." By 1920, all the major retailers (except the ever conservative Strawbridge & Clothier) placed separate sales departments below ground that sold a combination of lower-priced and discontinued items in far less opulent settings than their main sales floors.[25]

The lower-priced basement departments solved at least two problems confronting the department stores in the early twentieth century: what to do with their underground floors and how to compete with the new chain stores. During the 1880s and 1890s, improvements in ventilating systems had allowed the merchants to open their basements to customers. Initially, the retailers had treated this below-ground space exactly like any other selling area within their buildings. The continued reassurances as to how often the air was changed in the basements that regularly appeared in the store guides, however, indicate that many existing bourgeois shoppers may not have perceived the lower level as quite the equal of the other floors. By allocating the basement to less-expensive goods targeted at lower-middle-class and working-class customers, the department stores could expand (or defend) their market share and more fully utilize their buildings. Presumably, the retailers believed that people looking for bargains were more tolerant of their surroundings than those paying full price. Cecil Holm's parents appeared happy to have exchanged opulence for value.[26]

The Center City department stores also hoped that the bargain basements could fend off the challenge of the chain stores. Also known as variety stores and "five-and-tens," retailers such as F. W. Woolworth and S. S. Kresge started in the late nineteenth century and grew rapidly during the first two decades of the twentieth. By 1925, Woolworth had 1,260 units nationwide and Kresge 233. These stores succeeded by selling a variety of goods at low prices for cash only, following in part the methodology of the early department stores. The chains operated smaller units (usually consisting of but one sales floor) than did the department stores. Woolworth and Kresge drew on neighborhoods and towns for their clientele, not on the entire metropolis like Wanamaker. Initially these stores served smaller cities and towns but Woolworth opened its first store in Philadelphia about 1896 and had five outlets in the city a little over a decade later. The chains did not place all of their stores in Center City but also located them in suburban towns and neighborhood shopping districts. (Woolworth had two in Germantown and one in West Philadelphia.) Shoppers could often walk from their home to their local five-and-ten, as Albert Edmunds did one afternoon to the Woolworth on nearby Lancaster Avenue in West Philadelphia. By offering a variety of inexpensive merchandise from convenient locations, the chain stores represented a challenge to the low end of the department store market.[27]

To help meet this test, the department stores not only offered less expensive goods and fewer services in their basements than on their main sales floors but also decorated the downstairs stores more simply. Plainness in architecture and display were more than just cost-saving measures; by the 1920s some department store executives had begun to fear their great retail emporia were too grand and their elaborate structures might be chasing away some customers instead of attracting them (figure 35 shows the opulence of the main sales floor of the John Wanamaker store in 1911). Wanamaker management, for example, worried: "Are there not classes of people we are not reaching?" Specifically, they thought that "poorer people are reported to prefer to deal with the 8th Street Stores [Gimbel Brothers, Lit Brothers, and Strawbridge & Clothier] rather than at Wanamaker's. The size and the beauty of this store seems to frighten them off. Similarly it is said that our sales in Kensington amount to almost nothing." Here, Wanamaker officials were using "Kensington" as a code for working class, since it was an industrial section of the city with a largely working-class population, both facts well known to any contemporary bourgeois Philadelphian. Wanamaker's concern clearly indicates that the store was moving beyond its once almost exclusively middle-class focus. It and its competitors wanted to reach the mass market that now included more working-class women and men.[28]

It was not just the working classes that the early twentieth-century department stores wanted to attract; the retailers also actively sought more elite customers who might look down on the basements and the traditional selling departments alike. While the stores were reworking their lower levels to attract a more mass market, the merchants also were revising their upstairs departments to encourage a more "class" market. During the early twentieth century, some retailers created new selling areas with higher levels of service to attract a more well-heeled clientele. John Wanamaker created the "London Shop for Men" in the 1911 store as a separate department to sell "clothes which are different, which are exclusive, and which are correct." For female customers at Wanamaker, the metaphor crossed the channel to Paris. Scattered throughout the building, near their more pedestrian equivalents, were the "Little Gray Salons" that, according to Wanamaker, made "shopping a real delight." The store guide informed the discriminating customer (or at least the one with a bit more cash) that "these quiet little gray rooms are French in design, being furnished and finished like the charming shops in the Place Vendôme and the Rue de la Paix . . . and are planned to give seclusion from the usual shopping crowds and to enable women to select their purchases under the most ideal conditions of comfort, privacy and artistic atmosphere." In other words, Wanamaker wanted to insulate its upper-class customers from the hurly-burly confronted and created by its predominately middle-class clientele.[29]

The Philadelphia merchants added class to their selling space taxonomy with amazing rapidity. In 1908, John Wanamaker had only one department that sold ready-to-wear men's suits. By 1916, the same store had three: the

Figure 35. A retail palace: a sales counter on John Wanamaker's main floor in 1911. *Golden Book of the Wanamaker Stores.*

Down Stairs Store for working-class and lower-middle-class customers, the main department for the bulk of the bourgeoisie, and the London Shop for the elite and the upwardly mobile. Although none of its competitors defined as much space by class as did Wanamaker, by 1926 every department store in Philadelphia (except Strawbridge & Clothier) used class to demarcate some of their selling floors. Gimbels, Lits, and Snellenburg all had basement stores and Gimbels added custom tailoring to its men's department.[30]

The merchants created these new departments not simply because they had more selling space but as part of what John Wanamaker had termed the "science of merchandising." As with the daily newspapers, culture, not increased size, explains the new modes of spatial use. For example, the Wanamaker store had no bargain basement until 1916, five years after its greatly enlarged new building opened. Until then, the firm used the underground space just as it had in the past (and exactly as Strawbridge & Clothier continued to do until 1929), as simply another sales floor. The use of class to refine the taxonomy of space within the department stores reflected both business and cultural imperatives. Without a doubt, it was in part a reaction to the extension of the mass market in the early twentieth century beyond the middle class both to the elite and to the working classes. Wanamaker and Gimbels, in particular, simply tried to attract the broadest possible range of customers to their stores and serve these diverse groups in the most cost-effective (and profitable) manner. Adding class (or gender or any other category) to the existing spatial divisions also made the taxonomy more precise and hence more scientific. The department stores regularly touted their efficiency in design in both guidebooks and advertisements, and this increasingly detailed arrangement was simply a further step in the science of merchandising.[31]

As in the late nineteenth century, the merchants' taxonomy extended beyond space to time. And, as with space, the retailers built on and refined the annual retail calendar that was in place by 1900. The stores kept the successful events like January White Sales and August Furniture Sales and tried to establish new ones, such as Gimbels' "Annual Shirt Sale" in May. Retailers also tried to create special events; for example when Wanamaker issued a card reading: "12/12/12, This Souvenir Card Certifies to the purchase of articles, to which this is attached, Twelfth Month, Twelfth, Nineteen Hundred and Twelve, and that such transactions after to-day are unduplicatable until December 12, 2012." In Philadelphia, perhaps the greatest innovation (and definitely the longest-lasting) was "Clover Days" at Strawbridge & Clothier. Clover Days were special because they were not tied to a particular season or department; they were recurring sales throughout both the store and the year. Strawbridge & Clothier used Clover Days to help balance the selling cycles by manufacturing retail excitement. What the firm was doing was in the mainstream of scientific management; in the words of one text: "The store that does not have things happening in it regularly is not in the current of modern merchandising."[32]

Clover Days helped Strawbridge & Clothier draw in customers during the quiet times in the sales cycle. Chalkley Matlack and his relatives often came to the city from their farm in New Jersey for a Clover Day. He went because he "enjoy[ed] spending money" and found "much fascination . . . in buying things." Significantly, all three of the Clover Days Matlack mentioned in his diary were during lulls in the selling season (post-Easter or summer and midweek).[33]

Clover Days represented a broader trend in early twentieth-century retailing: the attempts by the department stores not just to program the year but also to micro-manage the week. During the late nineteenth century, the firms first tried to balance out the selling year; in the early twentieth century, they created new daily rhythms to attempt to equalize customer traffic throughout the week. By 1910, the merchants tied sales and specials to specific days with increasing regularity. In that year, both Snellenburg's and Lits' declared that Fridays were "bargain days" and Snellenburg's even numbered its consecutive sales (for example, "The 488th Friday Bargain Sale"). Lits' also tried to draw in customers with "Tuesday Specials." Later, Gimbels' declared that most Tuesdays (evidently a slow retailing day in early twentieth-century Philadelphia) were "Subway Store Days" and regularly featured specials from the basement in their advertising. Although department stores often stressed low prices in their ads, it is significant that many of these attempts to create traffic on slow days were aimed at the stores' more down-market clientele (this is particularly evident in scanning the merchandise offered by Lits and Snellenburg in their advertisements but also notable in how and when Gimbels pushed its bargain basement). As the early twentieth-century merchants refined their taxonomy of space to include class in the mix, they did the same with time. On the surface, all these sales were simply attempts by merchants to balance the retail load. More significantly, they represented a shared belief that merchants—and, by extension, their middle-class audience—could control their world. Behind these merchandising methods was the middle-class faith that people could use logic and rationality to rule their environment.[34]

Not all attempts by department stores to control the retail cycle were successful, however. In addition to individual sales that did not generate as much business as planned, Wanamaker's aborted bid to close on summer Saturdays in 1914 was a notable failure. The Wanamaker story is particularly interesting because it illustrates both the strengths and weaknesses of the massive department stores during the early twentieth century. In the spring of 1914, John Wanamaker suggested to his aisle managers in both New York and Philadelphia that the stores close every Saturday from mid-June to mid-September (the same slow summer sales period during which retailers had been closing early on Saturdays since the late nineteenth century). He argued that this would allow his workers more time with their families and that any sales lost on Saturday could be made up during the other five days. Although Wanamaker did have a paternalistic concern for his employees, the size of his stores (and their high staffing requirements) probably also influenced his thinking. At that time, the forty-five-acre Philadelphia store employed nearly eight thousand people, and keeping it open on slow days must have been expensive. Wanamaker never instituted his Saturday closings, however, for fear of losing sales to other retailers. Although Wanamaker was Philadelphia's leading retailer, neither he nor the other department stores could exercise unfettered control over the market.[35]

The department stores were selling machines that became larger and more expensive to operate during the first decades of the twentieth century. The department stores' greatest asset—the massive size that allowed them to display an abundance of merchandise—also led to their greatest liability— the need for a large sales and supervisory staff. Through the retail calendar, the stores attempted to reprogram the shopping rhythms of their customers. If the merchants could better balance sales over the year and the week, they could better utilize their employees. The stores' desire to manipulate their shoppers' schedules, however, was not their only attempt at applying science to humans.

By the early twentieth century, department stores carefully classified not only time and space but also people. Although the merchants neither created nor were in the forefront of human taxonomy, they did reflect this popular trend in bourgeois American society. The classification of people, unlike that of space and time, led to results that were often far from benign.[36]

In the late nineteenth century, members of the African-American middle class had, at best, ambivalent relationships with the city's leading department stores. Surviving diaries indicate that black men and women usually shopped at either John Wanamaker or Strawbridge & Clothier and avoided the other firms. Only Strawbridge & Clothier tried specifically to reach the African-American community with targeted advertising. Blacks found limited employment opportunities at the stores: the only jobs open were as waiters, porters, or elevator operators. W. E. B. DuBois, in his path-breaking late nineteenth-century study of Philadelphia, confirmed the limited opportunities open to African-Americans when he stated that "nearly all the [black] clerks and salesmen are to be found in the Negro stores."[37]

During the early twentieth century, the relationship between the African-American community and the department stores became further estranged. Gimbel Brothers mounted an exhibit entitled "Pranks of the Pickaninnies" during the 1900 Christmas season that reflected the stereotyped, racist images that were part of turn-of-the-century popular culture. What job opportunities that had existed in the stores decreased. An article in an African-American newspaper reported favorably on Wanamaker's employment practices in 1912 and noted the "Wanamaker Store gives employment to 300 colored people." More telling than the gross number of positions were the locations of the jobs: "119 in the dairy [basement restaurant], 83 elevator operators, 29 in tea room, 21 in helps' lunch room, 3 in printing department, 3 in warehouse, 2 in stable, 10 maids and 30 porters." Not one of these three hundred people worked in a selling position. Two photographs in a 1912 edition of Strawbridge's employee magazine *Store Chat* illustrate this employment segregation by showing the retailer's elevator operators—all of whom were black. Two African-American postal workers claimed "that, because of our race, the very best that we could hope for [in the private sector] would be to find employment as waiters. We then recalled that since we have been in the postal service the leading hostelries of the city, such as Gimbles [sic], Snellingburgs [sic], . . . falling in line with the universal movement against Negroes, have ruthlessly drawn the line against colored help."[38]

This human taxonomy, however, applied not only to African-Americans but to other ethnic groups as well. John Wanamaker's official biographer made this explicit in his review of the merchant's employment practices: the store's policy "prevented, after the flood of foreign born, any serious modification in the racial and cultural background of the store family." The writer continued by noting that the employees are "gathered from a background of long residence in America and coming from homes where 'the fear of God, order, and industry reigned' (we are quoting Wanamaker), the people who surrounded him were of English, Scotch, Irish, German—and to a lesser extent Scandinavian and French—forbears." The biographer also remarked that "for certain kinds of work, such as running elevators and restaurant service, the best class of colored people was employed." The great department stores did not invent racism nor were they the first to apply science to race; rather the human taxonomy developed by Gimbels, Wanamaker, and Strawbridge was an indication of the wider use and misuse of science by bourgeois society as a whole. [39]

As with the daily newspaper, the story of the department store in early twentieth-century Philadelphia was one of continuity and change. The redefinition of retail time and space begun in the late nineteenth century was largely complete by 1926. Within Gimbel Brothers, Lit Brothers, N. Snellenburg, Strawbridge & Clothier, and John Wanamaker, order and efficiency reigned. Building on the middle-class Victorian faith in science and rationality, the merchants extended their attempts to control time from the seasons of the year to the days of the week and further refined their taxonomy of space by adding class to the mix. By the 1910s, Philadelphia's great merchants represented this bourgeois Victorian faith in science and rationality in full flower. But as with the daily newspapers, Philadelphia's department stores also contained a supreme irony: this middle-class belief in order allowed the merchants to respond to the expanding market by shifting their stores away from an almost exclusive focus on the women and men of the bourgeoisie. This once middle-class geography became multi-classed. As the members of the working classes gained disposable income, retailers could use the tools and techniques that they had borrowed from (and honed on) the bourgeoisie to reach these potential new customers.

On one level, the 1911 John Wanamaker store was the apogee of the Victorian middle-class department store. The roots for every service, every department, every sale, every event, can be found in the late nineteenth-century shops of Wanamaker and his competitors. Although far larger and far grander than its predecessors, even this movement toward massiveness and opulence had begun in Victorian Philadelphia. On a different level, however, by 1916 when Wanamaker opened its bargain basement, the store was qualitatively different from its Victorian antecedent. Like the lower levels of Gimbels, Lits, and Snellenburg, Wanamaker's "Down Stairs Store" represented a shift away from the department store as a largely middle-class space. For most of the remainder of the twentieth century, the department store would be a multi-classed space aimed at the mass market.

In was not just Philadelphia's newspapers and department stores that were changing in response to this shift to a mass market but also the overall geography of the city and the region. From the boardwalk at Atlantic City to the streets of West Philadelphia, the women and men of the middle class confronted these changes in the early twentieth century.

Chapter 7
One Great Big Stretch of Middle Class

> People who went to the shore never went to the Poconos or married out of
> their class and most of the people in Philadelphia are in one class. One
> great big stretch of middle class. The Main Line is a boundary and Ritten-
> house Square a place to get your bearings and Fairmount Park belongs to
> all of them. . . . So many things belong to Philadelphia and are Philadel-
> phia. The people in Philadelphia take them for granted. Scrapple, of course;
> the Reading Terminal Market, cottage cheese, bricks, cobblestones, squares,
> Billy Penn, Ben Franklin, Independence Hall, the Betsy Ross House, the
> Liberty Bell, the Zoo, cinnamon buns, pepper pot, Delaware shad, Connie
> Mack, the lamp-lighter, the eagle at Wanamaker's, passes instead of car
> transfers, Strawberry Mansion, the Penn Relays, the Mummers, people
> from the homes for the blind selling brooms, drivers stopping their cars to
> give you a lift because you're both folks, the interest in the University of
> Pennsylvania as if the entire population were alumni. Then there is "the
> old lake" and "the new lake" in Fairmount Park. They have names but no-
> body uses them.[1]

As with the pages of the city's newspapers and the floors of its
department stores, the story of the streets and neighborhoods of Philadelphia was a mixture of continuity and change during the early twentieth century. For many members of the bourgeoisie, like the actor and playwright
John Cecil Holm, the early twentieth-century metropolis was the zenith of
the middle-class city created in the Victorian era. He, and many others,
looked around and saw nothing but "one big stretch of middle class" from
the Jersey shore to Center City to West Philadelphia and on to the Poconos.
Of course, this vision of Philadelphia was never entirely accurate because the
women and men of the bourgeoisie shared all these spaces with either members of the elite or the working classes or, like Center City, both, throughout
the late nineteenth and early twentieth centuries.

What made this "great big stretch of middle class" so real to Holm was the continued physical expansion of the carefully defined Victorian city. As the bourgeoisie expanded in size, so did the number of its "bedroom communities," both within the city limits and outside them. What linked all these middle-class homes to the offices, shops, and amusement parks was an increasingly broad array of transportation options. Bourgeois women and men continued to ride the streetcars of the Victorian era but they could also move about the region on the new subways, electric suburban trains, buses, and, ultimately, automobiles. As Center City continued to decline in importance as a residential area (to the white, native-born middle class at least), it took on more functions as the retail, commercial, and entertainment hub for the growing region. Its stores and commercial structures stretched steadily skyward. Its paved streets, well lit at night, lined with telephone and electric cables, continued to define modernity. By the 1920s, the Victorian middle-class city had become the middle-class metropolis.

But all was not perfect for the residents of Holm's "one big stretch of middle class." As with the newspapers and the department stores, the streets and communities of early twentieth-century Philadelphia also underwent fundamental change as the market expanded to encompass more and more members of the working classes. As the average worker's income rose and the city transit fare remained constant, working-class families could move into once middle-class neighborhoods.

By understanding the spatial order of early twentieth-century middle-class Philadelphia, we can not only better understand everyday life but, by developing the transition from the Victorian city to the early twentieth-century metropolis, we also can better understand the cultural roots of the political moment known as the Progressive Era. As with the newspapers and the department stores, the reordering of the middle-class city along rational lines was largely complete by the end of the nineteenth century. As the twentieth century progressed, however, once largely middle-class areas like West Philadelphia came under increasing pressure as more and more non-white and working-class people moved into the area. The middle-class men and women of West Philadelphia fought to maintain their sense of order, first through private action and later through politics.

Before developing this fundamental difference between the late nineteenth and early twentieth centuries, we should explore in more detail the continuities between the Victorian city and its replacement. The key to the creation of the Victorian middle-class city was the availability of cheap, reliable transport: the bourgeois corridors. Steam railways, coupled first with horse-drawn streetcars, then cable cars, and finally electric trolleys, allowed members of the Victorian middle-class to separate home from work, shopping, and amusement and to effectively stitch these disparate pieces of the region into one seemingly seamless stretch of middle-class geography. Bourgeois city dwellers, like Headley Holm in West Philadelphia, used these same corridors, along with some important additions, to expand the middle-class metropolis in the early twentieth century. Holm, an English émigré, was a moderately successful electrician with business throughout the city. His son later recalled both his father's extensive use of transport and the ways in which West Philadelphians used these bourgeois corridors to define "their" city:

[My fathers's] store was on Lancaster Avenue near Forty-first Street [in West Philadelphia]. When you left [there] headed for another section of Philadelphia you said you were going 'out to so-and-so', or 'over to so-and-so', or 'downtown'. If you spoke of going 'up', that meant Frankford, Kensington, or Germantown. 'Out' could mean a great many places, including the Main Line, Swarthmore, Overbrook, Sixty-ninth Street, and so forth. 'Over' could be interpreted as almost any place in the neighborhood or as far away as Camden, New Jersey. However, 'downtown' meant just that. . . . My father went about his business by horse car, trolley car, and elevated. He never learned to drive a car. He went all over Philadelphia.

If his father's work had taken him to, in the words of one guidebook, "the most beautiful suburbs in America," like that of music teacher Septimus Winner or draughtsman Edwin Jellett, Cecil would have added "trains" to the list of his father's transportation options. During the first two decades of the twentieth century, the steel rails of the bourgeois corridors continued to tie together the expanding metropolis for hundreds of thousands of middle-class Philadelphians like Holm. As the women and men of Philadelphia's bourgeoisie traveled for work, shopping, and pleasure, they continued to reshape the geography of their city and its region.[2]

As with the newspapers and the department stores, these bourgeois corridors underwent subtle changes after the turn of the century. Although more middle-class Philadelphians purchased automobiles as the twentieth century progressed, throughout the period the bourgeoisie continued to rely primarily on public transport. Over time, however, as working-class incomes rose and transit fares remained constant, middle-class clerks found themselves more often sharing "their" trolleys and trains with factory employees. In 1907, after years of public demand, Philadelphia finally opened its first "rapid transit" line: the Market Street Subway-Elevated. Part of the logic that inspired the city to help extend this project was the hope that relatively inexpensive transport would benefit members of the working classes by allowing them to separate home from work, which had heretofore been a middle-class (and above) luxury.[3]

The spatial reorganization of Philadelphia begun by the women and men of the middle class during the Victorian period was extended during the early twentieth century. The exact nature of this geography, however, varied among the members of the bourgeoisie. Each person would have his or her own routes through the region and his or her own set of borders. These paths and frontiers would differ because of employment, residence, race, religion, wealth, sex, and personal interests. Recall how Cecil Holm, for example, defined his "great big stretch of middle class:" "The Main Line is a boundary and Rittenhouse Square a place to get your bearings and Fairmount Park belongs to all of them." In other words, Holm's Philadelphia consisted of Center City, West Philadelphia, and the park. Mary Smith, who grew up a few blocks from Cecil Holm in West Philadelphia, but whose father was a far more successful businessman than Holm's, probably would have extended her world into the eastern Main Line and Delaware County, based on the many trips her family made visiting friends and collecting flowers in these early suburbs. The only landmarks that Edwin Jellett, living in Germantown in northwest Philadelphia, would have shared with Holm and Smith were Center City and Fairmount Park; the park would have been the southern edge of Jellett's Philadelphia (and the northern of Holm's and Smith's).[4]

The geography of middle-class Philadelphia was made up of these overlapping, individual maps. Some locations, such as Center City and the Jersey shore, were visited by virtually every bourgeois woman and man in the region. Others, like Willow Grove Park, were common destinations for the vast majority of middle-class Philadelphians. Still others were hubs of a more local nature: the shops of Lancaster Avenue (like that run by Headley Holm) would be patronized primarily by people living or working in West Philadelphia while similar establishments on "Main Street" (Germantown Avenue according to city maps but not to the locals) would be the destination of women and men from Germantown, Mount Airy, and Chestnut Hill. These shared locations helped to define "their" city and region for the bourgeoisie.

Middle-class Philadelphians continued to use the nineteenth-century bourgeois corridors during the early twentieth century. The bulk of these routes were in place by 1901, and, except for city-sponsored subway and elevated projects, the physical expansion of the rail system effectively ended in 1912 when the Philadelphia & Western Railway opened its line to Norristown. Transportation companies, through the application of new technologies like electricity, and the women and men of the region, by choosing among the varying transit options, constantly reconstructed Philadelphia. Between approximately 1905 and 1925, the bourgeoisie could pick from the broadest range of transport alternatives in the region's history. During that period, trolleys plied most of the streets of the city and many of the main roads in the hinterland; Philadelphia opened its first subway-elevated line; motorized buses began operation throughout much of the metropolis; steam railroads still offered an extensive commuter service and a variety of other, longer distance trains throughout the region; and the private motor car became increasingly available to the middle class.

Perhaps the most ubiquitous form of transportation used by middle-class women and men in the city were the trolleys of the Philadelphia Rapid Transit Company. Formed in 1902 from the hated Union Traction Company, the PRT operated electric cars on nearly every major street in the city. A virtual monopoly within Philadelphia (only a handful of small lines, mostly on the fringes of the municipality, remained outside its control), the PRT also extended its routes into parts of adjoining Montgomery and Delaware Counties. The most significant of these suburban offshoots were the lines to the company-owned amusement park in Willow Grove. For the first decade of its existence, the PRT was disliked by many middle-class Philadelphians; not only was it the local example of a "traction trust" but it seemed unable or unwilling to improve service. In 1911 came new management, improved labor relations, and a fleet of state-of-the-art trolleys, and following all these changes, a far better public image.[5]

By the early twentieth century, the counties surrounding Philadelphia in both Pennsylvania and New Jersey also had extensive trolley systems. Unlike in the city, no one company ever gained control over the majority of these suburban and rural lines. There were, however, a number of significant corporate consolidations that resulted in certain parts of the region having a dominant carrier. In Delaware County, Pennsylvania, for example, the Philadelphia & West Chester Traction Company operated the most important routes to Ardmore, Media, Sharon Hill, and West Chester. A similar situation existed in Camden County, New Jersey, where the Public Service Railway owned the bulk of the network. Over a dozen major and minor firms provided trolley service to virtually every portion of suburban Philadelphia.[6]

The most important expansion of Philadelphia's transit system in the first decade of the twentieth century was the construction of the Market Street subway-elevated. Built by the PRT, this massive undertaking consisted of two modes: a self-contained, high-speed service and a shorter subway-surface line that used conventional trolley cars. The high-speed line started as an elevated railway along Delaware Avenue with stops for the Camden ferries of the Pennsylvania and Reading Railroads and then plunged underground to follow Market Street through Center City as far as the Schuylkill River, where it emerged as an elevated again. It ran above Market Street through West Philadelphia, eventually reaching the Sixty-ninth Street terminal of the suburban Philadelphia & West Chester and Philadelphia & Western systems. The conventional trolleys operated in a subway under Market Street between City Hall and the Schuylkill River and then continued as surface routes throughout West Philadelphia. This new rapid transit system connected the region's ferries, steam railroads, and suburban trolleys and relieved congestion on Center City streets (see figure 36 for a particularly bad example of a pre-subway Market Street "trolley jam"). The PRT put the subway-elevated system in service in sections beginning in 1905 with the subway-surface cars and ending in 1908 with the Delaware Avenue elevated. Over a decade later, the PRT began operation of a city-financed extension of the elevated to Frankford in 1922.[7]

Although the steam railroads opened no new passenger lines in the metropolitan region during the twentieth century, they continually refined their existing systems. Three companies operated all the trains in and around Philadelphia: the Baltimore & Ohio with one minor line in Delaware County, the Pennsylvania with two separate networks that served the entire region (one for New Jersey points from Camden and the other for Pennsylvania destinations primarily from Broad Street Station), and the Reading also with two systems serving smaller sections of both states. All told, over 1,000 daily trains served hundreds of stations in and around the city.[8]

Under increased competitive pressures, initially from trolleys and later from buses and automobiles, the railroads made some significant changes to their commuter systems during the early twentieth century. In general, the companies decreased service on many shorter lines and improved it on medium-distance ones. A very few lines, like the Pennsylvania's Kensington and Newtown Square branches, lost their passenger trains entirely. Most lightly patronized lines, however, simply had the numbers of trips cut. Service on the Reading's Gloucester branch in New Jersey decreased from twenty-four round trips in 1893 to nine in 1906. Both the Gloucester and Newtown Square routes loss patronage to nearby trolley lines that offered significantly

Figure 36. A "trolley jam": Market Street at Tenth on December 21, 1907. Courtesy of the Urban Archives of Temple University.

more frequent service at lower fares. The Pennsylvania Railroad concluded as early as 1904 that it usually could not compete effectively with trolleys for short-distance commuter traffic and "the policy of closing small local stations within about five miles of the main terminal be continued, as the class of local travel secured at these stations is rarely profitable."9

It was the same Pennsylvania Railroad, however, that made the most dramatic improvement to local train service in the Philadelphia region during the early twentieth century: electrification. Although the railroad had experimented with electric train service in southern New Jersey during the 1890s, its first successful, large-scale use of the technology was on its secondary Camden to Atlantic City line in 1906. In addition to the through city-to-shore trains, the line developed an intensive local service. In the late 1910s, the company electrified its two busiest Philadelphia commuter routes to Paoli and Chestnut Hill. For the Pennsylvania, the biggest immediate advantage of the electric trains was increased terminal capacity at its crowded Broad Street Station. The Pennsylvania's depot was one of the busiest in the world and had run out of expansion space. Because the electric multiple unit cars did not have separate locomotives that had to be transferred from one end of the train to the other at the station, the electric cars significantly lessened the number of switching moves required at the depot. To the middle-class passenger, however, the electric trains were cleaner, quicker, and quieter than their steam-hauled counterparts. Riding the red cars of the Pennsylvania became a pleasurable ritual on the Main Line; one regular commuter claimed the railroad "furnished a comfortable seat in a steady restful vehicle, with a breezy window in summer and warmth (generally too much) in winter."10

By the 1910s, motorized buses began to roam the streets of the Philadelphia area. The PRT and other transit companies on both sides of the Delaware River initially adopted buses to supplement and, by the 1920s, to replace their trolley routes. Buses offered transit companies more operating flexibility (a bus could detour around an obstacle that would delay a trolley) and lower capital costs (buses operated on public highways while trolleys needed privately maintained rails). In addition to the buses operated by the established, regulated transit companies, in 1915 a new form of public transport came to the region: the jitney. Jitneys were unregulated buses operated by private individuals, usually in competition with existing transit companies. The jitneys usually charged lower fares but often only operated during peak hours when they could be assured of heavy ridership. Although jitneys could be found throughout the metropolis, they were extremely popular in New Jersey, perhaps because that state had a particularly good public highway system.11

All of these forms of public transport began the twentieth century as largely—but never exclusively—middle-class corridors. Members of Philadelphia's elite, for example, had long shared the relatively high-cost steam trains with the bourgeoisie. Because the fare structure of the railroads was based on the distance traveled, wealthier Philadelphians could afford to live in more distant suburbs than their middle-class counterparts. These elite "borderlands" existed toward the end of many of the commuter lines. The bourgeoisie had also shared to some extent the streetcars and trolleys with working-class Philadelphians, but the relatively high fares of the Victorian era coupled with low wages had limited ridership for the average worker.[12]

As the twentieth century progressed, the women and men of the middle class increasingly found themselves sharing the trolleys, buses, and subways with their working-class counterparts. This was caused by a combination of higher working-class wages and the unchanging city transit fare of five cents. Throughout the early twentieth century, workers made real wage gains as their income outpaced inflation. The subway-elevated initially opened up much of far West Philadelphia to middle-class development, but by the 1920s, more and more better-off working-class families moved there to take advantage of the relatively inexpensive houses and the cheap and rapid transit. The low fares helped to make these parts of the bourgeois corridors increasingly less middle class by the 1920s.[13]

The transport technology that would eventually be used by the women and men of the middle class to remake again the geography of Philadelphia and its region was the private automobile. By 1926, the metropolis had already made significant strides in accommodating itself to the car: the Fairmount Parkway and the river drives provided auto-friendly access to Center City and the Delaware River Bridge linked the Pennsylvania and New Jersey highway systems. For the first third of the twentieth century, however, the automobile had little effect on the spatial patterns of the city or region. Most middle-class development still followed the railroad and trolley lines. Even for the bourgeois Philadelphians who could afford an automobile, the car remained more of a toy for weekend exploration than a family's primary means of transport. A large number of middle-class Philadelphians, like Headley Holm, never owned a car and relied on the region's extensive public transport network for all their travel needs.[14]

Bourgeois Philadelphians used this increasingly complex web of transport to refine and to expand "their" city in the early twentieth century. The most common destination for middle-class women and men continued to be Center City. They went there for a wide variety of reasons but the three most frequent remained business, shopping, and entertainment. This daily flow of bourgeois women and men to Center City contributed to its dramatic physical transformation; in this period the area developed a number of interconnected and overlapping specialized commercial, retail, and theater zones that served the entire region. All these changes began in the Victorian city but reached their apogee in the early twentieth-century metropolis.

By 1905, Philadelphia had developed two separate commercial districts. The late nineteenth-century business section of the city, Second to Eighth between Market and Walnut Streets, continued to house many firms, both large and small. Although John L. Smith's map shop remained at its Sixth Street location until he retired, as early as 1899 he noted the shift westward: "6th St. is dead for Business." By then, leading banks and insurance companies had begun to build new structures along a new commercial corridor centered on Broad Street (which replaces Fourteenth Street in the city's grid) a few blocks west. Smaller firms followed, taking up offices in the new towers. For example, J. Harper Smith, Mary's father and a coal merchant, moved his firm ten blocks west in 1904 from a bank building at Fourth and Chestnut (in the traditional area) to another bank building at Broad and Chestnut (in the new one).[15]

But much more than a few blocks separated the two commercial districts. The most obvious difference between the new twentieth-century Center City and its nineteenth-century predecessor was height. Through the early 1890s, six stories qualified as a tall building in the city. By 1901, John L. Smith, the map maker, could marvel over "15 Story Buildings" with "Elevators." A few years later, another bourgeois Philadelphian captured this rapid transformation in his memoirs: "In nothing, however, have I seen such changes as in our principal streets and thoroughfares. . . . The erection of the enormous '*sky scrapers*' in the vicinity of Broad, Market, Chestnut + Walnut Streets. Their towering height makes one dizzy. Yet they are occupied throughout." The speed of this shift can be seen by comparing the two photographs in figures 37 and 38 that were taken about a decade apart at the same location. The first print, made in approximately 1894, shows the skyline of the old city, while the latter, focusing on the then new North American Building, illustrates this new skyscraper zone. The only two landmarks shared by the images are City Hall in the background and the oddly shaped greenhouse in the foreground.[16]

Between and around these two commercial districts stretched the

Figure 37. Before the skyscraper: Broad Street from Walnut circa 1894. Courtesy of the Print and Picture Collection, Free Library of Philadelphia.

primary retail zone of Philadelphia. Here, in addition to the department stores, were a multitude of shops selling goods and services to middle-class (and, increasingly, working-class) women and men of the metropolis. After the commute to work, the most common reason for a member of the bourgeoisie to visit Center City was to go shopping. Eliza Smith, Mary's mother,

Figure 38. After: Broad Street from Walnut circa 1905. Courtesy of the Print and Picture Collection, Free Library of Philadelphia.

went "downtown shopping" from her West Philadelphia home at least once a week for decades.[17]

Middle-class women and men from all over the region also came to Center City to be entertained and to be informed. The West Philadelphia Smiths, Edwin Jellett of Germantown, Clair Wilcox while a student at Penn, and Chalkley Matlack from New Jersey made regular use of the cultural institutions located there. Theaters, lecture halls, and museums dotted the major streets of downtown. The 1912 edition of *The Wanamaker Diary* (in addition to providing space to record one's own activities and thoughts, this annual publication was a font of information for bourgeois Philadelphians) included fourteen pages of seating plans for the major theaters. Except for the Grand Opera House in North Philadelphia, all were located in Center City and the vast majority could be found on or near Broad Street. The twentieth century also saw many large movie houses constructed in downtown, principally along Market and Chestnut Streets. Within a few blocks of City Hall could be found virtually all of Philadelphia's leading indoor entertainment sites.[18]

For most members of the middle class, Center City Philadelphia in the twentieth century was a destination: a place to work, to bank, to eat, to shop, to be entertained, to be enlightened. Within downtown, fairly specialized zones quickly developed. Offices located primarily around the old State House and City Hall; stores between Eighth and Broad along Market; cultural institutions along Broad; movie houses on Market and Chestnut. All these clusters happened before zoning or planning and without government intervention. In the cultural geography of downtown could be seen the subtle reordering of the bourgeois city.[19]

Middle-class women and men, however, were not—nor had they ever been—the only Philadelphians to visit Center City. Some spaces, like the courts and government offices, had always been used by members of different classes. Others, like the department stores, became more multi-classed as the twentieth century progressed. Still others, like the Philadelphia Club, were—and remained—elite spaces, off-limits to all but the most upwardly mobile of the bourgeoisie. While others still, like the vaudeville houses and other "cheap amusements" on the fringes of downtown, attracted a much more working-class clientele.[20]

Although twentieth-century Center City was a distinctly heterogeneous space, there is little to indicate that bourgeois Philadelphians felt "their" downtown was under any threat. One reason, of course, was that the streets of Center City had long been multi-classed, and middle-class women and men were accustomed to sharing "their" streets with others. In addition, bourgeois Philadelphians could navigate easily from one middle-class location in downtown to another without encountering a vaudeville house or a working-class saloon. This bourgeois geography worked in part because unregulated capitalism—read high rents—had largely kept working-class destinations off the main streets of Center City and relegated them to byways—like Arch Street—that were, at most, liminal parts of the middle-class city.

Two other key components of the middle-class terrain in the region were the amusement parks and the New Jersey shore. The same bourgeois corridors that had helped create both areas as middle-class havens during the late nineteenth century continued to serve them (supplemented with buses and automobiles) in the early twentieth. Like Center City, virtually every bourgeois Philadelphian visited these sites during the early twentieth century, and like the department stores, they became increasingly multi-classed during the 1910s.

Amusement parks first began to serve middle-class Philadelphians in the last decade of the nineteenth century and continued to do so during the first three decades of the twentieth. At their peak, there were dozens in the metropolitan area, usually placed along a trolley or railroad line (or both) for easy access. From White City Park (near Chestnut Hill and served by the PRT) to Woodside Park (in Fairmount Park with its own trolley system) to Neshaminy Falls Park (in Bucks County alongside the Reading) to Burlington Island Park (in New Jersey, which had the distinction of being reachable by train, trolley, and boat), the region offered many different ways to escape the city heat. A quick visit to the most popular of them all should suffice to sketch the contours of this initially largely middle-class space.[21]

By far the most successful of these amusement parks in the late nineteenth and early twentieth centuries was Willow Grove Park, just outside the city limits in eastern Montgomery County. Owned by the PRT (and its predecessors), Willow Grove was located at a hub of an extensive trolley system with routes leading into the city and out to the countryside (see figure 39 for the newly constructed, well-ordered trolley terminal at the park in 1905). Both city residents and suburbanites could also reach the park by train as it was within walking distance of a Reading Railroad passenger station. No other amusement park in greater Philadelphia so successfully drew middle-class patrons from throughout the city and region.[22]

Willow Grove Park thrived as a middle-class haven for essentially two reasons: accessibility and respectability. It was easy to reach the park from

Figure 39. The well-ordered trolley terminal at Willow Grove Park when new in 1905. Courtesy of the Print and Picture Collec-

middle-class neighborhoods in North and West Philadelphia, but it was expensive enough (an additional zone on the trolley or a relatively high fare on the Reading) to discourage working-class Philadelphians from visiting very often. Another way in which the park's management actively encouraged the bourgeois tone was by enforcing a strict code of conduct and dress. Unlike the topsy-turvy world of Coney Island, Willow Grove Park was an oasis of middle-class restraint. Finally, the park's primary attraction, a free concert series that ranged from popular pieces like Sousa to more "high-brow" works such as Wagner, helped to establish Willow Grove as a bourgeois space in the metropolis. Eugenia Barnitz, then a child living in Germantown, regularly went to the park and recalled: "In the summers we loved to go to Willow Grove Park. . . . It didn't cost anything to listen to the music, and that was well worth listening to, under the baton of such worthy leaders as Victor Herbert, John Prior, John Philip Sousa, Walter Damrosch, and lots of others."[23]

From its opening in 1895, Willow Grove Park attracted middle-class Philadelphians by the thousands every night during its season from May to September. They came by trolley and train to try the rides and amusements, eat supper, listen to the concerts, and, most of all, escape summer in the city. Eugenia Barnitz remembered that she usually went to the park with "a group of boys and girls [by] open trolley. . . . Once in a while some one would buy a dollar's worth of tickets on the old scenic railway. . . . If we had enough money amongst us we might take a ride on the lake in a row boat." Often Mary Smith's entire family made the trek from West Philadelphia to Willow Grove by trolley "for supper and for the evening." Mary Roberts of Downingtown visited the park once while staying with friends in the city. She enjoyed the trolley ride and she and her companions "[t]ook our suppers [at the park and] had a lovely time." Septimus Winner spent an entire afternoon and evening (until 8:30 P.M.) at the park for a total cost of seventy-five cents and "had a grand outing." The following year, Winner made clear one of Willow Grove's main attractions in this emphatic entry in his diary: "*Hot, hot, very hot,* . . . took a trolley trip with Hanah to Willow Grove [in the] afternoon and eveng, . . . and [found it] cool out there!"[24]

Septimus Winner's 1897 visit helps to highlight how Willow Grove and some of the other amusement parks maintained a largely middle-class clientele for the first few decades or so of their existence: price. Although seventy-five cents seems cheap for eight hours of entertainment, it represented over one-half day's pay for the average Philadelphia factory worker. Because the park was located in the suburban zone, the twenty-cent per person round-trip trolley fare alone would quickly become a major expense for a working-class family.[25]

Not all amusement parks maintained the largely bourgeois patronage of Willow Grove during the early twentieth century. The popular Woodside Park, located in Fairmount Park, developed a far more mixed clientele as the century progressed. Accessible by the independent Fairmount Park trolley (which connected the main park entrances in West Philadelphia and North Philadelphia), Woodside quickly lost its middle-class tone. During the late 1890s, bourgeois Philadelphians like the Smiths of West Philadelphia, John L. Smith and Septimus Winner of North Philadelphia, and Edwin Jellett of Germantown all visited the park, although never as often as they went to Willow Grove. By the first decade of the twentieth century, although they frequently used a ride on the park trolley to escape the summer heat, these people often passed by Woodside without stopping. Significantly, the upper-middle-class West Philadelphia Smiths regularly visited Willow Grove but evidently never returned to Woodside after 1897. Woodside offered fewer concerts than Willow Grove and was much more a straight amusement park, like New York's Coney Island. Woodside was also significantly closer than Willow Grove to many working-class homes, allowing for quick visits. Overall, Woodside retained some middle-class clientele throughout the early twentieth century but was becoming a much more multi-classed space than Willow Grove.[26]

In addition to amusement parks like Willow Grove, bourgeois Philadelphians escaped the summer heat by visiting the towns of the New Jersey coast, from Cape May to Long Branch, easily reached by the passenger services of the Reading and Pennsylvania railroad systems. Throughout the early-twentieth century, dozens of trains left every day from stations in Philadelphia and Camden for all the major seaside resorts. The prime destinations for bourgeois Philadelphians, the south Jersey communities between Cape May and Atlantic City, had competing passenger services from both railroads. The Sunday "dollar excursion" trains drew thousands for inexpensive day trips to the shore. John Smith, a regular user of these services, once had to wait in line for thirty-five minutes just to buy his ticket because of the crowds. Residents of the railroad suburbs in New Jersey often spent summer Sundays watching the parade of trains (at times with people perched on the open vestibules of the cars because of the high demand) steam through their towns. In 1904, the Reading and Pennsylvania carried over two million passengers to Atlantic City alone.[27]

By the early twentieth century, the communities along the New Jersey coast began to develop different resort markets. Most of the towns tried to attract middle-class families for extended stays. Cecil Holm recalled " 'The shore' in Philadelphia means along the Jersey coast and it could be one of many places. In our case it meant Wildwood. Philadelphians journeyed to Asbury Park, Ocean City, Avalon, Stone Harbor, Sea Isle City, and other summer spots. Atlantic City was reserved in our eyes for New Yorkers and Cape May for senators, congressmen, and the Main Line." All the communities in Holm's list, except for Atlantic City and Cape May, were places to spend a week, a month, or the season. Outside of Atlantic City and Cape May, there were few large hotels; most summer visitors either owned or rented a house. Philadelphia newspapers ran summer rental advertising supplements before the start of the season and middle-class women and men took day trips to the shore to examine potential vacation sites. Eliza Smith and one of Mary's sisters went by train to Wildwood one summer Tuesday in 1908 to find a "cottage" for the family. That trip was unsuccessful and Mary's mother and father took the train to Cape May the following Friday and "rented Mr. Lafayette Bennet's cottage 915 Madison Ave. for $100 from Aug. 1 to September 15." The passenger services of the Reading and Pennsylvania allowed Mary's father to commute to work from the shore and her mother and sisters to continue their activities—both shopping and volunteer—in the city.[28]

Despite Cecil Holm's view, Atlantic City remained the leading destination for middle-class Philadelphians because of its combination of proximity and modernity. The fastest express trains made the sixty-mile trip in just sixty minutes. Rail service to Ocean City took over an hour and a half and that to Cape May and Long Branch, two and a half hours or more. Less time on the train meant more time at the beach or boardwalk and the brevity of the trip allowed Atlantic City to dominate the one-day excursion traffic. Atlantic City, however, offered more than ease of access; it was also the most up-to-date of the shore communities. It not only provided, in the words of a leading guidebook, the "cool breeze of the ocean to delight and refresh those who, turning from the heat and hurly-burly of the city, seek the charm and change of the seashore life" but also broad avenues, electric street lighting, and trolleys. The same tome assured the potential visitor that "The city is admirably lighted with electricity. The authorities spend nearly $40,000 a year for lighting. The ocean promenade and the principal avenues are lit with brilliant electric lights the year round." In essence, Atlantic City combined the advantages of modern urban living with those of the natural air conditioning of the seaside. One could escape the city without leaving its benefits behind. The composition of the photograph in figure 40 emphasizes the

Figure 40. Modernity and the Jersey shore: Atlantic Avenue in Atlantic City circa 1903. Courtesy of the Print and Picture Collection, Free Library of Philadelphia.

modernity of the resort: a broad street (precisely defined by utility polls on both sides) with a trolley and electric light carefully centered. Atlantic City offered all the advantages of West Philadelphia with a lot less heat and humidity.[29]

Then why did Cecil Holm claim that "Atlantic City was reserved in our eyes for New Yorkers?" Admittedly, New Yorkers did go there, and Atlantic City was the only southern New Jersey resort that had direct train service (on two competing lines) to New York City, but more likely Holm's remark was a subtle reference to the more cosmopolitan nature of Atlantic City than the other coastal communities. Simply put, Atlantic City more closely mirrored the ethnic, racial, and class structure of Philadelphia than that of any other shore town. All members of the bourgeoisie went there, including the African Americans and Jews who would have faced more open discrimination in the cottage rentals of Ocean City than in the variety of accommodations at Atlantic City. Samuel Meade Newburger, a Central High graduate and cigar salesman who lived at 1817 Spring Garden Street, regularly summered with his family at Atlantic City. In addition, the dollar-excursion trains made the resort accessible to working-class Philadelphians for day trips. In words calculated to ease middle-class concerns about this cosmopolitanism, a guidebook emphasized that this mixing of people was well-controlled: "The current of humanity on the Boardwalk moves constantly on, the rule of the road—keep to the right—being strictly observed. As a study of some of the most unique phases of human character, a stroll along this crowded thoroughfare in spring or summer is worth a year of ordinary life. Year after year this commingling of the young and the old, the high and the low, the rich and the poor, the grave and the gay, goes on in Atlantic City."[30]

Not all bourgeois Philadelphians, however, appreciated the diversity of Atlantic City's summer population. As early as 1908, John L. Smith (a regular for years at that point) commented that "there are many cheap Jews at Atlantic City now—a Class of People that I do not care for! I do not take much stock in Atlantic City with the Class of People that are there now." A decade later, Albert Edmunds expressed a similar concern: "Atlantic City is becoming so vulgarized that Americans will soon abandon it to jews and millionaires." Edmunds, an English émigré, used the term "Americans" to refer to the native-born, white Protestants who were members of the middle and upper-working classes. Both WASP males centered their comments on one specific "other:" the increasingly large, non-native-born Jewish population of the Philadelphia region. Given the strong linkage between New York City and early twentieth century Jewish immigration, Holm's reference may have been a more covert way to make exactly the same point.[31]

In the early twentieth century, the Jersey shore and the excursion trains that linked it with Philadelphia became less exclusively middle class and more multi-classed than they had been in the Victorian era. White, bourgeois Philadelphians became increasingly aware of the presence of others in their region as once largely middle-class spaces—the department store, the newspaper, the amusement park, the shore—accommodated the mass market.

Returning home from the shore, we can observe changes at work in middle-class neighborhoods like West Philadelphia similar to those we saw in Atlantic City. Bourgeois men and women remade many square miles of the metropolis through the continued extension of their homes throughout the region. What Cecil Holm meant by his "great big stretch of middle class" were the blocks of mostly row and semi-detached homes that covered so much of the city's landscape. Although Philadelphia's housing patterns were in reality quite complex, with working-class and elite dwellings often intermixed with bourgeois ones, Holm's overstatement is understandable because there were so many identifiable "middle-class" neighborhoods: most of West Philadelphia, large portions of North Philadelphia, and virtually all of Germantown and Mount Airy. Thanks to Fairmount Park, one could travel by trolley from Germantown to far West Philadelphia—a distance of approximately ten miles—and never see a significant tract of working-class homes.[32]

These bourgeois "bedroom communities" were simply continuations of late nineteenth-century trends on a far grander scale. Within the city, the closely packed homes of West Philadelphia, North Philadelphia, and Germantown extended outward from Center City along the bourgeois corridors. Outside Philadelphia, the early suburbs of Wayne, Pennsylvania, and Haddonfield, New Jersey, were soon joined by dozens of other railroad and streetcar communities: Cynwyd and Landsdowne in Pennsylvania and Haddon Heights and Collingswood in New Jersey.

The ideal of the railroad suburb is closely associated with the Philadelphia region. A 1916 guidebook proclaimed the city's immediate hinterland "a garden of beauty and charm, forming what with good warrant have been termed 'the most beautiful suburbs in America.' " The Pennsylvania Railroad's directory of suburban sites and services built on this concept by a cover illustration that touched many bourgeois images: a polite steam locomotive not making excessive smoke, a well-maintained station bordered by a park, detached houses surrounded by green hills, and a motor car stopped in front of the station serving as a supplement for—not a competitor to—the train.[33]

The reality, however, for most middle-class Philadelphians during the early twentieth century was very different from this quasi-rural idyll. Although suburban communities began to grow in size and number around the city in the 1890s, the vast majority of bourgeois women and men continued to live within the corporate limits of Philadelphia until well into the twentieth century. Between 1870 and 1910, the city and region grew in population at approximately the same rate and only starting in 1910 did the suburbs show significantly more rapid development (see figure 41). What was true for the population in general was equally correct for the bourgeoisie: it was not until 1910 that the railroad and streetcar suburbs grew at a faster pace than Philadelphia's middle-class neighborhoods. As late as 1920, nearly three-quarters of the regions's middle class lived within the city limits. The row house in West Philadelphia was a far more typical bourgeois experience than was a detached home in Cynwyd or Haddonfield.[34]

As transportation technologies and usages changed, time increasingly helped to delimit space. Although the Pennsylvania Railroad defined "suburban" Philadelphia in spatial terms (producing a booklet touting their regional passenger service entitled "Thirty Miles Around Philadelphia"), it was actually commuting time that established the geography of the middle-class metropolis. The key to understanding the housing patterns of Philadelphia's bourgeoisie is this intersection of distance and time: travel time. A resident of Philadelphia's "Main Line" (the suburbs west of the city along the Pennsylvania Railroad) gave this explanation in 1922 for the outside limits of commuting: "Forty minutes a day is not too long to spend on the trains, as a man who wants to keep up with these history-making times should spend at least that much on the current journals. For that purpose he is furnished a comfortable seat in a steady restful vehicle, with a breezy window in summer and warmth (generally too much) in winter." Philadelphia had so many suburban rail lines that it was easy to find a home within a short commute of Center City. In the early twentieth century, a typical middle-class train or trolley ride to work was between twenty and forty-five minutes. Residential development extended this "distance" out the different transportation lines, causing large gaps in the built-up sections of both the city and its suburbs. Until the construction of the subway-elevated, West Philadelphia beyond Fiftieth Street was "farther" (the trip by trolley took longer) than were suburbs served by steam railroads twice the actual distance. The same person

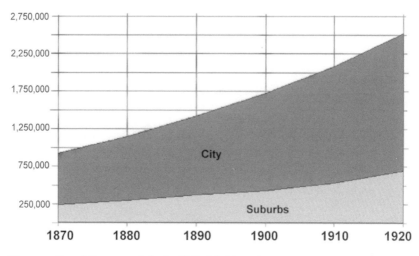

Figure 41. Population growth in the Philadelphia region.

observed that the trains of the Pennsylvania took "only twenty minutes from Bryn Mawr to Broad Street, less time than the city trolleys take from outlying West Philadelphia districts." A city report calling for additional rapid transit lines concurred: "[T]he bulk of the city's population lives in the 2, 3 and 4 mile zones, which is the territory served by the present surface electric railway system within 30 minutes from the center. The proposed subway and elevated lines will operate at an average speed of twice that of the surface lines, or say 16 miles per hour against 8 miles, so as to place most of the 6–mile zone within shorter time from City Hall than the present 4–mile zone." The map in figure 42 illustrates how the trains and the subway-elevated extended the commutation zone. Marked in light grey are the portions of Philadelphia and Camden Counties that could be reached from downtown in approximately forty minutes by trolley (or trolley and ferry in the case of Camden). The darker grey areas represent the residential districts that were accessible in the same travel time by steam train or subway-elevated (either alone or in connection with a suburban trolley). The forty-minute commutation limit included almost all of Philadelphia, parts of Delaware and Montgomery Counties in Pennsylvania, and sections of Burlington, Camden, and Gloucester Counties in New Jersey.[35]

The importance of travel time is illustrated by the building boom that took place in far West Philadelphia just before the Market Street subway-elevated opened. One middle-class Philadelphian observed: "Within the last

Figure 42. The forty-minute commute to Center City circa 1915.

two or three years, my walks have been much in West Philadelphia, say from *45th to 63rd + Spruce to Market*. Here row after row of houses have gone up like magic; they are built almost in the very fields. They are chiefly two stories + universally known as *Porch Fronts*. They are no sooner built, than occupied, even before the plaster is dry. In many streets, there is no paving or curbing, + the ground is like a ploughed field. . . . They rent for 16 to 18 dollars per month. They are poorly built of unseasoned materials." Typically less critical, John Smith visited the same area and noted the "many Improvements at 50 to 60th + Market St." Official city reports back up these observations: "The effect of the construction of the Market Street Subway-Elevated Line in West Philadelphia is very marked upon the number and increase of houses erected in this section of the city for the 5 years prior to the opening of this rapid transit line in 1907." The map in figure 43 shows the results of this construction frenzy in West Philadelphia north of Market Street between Fifty-third and Sixty-second Streets in 1910. The most striking features

Figure 43. Blocks of typical early twentieth-century, brick row houses in West Philadelphia from a 1910 city atlas. Courtesy of the Map Collection, Free Library of Philadelphia.

are the blocks of narrow, brick-built row homes that cover most of the terrain. This construction was common throughout much of the city.[36]

Not all middle-class Philadelphians lived in row homes, however, as the city offered a broad range of housing choices (especially for the upper-middle class). Mary Smith's family lived in a large, three-story, brick, semi-detached home at 4415 Pine Street in West Philadelphia built in the 1870s. Most of the houses in the immediate vicinity were similar and were occupied by members of the upper-middle class. Both Edwin Jellett and Eugenia Barnitz lived in stone, detached homes in the Germantown section of northwest Philadelphia. Germantown, a bastion of the bourgeoisie, contained in close proximity a mixture of all the middle-class housing styles available in the city: large and small detached and semi-detached homes and blocks of row houses. The Barnitz family residence, located one block from the Pennsylvania Railroad's Upsal station, was surrounded mostly by the large homes of the upper-middle class and the elite. Jellett and his mother owned a significantly smaller structure in a much less pretentious part of the community. Although there were a few mansions within walking distance of the Jellets' house, most of the buildings (regardless of whether they were free standing or attached) were modest in size.[37]

Although the vast majority of the bourgeoisie lived within the city during the first quarter of the twentieth century, suburban development began on both sides of the Delaware River in the 1880s and accelerated significantly in the 1910s. The population of Montgomery County, Pennsylvania, doubled between 1870 and 1920 while that of Delaware County, Pennsylvania, and Camden County, New Jersey, quadrupled during the same period. Most early growth took place within about an eight-mile radius of the city, because of both travel time and the higher railroad fares (which were based on distance, unlike the flat five-cent fare of the city's transit). Bedroom communities within this range included Bala, Cynwyd, Darby, Jenkintown, and Landsdowne in Pennsylvania; and Audubon, Bellmawr, Collingswood, Haddon Heights, Haddonfield, Magnolia, Runnemede, Westmount, and Westville in New Jersey.

Cynwyd on the Pennsylvania Railroad's Schuylkill Division was an archetypical railroad suburb for the Philadelphia region. Its explosive growth was made possible by the Pennsylvania Railroad's construction in 1884 of a line to Norristown and Reading. Although the Pennsylvania built the branch as part of its long competition with the Reading primarily to serve the anthracite industry, the line helped to create a suburbanized Cynwyd. Until then, the area had been known as Academyville and had consisted of mills, farms, and a few estates. Despite being only six miles from Center City in Lower Merion Township, it had a small population, primarily because the nearest train station (over a mile away in Merion) was too far a walk for a convenient daily commute. After completion of the branch, real estate speculators (including officials of the railroad) began to subdivide the farms and estates and build the infrastructure necessary to support suburban development. Growth came quickly in the early twentieth century, as fields turned into lots. The population expanded from 500 in 1900 to about 1300 in 1912. By 1916, according to the Pennsylvania Railroad, Cynwyd was "one of the most rapidly growing and most popular suburbs of Philadelphia." At that time, the railroad offered twenty-two weekday trains to the city with running times between eighteen and twenty-one minutes (well within the region's travel time equation). In addition to good transportation, it was the provision of other "urban" services that made Cynwyd's growth possible. The railroad guide continued: "All modern conveniences in the way of gas, electricity, Springfield water and underground drainage are supplied to its residents."[38]

Cynwyd and Philadelphia's other suburbs were more than simple creations of the railroads and trolley companies; they were the products of combined technological and economic changes in the late nineteenth century that made it possible to extend the full range of city amenities to nearby communities. For Cynwyd and Landsdowne and Haddonfield to attract middle-class families from Philadelphia's neighborhoods, the communities had to develop both physical and social infrastructures. The Pennsylvania Railroad acknowledged this when it touted "The charm of this suburban life, with its pure air, pure water and healthful surroundings, combined with the educational advantages provided, churches, stores and excellent transit facilities to and from the city, is manifest."[39]

In Cynwyd, all the pieces came together during the first decade of the twentieth century. A 1910 real estate sales brochure from one of the town's larger developments claimed that "the resident in Cynwyd finds every city convenience and every country comfort. Pure air, Springfield water, gas, electric lights, telephone service, and pleasant surroundings." The tract (and much of the community) consisted of "macadamized roads . . . and cement sidewalks." Within the village could be found one Roman Catholic and four Protestant churches along with two schools and a number of social clubs. Paved roads not only benefitted the growing number of automobile owners (some of whom were middle class) but were important amenities for non-motorists as well. Until 1917, the two main highways along the Main Line were private turnpikes and although the state and township provided a system of secondary roads, the local efforts were clearly deficient. After a drive with a friend through the area, Albert Edmunds complained that the driver "avoided toll-roads and preferred inferior paving to avoid two cents toll!" Until the township began paving streets, dust during the hot and dry summers was a serious problem. One resident recalled that the turnpikes "kept down" the dust "by sprinkling wagon that wet them down two or three times a day—all else was dust inches deep."[40]

By 1920 Cynwyd's infrastructure was complete. The township provided paved roads, sewers, schools, and police. The community equipped a volunteer fire department. A civic association, churches, a library, and clubs made up the town's social networks. Cynwyd, along with dozens of other suburban communities, offered most of the amenities of city life. And what was lacking was but twenty minutes away by train.[41]

The railroad schedules for these bourgeois corridors helped to highlight the continued scientific reordering of the middle-class environment in early twentieth-century Philadelphia. The coming of Daylight Saving Time, a well-studied event, was only a very minor part of this redefinition. By the early twentieth century, the railroads serving the city realistically hoped that their passengers could become so in tune with the rhythms of railway time that the suburban timetable would become superfluous.

Before exploring some of these more arcane changes, it would be useful to start with the obvious: the shift to Daylight Saving Time affected middle-class Philadelphia more than did the creation of Standard Time three decades before. Unlike the "day of two noons," the "spring forward, fall back" changes wrought by Daylight Saving Time did get mentioned in bourgeois diaries. Mary B. Smith in West Philadelphia noted (in relief) when "*Real* time [was] established again" in the fall of 1918. In part this is because the semiannual shift of a full hour was far more obvious than the onetime adjustment of a few minutes that took place in 1883. Equally as important, however, was how much more central railroad time had become for middle-class women and men. The trains running to their schedules helped set the cadence of daily life for the bourgeoisie. In a wonderful irony, it was the railroad companies (the very entities that had developed standard time just a few decades earlier) that had trouble adapting to the government-imposed Daylight Saving Time. In 1919, John L. Smith noted that the "RRds upset by [the] new Time" on the first day of the spring shift. As was true of the railroad timetable in the 1890s, the increasingly precise human definition of time on paper did not always translate into more accurate timekeeping in reality.[42]

Middle-class time took on many more classifications than just the well-known division between "Standard" and "Daylight." In early twentieth-century Philadelphia there existed what could be termed "Suburban" time as well. The Reading Railroad issued in 1910 a "Philadelphia Suburban Trains" booklet that contains schedules for six of its commuter lines. Four of the timetables list all stops along the branches but the other two are combined schedules for portions of the Reading's busy route through North Philadelphia to suburban Montgomery County. Within this folder, the Reading recognized at least two things: the importance of the travel time equation and the existence of passengers who used multiple commuter routes. The first is clear from the decision of the Reading to end its main stem service at Glenside (about thirty-five minutes from the city even though most of the trains continued to more outlying points, like Doylestown and Lansdale). The second is apparent because the Reading not only bundled its inner suburban network together in one folder but printed 20,000 copies of the booklet. The railroad obviously felt many people used more than one line on a regular basis (otherwise it would not have been cost effective to print the combined timetable as either a supplement to or a replacement for the route-specific ones). This small folder also carves out an intermediate niche in the hierarchy of timetables on the Reading. The railroad, like most of its competitors, had developed by the late-Victorian period two types of printed schedules: ones for specific routes (the Chestnut Hill branch, for example) and ones for the entire railroad (known as "system timetables"). But with "T. T. 7" (as the well-ordered railroad designated this folder), the Reading recognized something in between: suburban trains and, with them, suburban time.[43]

Suburban time is a way of rethinking the physical relationships in the metropolis by using the bourgeois corridors as a "map." In a city as heavily dependent upon trains and trolleys as was middle-class Philadelphia, geography had a different meaning than it did in the walking city of the early nineteenth century or the automobile version of the late twentieth. Because railroad trains were faster than trolleys and both were (usually) speedier than foot, it was not a straight line that was always the shortest distance (at least in time) between two points. This relationship between Center City and suburbs has already been explored, but there was an equally important intra-"suburban" traffic (people traveling between one outlying station and another). The Reading's "Philadelphia Suburban Trains" booklet catered for this service: allowing a rider to plot a trip from a station on one branch (say Germantown on the Chestnut Hill line) to a depot on a different branch (say Manayunk on the Norristown line) without using more than one timetable or traveling via Reading Terminal in Center City. In fact, because of the radial nature of most of Philadelphia's rail lines, the difference between "railroad geography" and that found in nature (and printed on maps) is even more dramatic for trips like these. Simply put, places that were physically close to each other (Manayunk and Germantown are good examples) could be very far apart by train. When Germantown resident Edwin Jellett visited friends in suburban Schwenksville, he had to take a complex combination of trolleys or trains to complete the twenty-mile journey. The trip took approximately three hours regardless of what mix of transport he tried. The trolleys were more direct yet slower, while the faster trains required Jellett to begin his westward journey by going southeast for nearly six miles toward Center City.[44]

Perhaps the most fascinating development of railroad time during this period was the attempt by the companies to do away with printed timetables altogether by having their middle-class passengers internalize their train schedules. As timetables became more complex in the late nineteenth century, railroads continuously battled to simplify them. Chapter 2 highlighted the "pocket timetable" that left out many details and most stops to concentrate on just the busiest stations as one such mechanism. The railways took this idea a step further by developing interval scheduling that would allow regular passengers to know when the trains ran without even consulting a timetable. At its base, interval scheduling is fairly simple: at a set interval (every five, ten, fifteen, twenty, thirty, sixty minutes) a train leaves one station for a specific destination. If the departure times are easy to remember— "every hour on the hour" or "quarter of and quarter after"—and remain constant throughout the day, a regular passenger would no longer need to consult a timetable. An early example of such a schedule was the Pennsylvania Railroad "Main Line" local service. By 1886, trains left Broad Street Station for Bryn Mawr every half hour from 6:15 A.M. to 10:45 P.M.[45]

By the early twentieth century, all of Philadelphia's railroads had adopted interval timetables for some of their busiest routes. This was in line with national trends; a leading contemporary text on railroad management concluded that "the uniform time-table [another name for such scheduling] on suburban lines has much in its favor." Sometimes the interval was highlighted by the company: the cover of the Baltimore & Ohio's New York timetable proclaimed "Every other hour on the even hour, New York to Philadelphia & Washington." More impressively, the Reading in its 1916 *Official Guide* listing heralded: "Your Watch is Your Time-Table! New York and Philadelphia, Every Hour on the Hour." More typically, the passenger had to glean the interval by reference to the actual train times. The 1906 Reading *Official Guide* listing for the same service includes a similar interval schedule but with none of the hype. As in 1886, the Pennsylvania Railroad in 1906 continued to do nothing to call attention to the rhythm of its Main Line local services.[46]

Although the Reading claimed that "Your Watch is Your Time-Table!," in fact it was you and your memory that took the place of the printed schedule. The interval timetable was another attempt by middle-class commercial institutions—the railroads—to impose rational order over what had not that long before been nature's time. The railroads both recognized and utilized the fact that riding their trains had become an important ritual in everyday middle-class life. At approximately the same moment that Frederick Taylor attempted to scientifically remake the workplace and John Wanamaker the retail store, the railroads tried to do the same with their most difficult cargo: passengers.

By the early twentieth century, the middle-class residential communities of West Philadelphia and Germantown, of Cynwyd and Collingswood, were neat, well-ordered places in the bourgeois metropolis. Middle-class women and men used the trains and the trolleys, the buses and the cars, to develop a taxonomy of space for their region: amusement at Willow Grove and the Jersey shore; business, shopping, and entertainment in Center City; and home on quiet, tree-lined residential streets surrounded by similar people. In this spatial arrangement, people not like oneself lived elsewhere, often in their own recognizable communities. Sometimes class was not enough; certain members of the middle class who were neither white nor "old-stock" also found themselves excluded. Although this order had just been developed in the late nineteenth century, for many bourgeois Philadelphians "their" city seemed timeless and permanent. Just after the turn of the century, however, change came to the fringes of some middle-class neighborhoods. At first, some bourgeois women and men tried to keep the others at bay by small-scale, private actions. By the 1910s, the people wanting restrictions increasingly saw local government—through planning and zoning—as the way to control "undesired" growth. These efforts to control change in the region highlight the fragility of the world that middle-class Philadelphians had made for themselves.

For members of the middle class living in North Philadelphia and Haddon Heights, the broad cityscape included places that were not part of their bourgeois metropolis, such as largely working-class neighborhoods like Kensington and the immigrant sections of Center City and South Philadelphia. Most middle-class women and men avoided these spaces—or only went on business—but some sought out these alien Philadelphias. John L. Smith regularly explored these areas for his amusement. His words reflect the distance that he (and many other members of the white, native-born bourgeoisie) put between himself and other Philadelphians. One Sunday he "went down town to Lombard St South St to see How they live there the streets were full of Italians I was surprised + I asked Policeman he said they were about going away to work for week but they all came back to spend Sunday at home." A few years later Smith made another visit to the immigrant-filled wards of Philadelphia and "saw stores full of Jew women buy live Fish they has in tanks . . . well this was new to me—+ I was well Pleased with my visit + will go again." "Chinatown," a small section of Center City with a large Asian concentration, was also a regular destination for bourgeois women and men because of the restaurants and shops located there.[47]

Overt racial discrimination restricted the housing opportunities for the African-American bourgeoisie during the early twentieth century and, ironically, helped to destabilize white middle-class neighborhoods as well. Because prejudice forced African Americans to pay more for housing than whites, there was always a financial incentive to sell or rent to a black person. James Stemons, an African-American postal clerk and newspaper editor, highlights this in his complaint that "House rent in decent localities is something frightful for colored people in this city. Because of my station in life I cannot afford to live in an alley or in a location that is not nice." Stemons' prose—his "station in life"—also nicely reflects how he shared a similar worldview with other members of the middle class regardless of race. Even blacks wealthy enough to buy their homes, like the highly successful caterer Albert E. Dutrieuille, tended to live in Center City and South Philadelphia, and not the neighborhoods that made up Cecil Holm's "one big stretch of middle class." Once African Americans began moving into the traditional bourgeois neighborhoods, however, "white flight" often took over. In 1917, the librarian Albert Edmunds expressed his racism quite blatantly when he "[w]rote to real-estate agents about negro encroachment on Wiota Street, as I saw an ape on a bicycle examining a house just vacated." Although particularly virulent in his remarks, Edmunds demonstrated a common white middle-class concern and reaction to blacks moving into even the fringes of bourgeois West Philadelphia (Edmunds' block consisted of small row houses not far from the railroad tracks). A few weeks later, Edmunds complained that "Another black family has moved in, and the once sweet little Wiota

Street has become a repulsive slum. The Wests are going to move, and doubtless all decent people will follow. I now call this whole section of West Philadelphia Baboonville. At Fortieth and Market the ape cars cross, going to and
from Lombard Street, and the corners are always dense with baboons waiting
for them." Two black families were enough to destabilize a block for not just
Edmunds but also the Wests.[48]

Race was not the only factor that could upset the fragile middle-class
taxonomy of space: apartments were another. Precisely why bourgeois
Philadelphians so feared large rental developments in their neighborhoods is
difficult to pin down—perhaps it was an issue of class or one of strain on infrastructure or just one of change—but they did dislike the structures. One
elderly, middle-class man noted with disapproval in 1904 the "rapid multipli-
cation of '*Apartments*.' . . . They may be seen in all our leading streets and
thoroughfares. The old idea of everyone dwelling under his own vine + fig
tree is fast disappearing, + with it, of course, the once hallowed idea of
'*home*.' " It was the construction of an apartment building "next door" that
helped to encourage members of Mary Smith's family to leave Pine Street in
West Philadelphia.[49]

The breakup of Mary Smith's household illustrates the brittleness of the
early twentieth-century middle-class world. When the Smiths moved to the
4400 block of Pine Street in the 1890s it was the epitome of bourgeois respectability: large homes, often filled with children, staffed with servants,
and owned by their white-collar occupants. The Smiths' neighbors included
a drug manufacturer, a contractor, a commission merchant, a secretary for a
coffee company, and an editor. Close enough to Center City that J. Harper
Smith had a convenient commute by streetcar and Eliza (J. Harper's wife and
Mary's mother) could keep up with her many activities, it was also far from
the noisy railroads and factories that touched the fringes of middle-class
West Philadelphia. In the early 1920s, both J. Harper and Eliza died, leaving
Mary, two of her unmarried sisters (Helen and Beth), and her married sister
Edith and her husband and children in the large house. Starting in 1923,
members of the Smith family attended meetings "in the interest of zoning in
West Phila." The largely unchecked private enterprise that characterized
American real estate development and that had created their environment
now threatened it. In 1925, this vague menace became real: the Smiths
learned that an apartment building was to be constructed next door to their
house. Before long, Edith and her husband Harry (who worked at that bastion of bourgeois respectability, the John Wanamaker department store)
started looking for houses in the trolley and railroad suburbs (Yeadon,

Drexel Hill, Landsdowne, and Glenside) while Mary, Beth, and Helen scoured the city for apartments (Center City, West Philadelphia, and Bala). It is more than just irony that, although the sisters objected to an apartment next door, they were willing to live in one elsewhere; it is also a reflection of the middle-class taxonomy of space: apartments did not belong in the 4400 block of Pine Street. Edith, Harry, and their children eventually moved to Glenside in Montgomery County, a community well served by both the streetcars of the Philadelphia Rapid Transit and the trains of the Reading Railroad. Mary, Beth, and Helen ended up moving just a short distance to "406 South 45th Street for a six-months' stay." For the next decade they would "winter" at this location, returning to Pine Street in the summer. In 1951, with Helen in a nursing home, Mary and Beth finally sold the house and, in the story's final turn, moved to an apartment.[50]

The Philadelphia bourgeoisie objected to apartments and African Americans in their neighborhoods in part because it violated the carefully arranged taxonomy of the metropolis they had devised in the late nineteenth century. The scientific redefinition of the region seemed firmly in place at the turn of the century. Home was separated from work and other special-ized areas and the residences of the white middle class were insulated from those of the working classes and others. By the 1910s, the same free-market capitalism that had allowed Eliza and J. Harper Smith and the other middle-class women and men of the city to create places like West Philadelphia now endangered their carefully constructed classification of space. Often "be-trayed" by members of their own class, the upholders of order first tried per-suasion: talking to neighbors and letters to real estate agents. When that failed, the bourgeoisie turned to another of their creations, bureaucratic regulation, to maintain their grammar of space. Initially with city planning and later with zoning, middle-class Philadelphians tried to enforce their visions of the metropolis on other recalcitrant city dwellers.[51]

In Philadelphia, as in many other cities, planning focused on maintain-ing the centrality of downtown and beautifying the civic landscape. The mu-nicipality adopted transit and highway schemes to improve access to Center City during the first two and a half decades of the twentieth century. The city extended the Market Street subway-elevated to Frankford in the northeast and started construction on a greatly expanded underground rail system. In addition, local and state governments improved the highway infrastructure throughout the region by taking over private turnpikes, paving and building roads at a faster rate, and constructing a bridge over the Delaware River link-ing Philadelphia with Camden. The Benjamin Franklin Parkway (figure 44)

Figure 44. The city beautiful: the Parkway circa 1924. Courtesy of the Urban Archives of Temple University.

not only improved automobile access to Center City but also gave downtown a grand entrance that could be lined with museums and monuments. The parkway was also Philadelphia's most complete expression of the nationwide City Beautiful movement. Outwardly the movement was an attempt to improve American cities by beautifying them, but many of its middle-class and elite supporters believed that beauty could be an effective social control device for the lower classes. Not only would the picturesque parkway draw back to the city elite and upper-middle-class families that had left for the suburbs, but the classic and tranquil surroundings of the parkway would also uplift and calm members of the city's working classes. Although Philadelphia, like most American cities, only completed a small fraction of its ambitious plans from this period, it made significant progress and spent much money on reinforcing Center City's role as the leading business, retail, and cultural hub for the region.[52]

Even though planning maintained part of the taxonomy of space, it did little for West Philadelphia and the other neighborhoods and, beginning in the 1910s, the middle class turned to zoning to uphold the remainder of their geographic sensibilities. Zoning, with its plans, maps, and "conforming" and "non-conforming" uses, was the bourgeoisie's scientific classification of space enacted into law. By the early 1920s, good-government experts considered zoning a necessity even in the suburbs. A report prepared for suburban Lower Merion Township concluded that the municipality's building code "should be supplemented by the application of zoning regulations which will prevent improper uses of property." The battle for land use regulations within Philadelphia was a long one; although agitation among the middle class began in the 1910s and progress was made in the 1920s, the city did not adopt a zoning plan until the 1930s. As with other concerns, the women and men of Philadelphia's bourgeoisie turned to government regulation in land use only after capitalism coupled with self control had failed. When the logic of the market came into conflict with their rational classification of the world, the middle class tried to strike an uneasy—and ultimately untenable—balance with zoning.[53]

In the long run, the world that many middle-class Philadelphians had created mentally and physically in the late nineteenth century proved too fragile to survive the changing dynamics of the free market. Individual decisions and largely unregulated capitalism had created the very bourgeois 4400 block of Pine Street in West Philadelphia; those same factors began to undermine that middle-class Victorian order in the 1920s. Although change was at the heart of the expansion of bourgeois Philadelphia during the late nineteenth and early twentieth centuries, the Smiths (and many of their neighbors) seemed to hope that somehow, once established, the middle-class taxonomy of space would become static. Not only would the retail zone always be the retail zone, but the blocks of middle-class homes would always be such. City planning might ensure that Center City would retain the functions it developed in the Victorian era, but the Smiths would need zoning and other regulations to keep apartments out of their quiet block of Pine Street.

In the case of the Smiths, political activism came when a very specific part of middle-class Philadelphia was threatened: their neighborhood. At the heart of their particular problem was a broader, early twentieth-century middle-class concern: the conflict between the ordered, rational worldview of the bourgeoisie and other conceptions of the city, nation, and world. It is not surprising that middle-class politicians and reformers during the period historians have called the Progressive Era focused on rationality and science, as they and their parents had largely remade their lives along the same lines during the preceding decades. During the Progressive Era, members of the middle class were not searching for order—for it was already there for them—but instead seeking to convince others to retain that order.

Postlude: Albion and I Went to the Sesqui

Monday, August 23, 1926: Showd city to Pardoes—Billy Penn—Independence Hall—Sears Roebuck—Bridge—Collingswd. . . . Albion & I went to the Sesqui—spend 3 hrs. in machinery bldg. saw ¼ of it. Huge. Sesqui is huge.[1]

Cyril Harvey was the headmaster of the Haddonfield Friends School in suburban New Jersey. He was in his twenties, married to fellow Friend Ruth, and the father of a baby girl (Dorothy Alice, born at 7 A.M. on April 19, 1925, weight seven pounds). His family lived in nearby Delaware County, Pennsylvania, and he often visited them. Harvey was something of a technological enthusiast: he loved all the latest inventions and gadgets. He was an active amateur photographer, but his greatest love (other than Ruth and Dorothy Alice)—and one of his largest expenses—was the radio. Harvey was always upgrading his equipment by either purchasing enhancements for his existing radio or buying an entirely new one when "progress" (or marketing) made his old set obsolete.

In the spring of 1926, however, he found a new image of modernity on which to lavish his money: the automobile. Like many other middle-class Philadelphians in the early twentieth century, the motor car began to replace the train or trolley as Harvey's primary form of leisure transport. The completion of the Delaware River Bridge that year meant that Harvey could easily drive to Delaware County and the motorists of Delaware County could go from home to the Jersey shore without the long wait at the ferries. The ties that bound bourgeois Philadelphia were now increasingly roads of asphalt and concrete and not rails of steel.

The Pardoes were friends of the Harveys from upstate Pennsylvania. They had come to the city for the Sesqui-Centennial International Exhibition (as the Sesqui was formally named). Cyril Harvey was a good host; he took them to many of the typical (and a few not so) Philadelphia tourist sites on a cloudy but surprisingly mild Monday in August. Despite the clouds and occasional showers, they went to the observation deck located at the feet of the statue of William Penn atop City Hall tower to see the impressive growth of the region. Had the day been clear, they would have been able to see Haddonfield but even in the clouds and drizzle they could see the new bridge, the many skyscrapers, and the new highways (including the parkway cutting its way diagonally across William Penn's grid). No trip to the city would be complete without a visit to Independence Hall and a quick touch of the Liberty Bell in its lobby and Harvey obliged. The one atypical site they visited was the Sears, Roebuck store in Camden, New Jersey. Most guides would have taken visitors to the more impressive stores along Market Street in Philadelphia— John Wanamaker, Strawbridge & Clothier, or Gimbel Brothers—but parking was undoubtedly more convenient at the Sears store.

Harvey and Pardoe returned to Philadelphia by car that afternoon to visit the Sesqui (see figure 45 for the giant Liberty Bell at the entrance to the fair). They missed the big event of the day: heavyweight champion Jack Dempsey had toured the grounds and took lunch at the Alpine Haus with the mayor early in the afternoon. The combination of Dempsey's appearance and the unseasonably cool weather drew a large crowd that day—estimated at over 30,000. Harvey and Pardoe went to one of the main buildings, the somewhat preposterously titled "Palace of U.S. Government, Machinery, Mines, Metallurgy, and Transportation." It contained a combination of history and modernity mixed with the Babbit-like boosterism that characterized both the Sesqui and much of middle-class culture in the Jazz Age. Harvey enjoyed his all-too-brief visit.

After retrieving his car from the muddy parking lot by the main gate, he and Pardoe headed home. The Sesqui was located in far South Philadelphia, down by the Naval Base. Harvey drove up Broad Street to City Hall, and shortly thereafter turned right onto Race Street. The trip would have been relatively fast through South Philadelphia but would have slowed down considerably in Center City. Traffic control was in its infancy in the metropolis and the rights-of-way among the motor cars, trolleys, pedestrians, and horse-drawn vehicles were subject to constant renegotiation (which is a polite way of saying that accidents were common). Harvey drove over the Delaware River Bridge, a structure he had declared a "great bridge" after he used it for the first time earlier that year. Philadelphians were incredibly proud of the structure, then the world's longest suspension bridge. Once Harvey paid his toll, he and Pardoe sped out on the more automobile friendly highways of New Jersey, home to Haddonfield.[2]

Figure 45. The new age: trucks parading in front of the massive Liberty Bell at the Sesquicentennial. Courtesy of the Print and Picture Collection, Free Library of Philadelphia.

Conclusion: The Trouble with History

The trouble with History [is] the things you want to know, they dont talk of + the things I saw + I know of he describes Incorrectly.[1]

John L. Smith recorded these words in his diary after reading one of the many newspaper articles published between 1911 and 1915 commemorating the fiftieth anniversary of the Civil War. As with many other veterans, the conflict had been a defining moment in Smith's life. Until his death in 1921, he was a vigorous consumer of Civil War history. On this day in 1911, Smith was clearly unhappy with both the structure and the details of the narrative. Since reading these words one hot summer day while researching this project, his entry has served as a warning to me as I constructed my version of late nineteenth- and early twentieth-century Philadelphia. My hope is that Smith would have recognized the middle-class city that he once inhabited.

As Smith reminds us, however, writing history is about much more than just getting the facts right; historians must "talk of" the "things" that their readers "want to know" about. In other words, for a historical narrative to have value or power it must place the facts in broader context. For me, this tale of late nineteenth- and early twentieth-century middle-class Philadelphia has at least two settings worth exploring.

First, I hope that this case study of the Philadelphia bourgeoisie will remind historians of the importance of unifying social and political history. Although this work is only a tentative first step, I think it amply illustrates the rewards for doing this. Despite many calls for integration, the social and political histories of the period continue along parallel trajectories. The stories of everyday life in the late nineteenth and early twentieth centuries, as developed by social and cultural historians, are, like mine, replete with tales of order, rationality, and what the Victorian middle class would have called science. The narratives of all the myriad Progressive Era attempts at reform—on the local, state, and national levels—written by political historians and political scientists are also full of examples of order, rationality, and science. For decades, both political and social historians have told broadly similar accounts of the period. Yet when political historians look for the roots of the Progressive Era's well-known search for political order, they usually confine their examinations to the words and deeds of politicians and their powerful friends. Social and cultural historians can be just as blind; all too often we ignore the politics of our subjects entirely. But people do not divide their lives so cleanly along disciplinary lines. John L. Smith, mapmaker and regional explorer, who read the *Public Ledger,* rode the Pennsylvania Railroad, and shopped at Gimbels, was also a lifelong Republican who voted in virtually every election and often for "reform" candidates. To understand Smith's politics, and perhaps even why he voted for Woodrow Wilson in 1912, we have to understand his broader worldview. To discover how he made sense of his life, including his politics, we must turn to the rituals and rhythms of the world Smith inhabited: middle-class Philadelphia.[2]

Since its publication thirty-six years ago, Robert Wiebe's *The Search for Order* has shaped historians' views on the roots of Progressive Era reforms. According to Wiebe, what motivated the political elite to create a well-ordered, rational governmental bureaucracy were fears of change and social disorder. Although fear may have motivated the politicians examined by Wiebe, if we look at John L. Smith and his colleagues in the Philadelphia bourgeoisie, we see similar changes, almost identical searches for order, throughout everyday life and not just in politics. These searches for cultural order, however, were not driven by fear but instead by a faith in progress and the future.

If my understanding of middle-class culture is correct, then the roots for this political search for order may have far more to do with how bourgeois Philadelphians (and Americans) made sense of their world than in any specific political or social threat. If, as I argue, almost all of middle-class life revolved around institutions—both commercial and not-for-profit from museums to libraries to department stores to newspapers to railroads—that used logic and order and (in the language of the time) "science" to reorder the world, why should members of the bourgeoisie not use the same paradigm to understand politics? As part of a broad faith in the future and a hope for continued progress, the middle-class women and men of Philadelphia participated in the "scientific" reconstruction of almost every aspect of their city and the nation between 1876 and 1926. For me, the multitude of Progressive Era reforms are but one small part of this complex cultural matrix.

The second context for this study focuses on the legacy of the late nineteenth- and early twentieth-century middle-class metropolis seventy-seven years later. The construction of the Delaware River Bridge in 1926 is an appropriate ending point for this particular vision of Philadelphia (figure 46), for it was a symbol of a new age; one in which the automobile largely replaced the train and the trolley. This shift was most noticeable in southern New Jersey, where streetcar service ended in the 1930s and, in the face of rapidly declining patronage, the Pennsylvania and the Reading Railroads would merge their lines to the Jersey shore.

The trains and trolleys were not the only staples of Victorian middle-class life to come under pressure in the 1920s. It was then when the first crack in the retail dominance of the Center City department store also appeared. Although Strawbridge & Clothier dramatically enlarged its Eighth and Market Streets store in the late 1920s (making it competitive in both size and amenities with those of John Wanamaker and Gimbel Brothers), it also began the construction of the first two suburban branch stores in the region: Ardmore and Jenkintown. The Great Depression ended the ambitious expansion plans of Gimbel Brothers (which, if completed, would have made its store "the largest in the world" yet again), and John Wanamaker's massive (and very upmarket) men's store, which opened on Broad Street during the slump, was also a failure.

The trends present in Philadelphia's newspaper industry that developed in the 1920s continued through mid-century. Instead of the thirteen daily journals that served the city in 1900, by 1948 there remained but three. None of the members of the genteel metropolitan press that had so defined Victorian Philadelphia had survived; the last to go was the *Public Ledger* in 1934. Of the surviving titles, two were general circulation broadsheets (one morning and one afternoon) and the other was an afternoon tabloid.

Change in a large city like Philadelphia seems almost inevitable. Throughout its history, the people of the city and its region both created and adapted to new opportunities. Philadelphians quite regularly transformed their region throughout the last four centuries, using money and technology to develop new urban visions. The city of the late nineteenth- and early twentieth-century middle class was but one of these dreams. The roots of this scientific reconstruction of the metropolis antedated the Centennial and

Figure 46. The symbol for the new age: the Delaware River Bridge when new in 1926.
Courtesy of the Philadelphia City Archives.

its legacy extended beyond the Sesquicentennial, but it was during that fifty-year period that the bourgeoisie's taxonomy of time and space was most apparent.

What is left of this urban vision today, seventy-seven years after the Sesquicentennial? At first glance, one is tempted to say very little. Of all the names that so defined the commercial culture of the middle-class city between 1876 and 1926, only two survive in 2003: *The Philadelphia Inquirer* and Strawbridge's. Neither is still owned by Philadelphians; the newspaper is part of the Knight-Ridder chain and the department store is a division of the May Company. Gimbel Brothers, after years of absentee ownership and indifferent management, folded in 1986. John Wanamaker, the epitome of bourgeois commercial culture in the city, went through a variety of owners before being purchased in 1995 by the May Company. The new owner found little value left in the name and quickly renamed the stores "Hecht's." A year later, to the shock of many Philadelphians (middle-class and otherwise), Strawbridge & Clothier, the region's last locally owned department store, sold itself to May. This time, however, the acquirer realized the benefit of a local name and retitled all its stores in the Philadelphia region "Strawbridge's" (including its former Wanamaker units). Today there are only two department stores left on Market Street in Center City, and both are owned by the May Company. These two department stores are no longer the retail hub of Center City, let alone the region.

In 2003, the once highly competitive newspaper market consists of but two titles: *The Philadelphia Inquirer* and the *Philadelphia Daily News*. Both are owned by the Knight-Ridder chain. *The Inquirer* is a morning broadsheet that has national pretensions and the *News* is a working-class tabloid. Neither seem closely related to the genteel metropolitan press of the Victorian city. *The Evening Bulletin*, that great early twentieth-century journalistic success story, folded in 1982 shortly after being sold by the McLean family to an oil company with media ambitions.

As for the railroads and transit companies, none of the names from the late nineteenth and early twentieth centuries survive today. The title of Philadelphia's greatest corporation, the once seemingly omnipotent Pennsylvania Railroad Company, vanished in 1968 when it merged to form the ill-fated Penn Central. The 1970 bankruptcy of the Penn Central helped motivate Congress to address the northeastern railroad crisis, which in turn led to the creation of the Consolidated Rail Corporation in 1976. Conrail not only took over most of the old Pennsylvania but also its erstwhile rival, the Reading, as well. In 1999, Conrail was divided between two of its competitors, CSX and Norfolk Southern, and for the first time in 170 years no major railroad called Philadelphia home. By 2003, little of the Victorian railway infrastructure is recognizable. Neither Broad Street Station nor Reading Terminal survive as operating depots. Broad Street had been pulled down in the 1950s as part of an urban revitalization scheme and Reading Terminal ended its days as a passenger depot in the mid-1980s. The structure (with its exquisite train shed) has been converted into part of a state-funded convention center. A truncated Conrail operates a pared-down freight system in the region for its out-of-town owners. Amtrak, another federal creation, runs the intercity passenger trains while the Southeastern Pennsylvania Transportation Authority, a state-created, regional agency, provides local train, bus, and trolley service.

Perhaps even greater changes have taken place in the fabric of the region. Again, at first glance, it looks like little of the well-ordered early twentieth-century middle-class city survives in 2003. Population has steadily shifted from the city to the suburbs since 1926. Philadelphia's population remained essentially stagnant from 1930 to 1970 and has declined since while the suburbs have undergone steady growth. In 1920, approximately three-quarters of the region's two-and-a-half-million people lived within the city limits; in 2000 the city contains only about thirty percent of the five-million residents of the metropolitan area. West Philadelphia and North Philadelphia, once massive stretches of middle-class homes, now house few members of the bourgeoisie. Today, the vast majority of the region's middle class live in the Pennsylvania and New Jersey suburbs.

Those same suburbs contain much of the region's commercial and shopping districts. King of Prussia in suburban Montgomery County not only includes one of the nation's largest shopping malls but also scores of office buildings. In a wonderful irony, one of the early twentieth-century bourgeoisie's favorite destinations, Willow Grove Park, became a shopping mall in the 1980s, so it still serves as a middle-class node today.

Although it is tempting to conclude that little of the Victorian bourgeoisie's taxonomy of space and time remains, I do not think it would be accurate. In fact, if we look again at Philadelphia and its region in 2003, the actual persistence of some underlying concepts developed a century ago by the women and men of the Victorian middle class is striking.

First, the reconceptualization of time initiated in the late nineteenth century is still present today. Time—on both the large and the small scale—remains divorced from nature. Men and women have used heating and air conditioning to help control the seasons much as their grandparents used the light bulb to extend the day. Retailers' attempts to influence the calendar have become more precise as computers have allowed the tracking of massive amounts of sale data. Stores still use technology to extend the selling day, much as John Wanamaker and his colleagues did 100 years ago.

Even the middle-class taxonomy of space has survived to a large degree on many levels. Not only do department stores still exhibit the same classification of space as they did in Victorian Philadelphia but so do the warehouse-like superstores and the shopping malls. The large enclosed malls are truly the inheritors of the middle-class clientele and ideals of the late nineteenth- and early twentieth-century department stores. Carefully placed at highway junctions, much as their predecessors were at streetcar nodes, large shopping malls draw on regional markets. Like the Victorian department stores, the malls have carefully defined interiors—individual stores instead of departments—and offer a full range of services to keep the customer in the structure for as long as possible. Bank cards now supply the same credit facilities for multiple merchants that the individual store account once did, and the automobile provides the delivery service previously the province of the retailer.

Major metropolitan newspapers like the *Inquirer* and the *Daily News* continue to be departmentalized. Where once sports occupied a page (or at most three) in the *Public Ledger* or *The Evening Bulletin,* it now takes an entire section in the modern daily. Although Philadelphia's Victorian editors and readers would find the size of today's *Inquirer* surprising (as would they find the lack of choice among titles), they would recognize the basic layout. As with the surviving department stores, the design of Philadelphia's remaining newspapers owes much to their Victorian antecedents.

Another major survivor is the late nineteenth-century middle-class geography of the region. As expressed by the city's (and outlying municipalities') zoning ordinances and master plans, the Victorian taxonomy of space largely remains the guiding concept for the metropolis' land use. Home—for the bourgeoisie of 2003, almost invariably in the suburbs—is still separated from work, shopping, and amusement. Industry, as it so often was in the Victorian city, is confined to the fringes of the middle-class world. Although zoning did not keep West Philadelphia a bourgeois haven, as many of its supporters had hoped, government and private action did keep many suburbs largely residential and mostly white and middle class. Even the locations would not totally surprise the Victorian bourgeoisie; although only a few of today's suburbanites ride the surviving commuter trains, the modern suburbs essentially follow the late nineteenth-century rail corridors. The white-collar office, the most common work destination for Philadelphia's modern bourgeoisie, tends to exist in well-defined commercial areas from the new skyscraper zone in Center City to suburban office developments located along limited-access highways.

These limited-access highways and the upmarket automobiles that use them are the new bourgeois corridors of the metropolis. Playing the same roles as the trains and trolleys once did, automobiles now transport the women and men of Philadelphia's middle class from one bourgeois location to another. In the Victorian city, the middle class rode the streetcars as the working classes walked; today, the working classes ride the busses and remaining trolleys as the bourgeoisie drives.

Over 100 years after the Victorian middle class remade their Philadelphia in a new, scientific image, a surprisingly large legacy remains. As with Victorian bourgeois culture itself, this legacy is a very mixed one. Most of what is left is quite benign, attempts to rationally classify space and time in the name of "efficiency" and "progress"—if no longer "science." But often the political inheritance was and is not benign: public laws and private agreements have been and continue to be used to keep others out. Members of today's middle class battle to keep low-income housing and light industry out of suburban Pennsylvania and New Jersey, much as their predecessors once did in West Philadelphia and Germantown.

I believe that by better understanding the cultural roots of the Progressive Era, we learn not only about Victorian middle-class society in the city but also about the nature of our own comprehension of the transformations affecting late twentieth- and early twenty-first-century America. Fin-de-siècle Philadelphians' understandings of time and space changed not because of technological or demographic imperatives, but because their paradigm for order had shifted. Once change is divorced from inevitability, it and its consequences become human actions subject to political debate and societal control.[3]

Appendix

What follows is some basic demographic information about the sixty-three middle-class women and men whose papers I used for this study. A blank in any column indicates that I do not know the relevant information; an entry followed by a question mark shows that, although I am not certain of the data, I have enough information to make an assertion that I believe to be correct.

Name	Birth–Death	Sex	Race	Religion	Home	Work
William G. Armstrong	–1888?	M	W		Philadelphia	Engraver
Mary Brown Askew		F	W		Burlington, N.J.	
Eugenia L. Barnitz	1882–	F	W		German-town	Student
Moses Behrend		M	W	Jewish	Center City	Student
Leo G. Bernheimer	1876–	M	W	Jewish	North Philadelphia	Student
Anna E. Broomall	–1931	F	W	Friend	Delaware County	Medical doctor
Fred Caravelli		M	W	Roman Catholic	Philadelphia (then N.J.)	Student then barber
James J. Cleary		M	W		Philadelphia	Salesman

Name	Birth–Death	Sex	Race	Religion	Home	Work
Helen M. Cochran		F	W		Chester, Pa.	Student
Harriet C. Crothers	–1889	F	W	Episcopalian	Center City	
Laurence A. Deering		M	W	Roman Catholic	Center City	Priest
J. William Dow		M	W		Haddonfield, N.J.	Student
Albert J. Edmunds		M	W	Protestant	Philadelphia	Librarian
Howard Edwards	1833–1925	M	W	Friend	Philadelphia	
William B. Evans		M	W		Yeadon, Pa.	Grocer
Edith Shelhom (Garwood)	1895?–	F	W	Methodist	N.J.	Student, then farmer
W. E. Garwood		M	W		N.J.	Farmer?
Alexander B. Geary	1870–1952	M	W		Wallingford, Pa.	Lawyer/ politician
Mrs. Bennett H. R. Gilbert		F	W		Haddonfield, N.J.	Student
Harry Goff	1905–	M	W		Haddon Heights, N.J.	Student
Cyril Hingston Harvey		M	W	Friend	Pa. (then N.J.)	Teacher
William Souder Hemsing	1866–1940	M	W	Protestant	Souderton, Pa.	Clerk
[Robert?] Hinch		M	W	Roman Catholic	Philadelphia	Huckster?
John Cecil Holm		M	W	Methodist?	West Philadelphia	Student

Name	Birth–Death	Sex	Race	Religion	Home	Work
Edwin C. Jellett	1860–1917	M	W	Episcopalian	German-town	Draughts-man
C. W. Kirven		M	W		Delaware County	Farmer small business-man
Mrs. Tucker C. Laughlin	1859–91	F	W		German-town	Seamstress
Edwin W. Lehman		M	W		West Philadelphia	Retired
William E. Lockwood		M	W		Chester County, Pa.	Railway equipment sales?
Sylvia Smith Long		F	W		Haddon-field, N.J.	Student
Dick Luckenbach	1907–	M	W		Haddon Heights, N.J.	Student
Susan R. MacManus		F	W		West Philadelphia	Housewife
Paul V. Magee		M	W		Haddon-field, N.J.	Student
T. Chalkley Matlack	1858–	M	W	Friend	Philadelphia (then N.J.)	Teacher, then farmer
Charles K. Mills		M	W		Philadelphia	Doctor/professor
Margaret Moffat		F	W		Philadelphia	Student, then chemist
Henrietta Ulman Newmayer		F	W	Jewish	Philadelphia	Housewife
Sam H. Newsome	1903?–	M	W		Chester, Pa.	Student

Name	Birth–Death	Sex	Race	Religion	Home	Work
George T. Parry		M	W		North Philadelphia	Shop-keeper
Elizabeth Broomell Passmore	–1931	F	W	Friend	Chester County, Pa.	Widow and farmer
Josiah S. Pearce	1841–1915	M	W	Christian	Ardmore, Pa.	Banker and politician
James A. Pennypacker	1899–	M	W		Haddonfield, N.J.	
William J. Phillips		M	W		Cynwyd, Pa.	Student
Mary Roberts		F	W	Christian	Downingtown, Pa.	Teacher
Mildred Schwaemmle	1907–	F	W		Haddon Heights, N.J.	Student
Sarah P. Sellers		F	W	Friend	Delaware County	
Bernice Dutrieuille Shelton	1903–	F	B	Roman Catholic	Philadelphia	Student
Robert L. Sinclair		M	W	Presbyterian	West Philadelphia	Lawyer?
H. Sidney Smith	1877?–	M	W		Chester, Pa.	Mill worker
John L. Smith	1846–1921	M	W	Episcopalian	North Philadelphia	Mapmaker
Mary B. Smith		F	W	Presbyterian	West Philadelphia	Student
David Ludlow Stackhouse		M	W		Haddon-field, N.J.	Student
James Samuel Stemons		M	B		South Philadelphia	Editor/ postal clerk
William E. Stokes		M	W	Presbyterian	West Philadelphia	Lawyer

Name	Birth–Death	Sex	Race	Religion	Home	Work
Mary Taylor	1845–1918	F	W		Jenkintown, Pa.	
Clemens Titzck, Jr.		M	W		Haddon Heights, N.J.	Student
Margaret Twist		F	W	Roman Catholic?	Delaware County, Pa.?	Student, then housewife
Laura Waite	1891–	F	W		Ridley Park, Pa.	Student
Anna Wallin	1872?–	F	W		Philadelphia	Music teacher
Jacob C. White, Jr.	1837–1902	M	B	Protestant	Center City	Principal
Clair Wilcox		M	W		West Philadelphia	Student
John A. Wilson	–1896	M	W	Protestant	West Philadelphia	Engineer
Septimus Winner	1827–	M	W		North Philadelphia	Music teacher/ shopkeeper

Notes

Introduction

1. J. Loughran Scott, *Quaint Corners in Philadelphia*, 2nd ed. (Philadelphia: John Wanamaker, 1899), pp. v–vi.

2. A recent work that looks at images of modernity in nineteenth century London is Lynda Nead, *Victorian Babylon: People, Streets and Images in Nineteenth-Century London* (New Haven: Yale University Press, 2000). Because the suburbs were so intimately connected to the city during this period, I apply the label "Philadelphians" not only to city dwellers but also to those people who lived in its immediate hinterland and who had ties to the metropolis. The map in figure 1 is based on the ward maps contained in John Daly and Allen Weinberg, *Genealogy of Philadelphia County Subdivisions* (Philadelphia: City of Philadelphia, 1966). I thank Ward J. Childs, City Archivist, for permission to use this map. On the elite, see E. Digby Baltzell, *Philadelphia Gentlemen: The Making of a National Upper Class*, 2nd ed. (Philadelphia: University of Pennsylvania Press, 1979).

3. Throughout this work the term "bourgeoisie" will be used interchangeably with "middle class."

4. For a recent examination of a shared transatlantic culture in politics, see Daniel T. Rodgers, *Atlantic Crossings: Social Politics in a Progressive Age* (Cambridge, Mass.: Belknap Press, 1998). In fact, this shared culture extended beyond the usually studied transatlantic world of the United States, Canada, and Europe to the bourgeoisie in many of the European colonies throughout the globe. See, as examples, Asa Briggs, *Victorian Things* (London: Penguin Books, 1990); Nicholas Faith, *The World the Railways Made* (New York: Carroll & Graf, 1990), and Wolfgang Schivelbusch, *The Railway Journey: The Industrialization of Time and Space in the 19th Century* (New York: Berg, 1986). A recent work that links science and technology with the Victorian worldview is Michael Freeman, *Railways and the Victorian Imagination* (New Haven: Yale University Press, 1999), especially the introduction and chap. 2.

5. For transnational accounts of the Victorian city, see Asa Briggs, *Victorian Cities* (London: Odhams Books, 1963), and H. J. Dyos and Michael Wolff, eds., *The Victorian City: Images and Realities*, 2 vols. (Boston: Routledge & Kegan Paul, 1973).

6. Unlike the 1893 Columbian exhibition, surprisingly few scholars have examined the Centennial. In part, the Centennial is ignored because of a slight by the prominent critic Lewis Mumford in *The Brown Decades: A Study of the Arts in America, 1865–1895* (1931; reprint, New York: Dover Publications, 1955), p. 14. Mumford saw the Centennial as an example of what was wrong with Victorian America and Chicago's fair as the start of the end of the "brown decades." See Thomas J. Schlereth, *Artifacts and the American Past* (Nashville: American Association for State and Local History, 1980), chap. 6, for an interesting essay on how the Centennial could be studied. A book that considers the fair as part of a broader trend of social control is Robert W. Rydell, *All the World's a Fair: Visions of Empire at American International Expositions, 1876–1916* (Chicago: University of Chicago Press, 1984). Three works that have focused on the Centennial are Bruno Giberti, *Designing the Centennial: A History of the 1876 International Exhibition in Philadelphia* (Lexington, Ky.: University Press of Kentucky, 2002), Richard R. Nicolai, *Centennial Philadelphia* (Bryn Mawr, Pa.: Bryn Mawr Press, 1977), and John Maass, *The Glorious Enterprise: The Centennial Exhibition of 1876 and H. J. Schwarzmann, Architect-in-Chief* (Watkins Glen, N.Y.: American Life Foundation, 1973). On the role of deception in nineteenth-century middle-class society more generally, see James W. Cook, *The Arts of Deception: Playing with Fraud in the Age of Barnum* (Cambridge: Harvard University Press, 2001).

7. Good introductions to Gilded Age historiography can be found in the essays in Charles W. Calhoun, ed., *The Gilded Age: Essays on the Origins of Modern America* (Wilmington: SR Books, 1996). For a more synthetic work, see Sean Dennis Cashman, *America in the Gilded Age: From the Death of Lincoln to the Rise of Theodore Roosevelt,* 3rd ed. (New York: New York University Press, 1993).

8. Historians' understanding of Progressive Era politics has changed radically in the last three decades and a new synthesis is just beginning to be sketched out. Peter G. Filene, "An Obituary for 'The Progressive Movement,' " *American Quarterly,* 22 (Spring 1970), pp. 20–34. For a review of the historiography, see Daniel T. Rodgers, "In Search of Progressivism," *Reviews in American History,* 10 (December 1982), pp. 113–32, and for an attempt at synthesis, see Richard L. McCormick, *The Party Period and Public Policy: American Politics from the Age of Jackson to the Progressive Era* (New York: Oxford University Press, 1986), chap. 7.

9. For a discussion of the system of classification, see Maass, *The Glorious Enterprise,* pp. 112–14. The specific examples comes from John D. McCabe, *The Illustrated History of the Centennial Exhibition* (1876; reprint, Philadelphia: National Publishing, 1976), p. 195. The pagination is different in the reprint than in the original (held by the Historical Society of Pennsylvania, among others). As it is far easier to find copies of the reprint, I will use its pagination throughout this work.

10. McCabe, *The Illustrated History of the Centennial Exhibition,* p. 297. The system of judging is also discussed in the contexts of international exhibitions and professionalization in Giberti, *Designing the Centennial,* chap. 1.

11. For reactions to these sweeping changes, see Samuel P. Hays, *The Response to Industrialism, 1885–1914* (Chicago: University of Chicago Press, 1957); Thomas J. Schlereth, *Victorian America: Transformations in Everyday Life, 1876–1915* (New York: HarperPerennial, 1991); and George Cotkin, *Reluctant Modernism: American Thought*

and Culture 1880–1900 (New York: Twayne Publishers, 1992). Cotkin's use of Darwinism as part of the definition of modernity and modernism has heavily influenced my own thinking. On antimodernism, see T. J. Jackson Lears, *No Place of Grace: Antimodernism and the Transformation of American Culture: 1880–1920* (Chicago: University of Chicago Press, 1983). On the home, see Richard Sennett, *Families Against the City: Middle Class Homes of Industrial Chicago, 1872–1890* (Cambridge: Harvard University Press, 1970). On the movement to the suburbs, see Sam Bass Warner, Jr., *Streetcar Suburbs: The Process of Growth in Boston, 1870–1900*, 2nd ed. (Cambridge: Harvard University Press, 1978), and Kenneth T. Jackson, *Crabgrass Frontier: The Suburbanization of the United States* (New York: Oxford University Press, 1985). The classic political interpretation is found in Robert H. Wiebe, *The Search for Order, 1877–1920* (New York: Hill and Wang, 1967), and a valuable analysis of it is Kenneth Cmiel, "Destiny and Amnesia: The Vision of Modernity in Robert Wiebe's *The Search for Order*," *Reviews in American History* 21 (June 1993), pp. 352–68.

12. Another work that looks at this transformation from a cultural perspective is Alan Trachtenberg, *The Incorporation of America: Culture & Society in the Gilded Age* (New York: Hill and Wang, 1982). His interpretation focuses on the cultural effects of the emergence of the modern business corporation. Although Trachtenberg's view and my argument are consistent with each other, we differ on the basis of the middle-class metaphor. To me, the corporation is just another example of science applied to society and not an independent variable.

13. On museums, see Steven Conn, *Museums and American Intellectual Life, 1876–1926* (Chicago: University of Chicago Press, 1998). Examples of classification in American Victorian life are included in the following works: Kenneth L. Ames, *Death in the Dining Room & Other Tales of Victorian Culture* (Philadelphia: Temple University Press, 1992) (home interiors); Burton J. Bledstein, *The Culture of Professionalism: The Middle Class and the Development of Higher Education in America* (New York: W. W. Norton, 1976) (the professions); Daniel Bluestone, *Constructing Chicago* (New Haven: Yale University Press, 1991) (office buildings); M. Christine Boyer, *Manhattan Manners: Architecture and Style, 1850–1900* (New York: Rizzoli, 1985) (city streets); John P. Comaromi and M. P. Satija, *Dewey Decimal Classification: History and Current Status* (London: Sterling Publishers, 1989) (library cataloging); John F. Kasson, *Amusing the Million: Coney Island at the Turn of the Century* (New York: Hill & Wang, 1978) (urban space); Lawrence W. Levine, *Highbrow, Lowbrow: The Emergence of Cultural Hierarchy in America* (Cambridge: Harvard University Press, 1988) (culture); Dorothy Ross, *The Origins of American Social Science* (New York: Cambridge University Press, 1991) (social science); and Daniel Nelson, *Frederick W. Taylor and the Rise of Scientific Management* (Madison: University of Wisconsin Press, 1980) (management). Temporal changes are examined in Stephen Kern, *The Culture of Time and Space, 1880–1918* (Cambridge: Harvard University Press, 1983), and Michael O'Malley, *Keeping Watch: History of American Time* (New York: Viking, 1990).

14. The term "bourgeois corridors" is a play on John Stilgoe's interpretation of rail lines as "metropolitan corridors" in which the modernity and urbanity of the trains were often juxtaposed with rural (and semi-rural) settings. John R. Stilgoe, *Metropolitan Corridor: Railroads and the American Scene* (New Haven: Yale University Press, 1983).

15. I owe an intellectual debt to Alex Roland of Duke University, who urged me to take the Victorians seriously when they claimed to be acting scientifically (at least so far as they defined the term).

16. *Oxford English Dictionary*, 2nd ed. (New York: Oxford University Press, 1989), p. 1674. Raymond Williams develops a slightly different evolution of the term "science" but comes to a broadly similar conclusion. Raymond Williams, *Keywords: A Vocabulary of Culture and Society* (New York: Oxford University Press, 1976), pp. 232–35.

17. An introduction to the historiography of Victorian science and technology can be found in James Roger Fleming, "Science and Technology in the Second Half of the Nineteenth Century," in Calhoun, *The Gilded Age*, chap. 2. For the methodology of the life sciences in the nineteenth century, see Garland Allen, *Life Sciences in the Twentieth Century* (New York: Cambridge University Press, 1975), chap. 1, and Lois N. Magner, *A History of the Life Sciences* (New York: Marcel Dekker, 1979), chap. 12 (in particular pp. 342–48). An article that illustrates the pervasiveness of the life sciences in nineteenth-century middle-class culture is Daniel Goldstein, "Yours for Science: The Smithsonian Institution's Correspondents and the Shape of the Scientific Community in Nineteenth-Century America," *ISIS* 85 (1994), pp. 572–99. Dorothy Ross notes that the social sciences borrowed their methodology from the same Newtonian and Baconian models as used by life sciences in *The Origins of American Social Science*, pp. 17–18 and 59–60. The quotation on the life sciences comes from Magner, *A History of the Life Sciences*, p. 343.

18. A concise introduction to the American reception of Darwin can be found in Cotkin, *Reluctant Modernism*, chap. 1. A more detailed account is Jon H. Roberts, *Darwinism and the Divine in America: Protestant Intellectuals and Organic Evolution, 1859–1900* (Madison: University of Wisconsin Press, 1988). Others who have considered Darwin as a trope for the period include Robert Young, *Darwin's Metaphor: Nature's Place in Victorian Culture* (New York: Cambridge University Press, 1985), and George Levine, *Darwin and the Novelists: Patterns of Science in Victorian Fiction* (Cambridge: Harvard University Press, 1988). For a discussion of the effects of Darwin on American racial thought (effectively creating a taxonomy of race), see John Higham, *Strangers in the Land: Patterns of American Nativism, 1860–1925*, 2nd ed. (New Brunswick, N.J.: Rutgers University Press, 1988), pp. 133–36. On the rise of science as authority in Victorian America, see Charles E. Rosenberg, *No Other Gods: On Science and American Social Thought*, rev. ed. (Baltimore: Johns Hopkins University Press, 1997), and Ross, *The Origins of American Social Science*, pp. 53–64. For examples of college science courses using taxonomy, see the *University of Pennsylvania Catalogue and Announcements, 1887–88* (Philadelphia: University of Pennsylvania, 1887), p. 42, and *Catalogue of the University of Pennsylvania, 1897–98* (Philadelphia: University of Pennsylvania, 1897), pp. 225–27. High school classes in the life sciences can be found in the *Catalogue of the Central High School of Philadelphia, 1898–1899* (Philadelphia, [1898]), p. 53.

19. Lawrence M. Friedman, *A History of American Law*, 2nd ed. (New York: Simon & Schuster, 1985), p. 617. This quote also appears in a leading undergraduate text, Hall, *The Magic Mirror*, p. 221. For examples of the views of Langdell on law as a science, see Hall, *The Magic Mirror*, pp. 219–21, and Ellen Condliffe Lagemann, *The*

Politics of Knowledge: The Carnegie Corporation, Philanthropy, and Public Policy (Chicago: University of Chicago Press, 1989), pp. 83 and 90. For discussions of the development of the Harvard case method, see, for a detailed presentation, Robert Stevens, *Law School: Legal Education in America from the 1850s to the 1980s* (Chapel Hill, N.C.: University of North Carolina Press, 1983), chaps. 3 and 4, and, for a quick overview, Hall, *The Magic Mirror*, pp. 218–21.

20. This view of suburbanization was first developed by Sam Bass Warner in his case study of Boston, *Streetcar Suburbs,* and later extended to the nation as a whole by Kenneth Jackson in *Crabgrass Frontier.*

21. For an example of a post-structural critique that explicitly develops the effects of the computers on information, see Jean-François Lyotard (trans. Geoff Bennington and Brian Massumi), *The Postmodern Condition: A Report on Knowledge* (Minneapolis: University of Minnesota Press, 1984).

22. My analysis is built on the theory that "culture" consists of the rhythms and rituals of everyday life. This understanding of culture comes from the work of the noted anthropologist Clifford Geertz and has been used by historians and scholars in other disciplines for decades. For example, James Carey, in his cultural studies of communication, urges us not to view human communication as mere "transmission"—words spoken to an audience—but instead as a ritual of shared meanings and symbols. For Carey, the audience, as much as the speaker, shapes the message. It is within this ritual of communication that the shared assumptions of a culture can be found. I was introduced to this approach by John Kasson of the University of North Carolina. Two essays that deal with the sources of this method are Suzanne Desan, "Crowds, Community, and Ritual in the Work of E. P. Thompson and Natalie Davis," chap. 2 (social history), and Aletta Biersack, "Local Knowledge, Local History: Geertz and Beyond," chap. 3 (anthropology), in Lynn Hunt, ed., *The New Cultural History* (Berkeley: University of California Press, 1989). See as examples, Roland Delattre, "Ritual Resourcefulness and Cultural Pluralism," *Soundings* 61 (1978), pp. 281–301, and Clifford Geertz, *The Interpretation of Cultures* (New York: Basic Books, 1973). My own work is heavily influenced by James W. Carey, *Communication As Culture: Essays on Media and Society* (Boston: Unwin Hyman, 1989), and Henri Lefebvre (trans. Eleonore Kofman and Elizabeth Lebas), *Writings on Cities* (Cambridge, Mass.: Blackwell, 1996). In addition to this study of ritual and rhythm, I drew on two other intellectual traditions. Each is a powerful way to understand the historical moment, and this study benefits from the combination of them. By far the most common among students of the city is a careful examination of system or structure in society; social scientists, social historians, and others use this method to find order in the seeming randomness of the world. They search for the underlying structures that link the minor events that fill most days for most people. Two good examples of urban studies are Christine Stansell, *City of Women: Sex and Class in New York 1789–1860* (Urbana: University of Illinois Press, 1987), and Theodore Hershberg, ed., *Philadelphia: Work, Space, Family and Group Experience in the 19th Century* (New York: Oxford University Press, 1981). Others, such as the philosopher Michel Foucault, conceptualize structure differently but still focus their studies on underlying systems. For an essay that examines Foucault, see Patricia O'Brien, "Michel Foucault's History of Culture," in Hunt, *The New Cultural History*, chap. 1. The final method I

use highlights the physicality of the human experience by examining the artifacts that have been left behind. "Artifact" in this sense is very broadly defined: it can range from a small item (a spoon or a railroad timetable) to a larger one (a trolley car) to a structure (both the interior and its setting) to topography (of a city block or an entire region). "Material culture" (the most common label for this approach when scholars apply it to items) can reveal the details for which no written texts survive. Artifacts alert historians to the possibilities of the historical moment; they help scholars fill patent gaps in the record and discover the latent ones. By holding an object or visiting a location, a student of culture can better understand what the written record describes and, perhaps more importantly, what it leaves out. If you believe as I do that culture can be found in the rituals of everyday life, often the only way to understand these rituals is to find the things that were used in them because many of these actions were so commonplace, their details may never have been recorded. While the use of artifacts to understand space may seem obvious, they are equally beneficial in reconstructing conceptions of time. From images (the clock faces that appeared on the cover of *The Official Railway Guide* to represent the then-new time zones) to printed words and numbers (multiple-edition newspapers and timetables) to larger things (clocks), time, too, has a physicality. The literature on the material culture (objects as artifacts) is well developed; either of the following works by Thomas J. Schlereth will serve as an introduction: *Artifacts and the American Past: Material Culture: A Research Guide* (Lawrence: University of Kansas Press, 1985) or *Material Culture Studies in America* (Nashville: American Association for State and Local History, 1982). The use of the built environment as an artifact by historians is far less common (especially outside of architectural studies). I was introduced to it by a work of military history: John Keegan, *The Faces of Battle* (New York: Viking, 1976).

23. The historian William Leach uses a different understanding of culture—effectively the transmission model—in his examination of Wanamaker in *Land of Desire: Merchants, Power, and the Rise of a New American Culture* (New York: Pantheon Books, 1993). For his theoretical assumptions, see the Preface and Introduction, pp. xiv–xv.

24. Overall, sixty-three archival collections and oral histories provided the guides for my tours of Philadelphia. A complete list is included in the appendix. For scholarship on diaries, see Alex Aronson, *Studies in Twentieth-Century Diaries: The Concealed Self* (Lewiston, N.Y.: Edwin Mellen Press, 1991); Margo Culley, ed., *A Day at a Time: The Diary Literature of American Women from 1764 to the Present* (New York: The Feminist Press, 1985); and P. A. Spalding, *Self-Harvest: A Study of Diaries and the Diarist* (London: Independent Press, 1949).

25. The surviving records vary greatly among the firms studied. For example, basic corporate and financial records for the city's two major railway companies, the Pennsylvania and the Reading, are largely complete whereas holdings of operational records are far spottier. The records of the street railroads are even more elusive; although much survives, not only are the holdings scattered among multiple archives but many are in private collections. For department stores, there are two outstanding archival collections for Wanamaker and Strawbridge & Clothier but little for the other major firms. The newspaper industry brings one of the greatest frustrations as

there are no major public collections of any of the corporate records of these important enterprises.

26. Karen Lystra, *Searching the Heart: Women, Men, and Romantic Love in Nineteenth-Century America* (New York: Oxford University Press, 1989), p. 5.

27. For Marx's view of the transitional nature of (what he defines as) the lower middle class, see the *Communist Manifesto* reprinted in Eugene Kamenka, ed., *The Portable Karl Marx* (New York: Penguin, 1983), p. 212. For an excellent conceptualization of the development of the middle class in the nineteenth century, see Stuart M. Blumin, *The Emergence of the Middle Class: Social Experience in the American City, 1760–1900* (New York: Cambridge University Press, 1989), esp. chap. 1. His discussion has helped to shape mine, although I more greatly emphasize culture than he does. On the importance of a close, historical analysis of class, see E. P. Thompson, *The Making of the English Working Class* (New York: Vintage Books, 1966). A very good (although now a little dated) bibliographic essay on the American middle class can be found in John S. Gilkeson, Jr., *Middle-Class Providence, 1820–1940* (Princeton, N.J.: Princeton University Press, 1986).

28. In addition to Lystra, *Searching the Heart*, other examples of cultural studies of the middle class include Karen Halttunen, *Confidence Men and Painted Women: A Study of Middle-Class Culture in America, 1830–1870* (New Haven: Yale University Press, 1982), and John F. Kasson, *Rudeness & Civility: Manners in Nineteenth-Century America* (New York: Hill and Wang, 1990).

29. An example of an otherwise strong study that largely ignores the role of women because of its focus on paid employment is Blumin, *The Emergence of the Middle Class*. Some of the many cultural studies that have highlighted the importance of the female members of the bourgeoisie are Leonore Davidoff and Catherine Hall, *Family Fortunes: Men and Women of the English Middle Class, 1780–1850* (Chicago: University of Chicago Press, 1991); Halttunen, *Confidence Men and Painted Women*; Margaret S. Marsh, *Suburban Lives* (New Brunswick, N.J.: Rutgers University Press, 1990); and Mary P. Ryan, *Cradle of the Middle Class: The Family in Oneida County, New York, 1790–1865* (New York: Cambridge University Press, 1981).

30. For an examination of the African-American middle class in the city, see W. E. B. DuBois, *The Philadelphia Negro: A Social Study* (Philadelphia: University of Pennsylvania Press, 1899). A brief overview of the formation of the middle class within immigrant communities can be found in John Bodnar, *The Transplanted: A History of Immigrants in Urban America* (Bloomington: Indiana University Press, 1987), chap. 4. For a comparison of Black and "new immigrant" residential and employment patterns, see Stanley Lieberson, *A Piece of the Pie: Blacks and White Immigrants since 1880* (Berkeley: University of California Press, 1980).

31. A listing of the diarists is included in the appendix. The three people who may have been members of the working classes are James Cleary, [Robert] Hinch, and Sidney Smith.

Prelude

1. John L. Smith diary.
2. This narrative is derived from the entries for January 30, April 2, April 30, May 7, May 9, May 10, May 15, June 14, July 3, July 20, and August 21, 1876, John L. Smith diary; *Gopsill's Philadelphia City Directory for 1877* (Philadelphia: James Gopsill, 1877), p. 1352; McCabe, *The Illustrated History of the Centennial Exhibition*, pp. 10–47, 94, 112–16, and 291–92; and the *Public Ledger*, June 14–15, 1876.

Chapter 1

1. *System of Steam/Street Railroads/ways of Philadelphia: A Complete Guide, with Maps* (Philadelphia: Allen, Lane & Scott, 1887).
2. John Cecil Holm, *Sunday Best: The Story of a Philadelphia Family* (New York: Farrar & Rinehart, 1942), p. 134. Holm, the son of a middle-class electrician, was describing the early twentieth century but this perception developed in the late nineteenth.
3. See Jack Simmons, *The Victorian Railway* (New York: Thames and Hudson, 1991), pp. 332–36, for what he terms "the liberation of women" by Britain's railways. The many varied journeys of the female members of the West Philadelphia Smith family were ably chronicled by Mary, born 1871, in the Mary B. Smith diary.
4. For an introduction to parliamentary and workmen's trains in Britain, see Simmons, *The Victorian Railway*, pp. 318–32. Although some American scholars have viewed the Interstate Commerce Act of 1887 as a watershed in governmental regulation, see, for example, Morton J. Horwitz, *The Transformation of American Law, 1870–1960: The Crisis of Legal Orthodoxy* (New York: Oxford University Press, 1992), pp. 222–23, Britain had far more thorough regulation in the Victorian era. For a nuanced view of the limits of America's early regulatory regime, see Morton Keller, *Affairs of State: Public Life in Late Nineteenth Century America* (Cambridge, Mass.: Belknap Press, 1977), pp. 422–30. The following two works by Federic W. Speirs provide a detailed look at the Victorian debate over street railway regulation: *The Street Railway System of Philadelphia: Its History and Present Condition* (Baltimore: Johns Hopkins University Press, 1897), and "Regulation of Cost and Quality of Service as Illustrated by Street Railway Companies," *Annals of the American Academy of Political and Social Science* (1900 annual meeting), pp. 63–76.
5. Other works arguing for a "social construction" of technology include Leo Marx, *The Machine in the Garden: Technology and the Pastoral Ideal in America* (New York: Oxford University Press, 1964); John F. Kasson, *Civilizing the Machine: Technology and Republican Values in America, 1876–1900* (New York: Penguin Books, 1977); Thomas P. Hughes, *American Genesis: A Century of Invention and Technological Enthusiasm* (New York: Penguin, 1989); and Carroll Pursell, *The Machine in America: A Social History of Technology* (Baltimore: Johns Hopkins University Press, 1995).
6. For information on commuting in the city, see Theodore Hershberg, Harold E. Cox, Dale B. Light, Jr., and Richard R. Greenfield, "The 'Journey-to-Work': An Em-

pirical Investigation of Work, Residence and Transportation, Philadelphia, 1850 and 1880," in Hershberg, *Philadelphia*, pp. 134–35 and 141–52. For a detailed look at antebellum Philadelphia, see Sam Bass Warner, Jr., *The Private City: Philadelphia in Three Periods of its Growth*, 2nd ed. (Philadelphia: University of Pennsylvania Press, 1987), chaps. 3–7.

7. On consolidation, see Russell F. Weigley, *Philadelphia: A 300-Year History* (New York: W. W. Norton, 1982), pp. 359–75, and Warner, *Private City*, pp. 152–57.

8. A description of Philadelphia's first rail service can be found in Weigley, *Philadelphia*, pp. 272–73. The increase in the importance of passenger traffic on the steam railroads is discussed in Jeffrey P. Roberts, "Railroads and the Downtown: Philadelphia, 1830–1900," in William W. Cutler, III, and Howard Gillette, Jr., eds., *The Divided Metropolis: Social and Spatial Dimensions of Philadelphia, 1800–1975* (Westport, Conn.: Greenwood Press, 1980), pp. 27–55. For the technological changes described here, see Brian J. Cudahy, *Cash, Tokens, and Transfers: A History of Urban Mass Transit in North America* (New York: Fordham University Press, 1990), chaps. 1–6 (horsecars to trolleys); Brooke Hindle and Steven Lubar, *Engines of Change: The America Industrial Revolution, 1790–1860* (Washington, D.C.: Smithsonian Institution Press, 1986), chap. 8 (locomotives and railroads in general); Thomas J. Misa, *A Nation of Steel: The Making of Modern America, 1865–1925* (Baltimore: Johns Hopkins University Press, 1995), chap. 1 (rails); and John H. White, Jr., *The American Railroad Passenger Car* (Baltimore: Johns Hopkins University Press, 1978), chap. 1 (passenger equipment).

9. For brief overviews of the development of the street railway system in Philadelphia see Hershberg, *Philadelphia*, pp. 141–42, and Charles W. Cheape, *Moving the Masses: Urban Public Transit in New York, Boston, and Philadelphia, 1880–1912* (Cambridge: Harvard University Press, 1980), pp. 157–62. A more extended history can be found in Alan Gin, "Transportation Innovation and Urban Residential Location" (Ph.D. diss., University of California at Santa Barbara, 1987), pp. 60–83. For a look at the development of street railways nationally, see Cudahy, *Cash, Tokens, and Transfers*, chap. 2.

10. A number of published guidebooks to the street railways of the city give some flavor for this period of competitive service. See, as an example, the *Official Street Railway Map and Guide Book of Philadelphia* (Philadelphia: E. P. Knoll, 1886), which lists the routes, fares, and transfer privileges of the various companies. Information about steam train service in 1880 can be found in the *Strangers and Citizens Hand Book and Official Guide to Railroads, Steamship and Steamboat Lines, Business Houses, and Places of Interest in Philadelphia, September 1880* (Philadelphia: Burk & McFetridge, 1880). See Chapter 2 for a discussion of Victorian railway station placement.

11. The (short) story of Philadelphia's cable cars can be found in Cheape, *Moving the Masses*, pp. 161–71. For the start of service on a variety of lines, see the entries for January 11, May 29, June 23, July 12, and September 22, 1894, and January 27, 1895, Mary B. Smith diary. Entry for May 29, 1894, Mary B. Smith diary.

12. Entry for December 20, 1893, Leo G. Bernheimer diary.

13. McCabe, *The Illustrated History of the Centennial Exhibition*, p. 42. *System of Steam/Street Railroads/ways of Philadelphia*.

14. For the 1880 statistic, see Hershberg, *Philadelphia*, p. 152, and for the changing

middle-class commuting patterns, pp. 134–41. For Smith's travels, see the entries for December 21, 1880 and February 1, 1887, John L. Smith diary.

15. For J. Harper Smith's home and work, see entries for December 17, 1895, August 29, 1896, and February 21, 1898, Mary B. Smith diary. For details of the house, see Richard Webster, *Philadelphia Preserved: Catalog of the Historic American Buildings Survey* (Philadelphia: Temple University Press, 1976), p. 218. The house still stands and is worth a visit as nearly the entire 1860s block is intact. The route information can be found in the *System of Steam/Street Railroads/ways of Philadelphia.*

16. On Lathrop Smith attending the Newton School, see the entry for February 22, 1896, Mary B. Smith diary. For Bernheimer's trips to Central, see, as an example, the entry for December 20, 1893, Leo G. Bernheimer diary. A typical trip to Penn can be found at the entry for October 2, 1894, Leo G. Bernheimer diary. The travel times are from the entry for September 25, 1895, Leo G. Bernheimer diary. The complaint about the delayed journey can be found at the entry for December 6, 1895, Leo G. Bernheimer diary.

17. Bernheimer often walked to Central. Entry for September 22, 1891, Leo G. Bernheimer diary.

18. For the cheap trains see the Philadelphia & Reading Railroad announcement, dated January 23, 1875, Reading collection (Hagley), box 1059, and J. Thomas Scharf and Thompson Westcott, *History of Philadelphia, 1609–1884,* vol. 3 (Philadelphia: L. H. Everts & Co., 1884), p. 2187. "Workmen's trains" on the Reading were very different from their British counterparts. The Reading priced its trains to attract lower-middle-class clerks and used the discount to help with rush hour capacity. No governmental body mandated the trains nor set the fares. Later, the Pennsylvania would respond with similar trains on competing lines. See George H. Burgess and Miles C. Kennedy, *Centennial History of the Pennsylvania Railroad Company, 1846–1946* (Philadelphia: Pennsylvania Railroad Company, 1949), pp. 413–14, for an explanation of how competition with the Reading spurred the construction of two lines in the Philadelphia area. The streetcar time for Germantown is from the entry for June 9, 1885, William G. Armstrong diary, and the train time is from the Reading Railroad Germantown & Chestnut Hill Branch timetable effective May 20, 1894. The story of Overbrook's development can be found in Marsh, *Suburban Lives,* pp. 92–103; and, in a rich, anecdotal, amateur history, Tello J. d'Apery, *Overbrook Farms* (Philadelphia: The Magee Press, 1936). See David R. Contosta, *Suburb in the City: Chestnut Hill, Philadelphia, 1850–1990* (Columbus: Ohio State University Press, 1992), chaps. 2–5, for the development of Chestnut Hill. Over 4,600 passengers used the Chestnut Hill line of the Philadelphia & Reading daily in the summer of 1901. Statement of Earnings of Trains, July 1901, Reading collection (Hagley), box 1.

19. On walking, see the entry for April 22, 1886, Edwin C. Jellett diary. For the train tickets, see the Cash Accounts for 1886 and 1888, Edwin C. Jellett diary, in which he lists his expenditures for the year.

20. The best source for the African-American middle class continues to be DuBois, *The Philadelphia Negro.* Another valuable source is Roger Lane, *William Dorsey's Philadelphia and Ours: On the Past and Future of the Black City in America* (New York: Oxford University Press, 1991). Of the black guides in my sampling, the

papers of James Samuel Stemons, a postal clerk and newspaper editor, in the Balch Institute for Ethnic Studies were the most illuminating on this issue.

21. The Philadelphia Social History Project estimated that 28% of streetcar riders in 1880 were shoppers. Hershberg, *Philadelphia*, p. 152.

22. Entry for December 12, 1877, John L. Smith diary. Entry for December 21, 1886, Edwin W. Lehman diary. For an example of out-of-town visitors touring department stores along with other sites, see Cousin Bertha's visit at the entry for December 28, 1894, Mary B. Smith diary. Starting in the 1880s and continuing at least until the late 1920s, the city's three largest dry goods/department stores issued many guides to their stores aimed at the out-of-town visitor; see, as examples, *Dictionary of Philadelphia and its Vicinity* (Philadelphia: John Wanamaker, 1887); *What We Look Like* (Philadelphia: Strawbridge & Clothier, [1887]); *A Little Hand-book of Philadelphia: Together with Certain Annals of the Wanamaker System* (Philadelphia: John Wanamaker, 1899); and *A Book About the Gimbel Store Philadelphia: The Largest Retail Store in the World* (Philadelphia: Gimbel Brothers, 1905).

23. Between 1876 and 1900, over 90% of retail visits (in which the destination was indicated) in my sampling were to Center City. The Wanamaker store estimated that, in 1880, twenty-five hundred people per hour used the main corridor on a typical day and as many as forty thousand shoppers per day used it during the Christmas season. Gibbons Card File Number 1, John Wanamaker papers.

24. Entry for December 22, 1888, Mrs. Tucker C. Laughlin diary. Entry for December 28, 1894, Leo G. Bernheimer diary. There are two ways to discover these regional shopping nodes. The detailed city atlases of the period allow scholars to locate these retail districts throughout the city by looking for clusters of stores. See, as an example, *Atlas of the City of Philadelphia: Complete in One Volume* (Philadelphia: G. W. Bromley & Co., 1895). Others are cited in the bibliography. The other method is to carefully read the surviving diaries and memoirs of middle-class Philadelphians. Perhaps the best way to obtain a feel for the texture and rhythm of these areas is to read Holm, *Sunday Best*. His father's shop was on Lancaster Avenue in West Philadelphia.

25. Entries for December 12 (sweeper) and December 14–15, 1888 (stove), and December 6, 1889 (buttermints), Mrs. Tucker C. Laughlin diary. For the strawberries, see the entry for March 14, 1888, William G. Armstrong diary.

26. The middle-class focus of period department stores is discussed in Susan Porter Benson, *Counter Cultures: Sales Women, Managers, and Customers in American Department Stores, 1890–1940* (Urbana: University of Illinois Press, 1988).

27. The Philadelphia Social History Project estimated that 25% of total rides in 1880 were for recreation. Hershberg, *Philadelphia*, p. 152.

28. Entries for December 15, 1894 (Art Alliance), and November 25 (theater), and November 26, 1897 (food exposition), Mary. B. Smith diary. Entries for January 26 (opera via the Reading), January 27 (Indian Rights Association meeting via the Reading), and May 17, 1883 (Academy of Natural Sciences via the Reading), and October 4 (Republican Party meeting via the Pennsylvania) and December 19, 1884 (Indian Rights Association meeting via the Pennsylvania), Edwin C. Jellett diary.

29. Entry for September 23, 1884, Edwin C. Jellett diary. William S. Hemsing, *The Diaries of William Souder Hemsing: An Intimate Look at Souderton, Pennsylvania,*

1885–1888, 1902–1906, 1918 (Souderton, Pa.: Indian Valley Printing, 1987), p. 248. Entry for October 27, 1898, Septimus Winner diary.

30. For a history of Willow Grove, see Ray Thompson, *Willow Grove Park: A Look Back in Time . . . To Another Era of Entertainment* (priv. pub., 1977). For a look at the variety of parks in southern New Jersey, see Shirley R. Bailey and Jim Parkhurst, *Early South Jersey Amusement Parks,* 2nd ed. (Millville, N.J.: South Jersey Publishing, 1990).

31. Entry for September 8, 1895, Leo G. Bernheimer diary. Eugenia L. Barnitz memoirs, p. 67.

32. The phrase is John Stilgoe's and refers to his interpretation of the trains and rail lines as uniquely urban and modern environments often juxtaposed with rural and semi-rural settings. Stilgoe, *Metropolitan Corridor.*

33. For "botanizing," see the entry for June 13, 1897, Edwin C. Jellett diary. Just a small sample of Jellett's many destinations includes the entries for March 19 (Burlington, N.J.) and October 15, 1882 (Mt. Holly, N.J.), October 12, 1884 (Radnor, Pa.), and May 22 (Valley Forge, Pa.), August 14 (Lumberton, N.J.), and October 23, 1887 (Limerick, Pa.), Edwin C. Jellett diary. An example of Smith's interest can be found at the entry for May 6, 1888, John L. Smith diary. In part, Smith's interest in "the improvements" was professional; he was a mapmaker. It was also motivated by a not uncommon middle-class penchant for suburban real estate speculation (although for Smith, the investments seldom paid off). For the story of his participation in an unsuccessful attempt to develop Cynwyd in suburban Montgomery County, see the entries for February 25, April 6, May 7, May 14, May 15, and May 23, 1889, John L. Smith diary.

34. For the elite summering on the Main Line, see Baltzell, *Philadelphia Gentlemen,* p. 202. See, for example, the entries for September 4 and 10, 1882, Edwin C. Jellett diary. Entries for August 13, September 3, and September 7, 1896, Mary B. Smith diary.

35. For well-illustrated accounts of the train services to the Jersey shore, see W. George Cook and William J. Coxey, *Atlantic City Railroad: The Royal Route to the Sea* (Oaklyn, N.J.: West Jersey Chapter, National Railway Historical Society, 1977), and Frederick A. Kramer, *Pennsylvania-Reading Seashore Lines: An Illustrated History of South Jersey's Jointly-Owned Railroad* (Ambler, Pa.: Crusader Press, 1980), pp. 4–21. For specific examples of all the activities listed here (including the price fixing), see the Atlantic City Railroad files in the Reading collection (Hagley), boxes 933–37.

36. A short entry on the blizzard can be found in *Bulletin Almanac 1976* (Philadelphia: Bulletin Company, 1976), p. 448. "Sunday Afternoon with Moses Behrend, M.D.: A Biographic Sketch," p. 7. Hemsing, *The Diaries of William Souder Hemsing,* pp. 293–94. Entry for March 13, 1888, William G. Armstrong diary. T. Chalkley Matlack memoirs, vol. 1, p. 21.

37. Entries for February 3 and December 27, 1880, John L. Smith diary. Entries for January 10 and 11, 1883, John A. Wilson diary. Entry for December 24, 1883, Septimus Winner diary.

38. Entry for February 7, 1895, Leo G. Bernheimer diary. Entry for February 13, 1899, Mary B. Smith diary.

39. "Narrow Escapes," *Public Ledger,* October 9, 1876, p. 1. Entries for March 20,

1893 (cable car), January 24, 1895 (delays), February 2, 1895 (injured friend), January 14, 1896 (witnessed slip), and March 12, 1896 (close shave), Leo G. Bernheimer diary. "Coroner's Inquests," *Public Ledger*, July 19, 1876, p. 1 (pedestrian). "Coroner's Inquests," *Public Ledger*, June 29, 1876, p. 1 (fall from platform).

40. Entry for August 25, 1880, John L. Smith diary. Two examples of delayed travel are the entries for November 3, 1884, Mary Brown Askew diary, and June 30, 1887, Edwin W. Lehman diary. Entry for April 19, 1892, Leo G. Bernheimer diary.

41. Hemsing, *The Diaries of William Souder Hemsing*, p. 275. Railroad workers, employed by the nations's first big businesses, were in the forefront of labor movement in the late-nineteenth century. For a quick introduction, see Eric Arnesen, "American Workers and the Labor Movement in the Late Nineteenth Century" in Calhoun, *The Gilded Age.*

42. Entries for December 17, 19, 23, and 24, 1895, Leo G. Bernheimer diary. Entry for December 18, 1895, Septimus Winner diary (took a furniture van to go shopping). Entry for December 17, 1895, Mary B. Smith diary. Further information on the strike can be found in Weigley, *Philadelphia*, p. 495, and the sources noted there.

43. Entry for December 17, 1895, Albert J. Edmunds diary. Entry for December 17, 1895, Septimus Winner diary.

44. Entries for December 17 and 24, 1895, Albert J. Edmunds diary.

Chapter 2

1. Christopher Morley, *Kitty Foyle* (1939; New York: Signet Books, 1950), p. 112. Morley, raised in the suburb of Haverford, began his writing career in Philadelphia as a popular columnist for *The Evening Public Ledger.*

2. Unlike in Britain, where scholars have been actively exploring the place of the railway in society for decades, few American historians have considered the effects railroad stations had on everyday life. Three recent examples of this large British canon on the railway in society are Jeffrey Richards and John M. MacKenzie, *The Railway Station: A Social History* (New York: Oxford University Press, 1986); Simmons, *The Victorian Railway*; and Freeman, *Railways and the Victorian Imagination.* An American essay that drew on earlier British works (with the added advantage of a focus on Philadelphia) is Roberts, "Railroads and the Downtown: Philadelphia 1830–1900." Other works that have looked at the cultural meanings of railroad stations are Stilgoe, *Metropolitan Corridor*; Schivelbusch, *The Railway Journey* (from whom I borrow the gateway metaphor); and Sally A. Kitt Chappell, "Urban Ideals and the Design of Railroad Stations," *Technology and Culture* 30 (1989), pp. 354–75.

3. Reading Terminal is probably best known for this farmers' market that outlasted the depot and continues to function to this day. Since the 1860s there had been a food market at Twelfth and Market Streets. In order to buy the land for their station, the Reading agreed to house this facility on the ground floor of the structure under the platforms. The Pennsylvania Railroad found this so humorous, they published a cartoon showing the president of the Reading as a butcher and promising, among other things, "A parlor car seat goes with every turkey sold." The history of the

market can be found in Carol M. Highsmith and James L. Holton, *Reading Terminal and Market: Philadelphia's Historic Gateway and Grand Convention Center* (Washington, D.C.: Chelsea Publishing, 1994), pp. 38–52.

4. See Roberts, "Railroads and the Downtown: Philadelphia 1830–1900," pp. 27–55, generally, for a discussion of the effect of stations (and their ancillary facilities) on the urban fabric, and, specifically, for the shift to more central locations, pp. 37–47. More detailed histories of these changes in location can be found in John H. Hepp, IV, " 'Such a Well-Behaved Station': The Philadelphia & Reading Railroad and its Passenger Terminals in Philadelphia, 1830–1900" (paper presented at the annual meeting of the Society for Industrial Archeology, Sacramento, Calif., 1996), and John H. Hepp, IV, "Before Thirtieth Street: A Century of Pennsylvania Railroad Passenger Terminals in Philadelphia" (paper presented at the Conference on the Sesquicentennial of the Chartering of the Pennsylvania Railroad, Strasburg, Pa., 1996). The basis for the maps in figures 9 and 10 is an 1876 map of the railroads in Philadelphia prepared by diarist John L. Smith in the collection of the author. Similar maps are held by the Historical Society of Pennsylvania and the Map Collection of the Free Library of Philadelphia.

5. The quote is from *Guide-Book to the West Chester and Philadelphia Railroad* (Philadelphia, 1869), p. 8, Delaware County Historical Society. For the movement of stations to outlying locations at mid century, see the *Fifth Annual Report of the Directors of the Pennsylvania Rail Road Company* (1852), pp. 16 and 37–38, and *The Tenth Annual Report of the President and Managers of the West Chester and Philadelphia Railroad Company* (1860), pp. 9–10.

6. See, as examples, the entries for November 21, 1881, and September 22, 1889, John L. Smith diary.

7. The following are the estimated travel times to the old State House: under ten minutes, Market Street (D on map 9) and South Street (E) ferries; fifteen to twenty minutes, Vine Street ferry (F); twenty to twenty-five minutes, WC&P (2), PRR (3), Main Line (4), and Green Street (5) depots; thirty to forty minutes, Prime Street station (1); and thirty-five to forty-five minutes, North Penn (6) and Kensington (7) depots. These estimates are based on information in Hershberg, *Philadelphia*, pp. 128–173; *Philadelphia and its Environs,* 2nd ed. (Philadelphia: J. B. Lippincott, 1873), p. 86; and a map in *Philadelphia Store News,* p. 3, John Wanamaker papers, box 75.

8. For the role of the railroad in the development of Haddonfield, see Marsh, *Suburban Lives.* The later development of the Main Line suburbs can be seen in J. W. Townsend, *The Old "Main Line"* (priv. print., 1922), p. 21.

9. Steam railroad schedules for 1880 can be found in the *Strangers and Citizens Hand Book and Official Guide to Railroads, Steamship and Steamboat Lines, Business Houses, and Places of Interest in Philadelphia* (Philadelphia: Burk & McFetridge, September 1880), pp. 45 and 50–63.

10. For the Centennial Exposition, the Pennsylvania Railroad built a new and larger West Philadelphia depot and the Philadelphia, Wilmington & Baltimore rebuilt and expanded its Prime Street station. A few years later, the Philadelphia & Reading planned to enlarge its terminal at Ninth and Green Streets to serve as a consolidated station for all its passenger services. As to Prime Street, see *Thirty-ninth Annual Report of the Philadelphia, Wilmington and Baltimore Railroad Company* (1877),

pp. 9–10. For West Philadelphia, see Pennsylvania Railroad board minute book no. 7 (January 26, 1876, meeting), p. 141. A reference to the Reading's plans and a copy of a privately held architectural drawing can be found in George E. Thomas, Michael J. Lewis, and Jeffrey A. Cohen, *Frank Furness: The Complete Works* (New York: Princeton Architectural Press, 1991), pp. 140 and 254. The Pennsylvania, however, had planned to build its Centennial station closer to downtown but dropped the project with some fanfare in 1876 (because of the high cost of acquiring the land) and did not publically resume work on it until 1879 (after the company had secretly purchased the needed right of way). See "Another Large Depot Improvement," *Public Ledger*, February 8, 1876, p. 1.

11. Information on travel time from *Philadelphia Store News*, p. 3. The "minor depots" reference is from *Rand McNally & Co.'s Handy Guide to Philadelphia and Environs Including Atlantic City and Cape May* (New York: Rand, McNally, 1900), p. 10. The Broad Street quote is from Burgess and Kennedy, *Centennial History of the Pennsylvania Railroad Company*, p. 433.

12. The details of the evolution of this station can be found in *Report of the President and Managers of the Philadelphia, Germantown and Norristown Railroad Company to the Stock and Loan Holders, November 3, 1851*, pp. 5–6; *Report of the President and Managers of the Philadelphia, Germantown and Norristown Railroad Company to the Stock and Loan Holders, For the Year ending September 30, 1858*, p. 4; *Report of the President and Managers of the Philadelphia, Germantown and Norristown Railroad Company to the Stock and Loan Holders, For the Year ending September 30, 1863*, pp. 6–7; *Report of the President and Managers of the Philadelphia, Germantown and Norristown Railroad Company to the Stock and Loan Holders, For the Year ending Sept. 30, 1864*, p. 6; and *Report of the Receivers of the Philadelphia & Reading Railroad Co.* (1882), p. 61. For an examination of the changing station styles, see Carroll L. V. Meeks, *The Railroad Station: An Architectural History* (New Haven: Yale University Press, 1956), chaps. 2–3, especially pp. 48–55 and 69–75. For illustrations of similar structures, see Lawrence Grow, *Waiting for the 5:05: Terminal, Station and Depot in America* (New York: Main Street/Universe Books, 1977), pp. 29 (Rochester, N.Y.), 31 (Baltimore), 32–33 (Savannah), and 39 (Baltimore). For similar developments in other cities, see Carl W. Condit, *The Railroad and the City: A Technological and Urbanistic History of Cincinnati* (Columbus: Ohio State University Press, 1977), and Richard C. Barrett, *Boston's Depots and Terminals: A History of Downtown Boston's Railroad Stations* (Rochester, N.Y.: Railroad Research Publications, 1996).

13. The package room held parcels (frequently from Center City retailers) for pick-up by outbound passengers and visitors' luggage as they explored the city. The plan appears as an attachment to John W. Royer to A. A. McLeod, November 23, 1886, Reading collection (Hagley), box 1025. The "non-smoking" policy is contained in Franklin B. Gowen to J. E. Wooten, March 2, 1883, Reading collection (Hagley), box 1025.

14. The story of Smith's "narrow escape" comes from the entry for September 4, 1881, John L. Smith diary. Others passengers were not as fortunate as Smith. See, for example, "The Fatal Accident at the West Chester and Philadelphia Railroad Depot," *Public Ledger*, August 9, 1876, p. 1. The guide book warning is in *Baedeker's United States, 1893* (1893; reprint, New York: De Capo Press, 1971), p. xxix.

15. Grade crossing fatalities were very common in the city. A few representative newspaper articles include "Fatal Railroad Accident," *Public Ledger*, June 2, 1876, p. 1; "Meeting of the Highway Committee," *Public Ledger*, June 6, 1876, p. 1; "The Pennsylvania Railroad—Fatal Accident—Coroner's Investigation in the Case of Matilda Cubler," *Public Ledger*, June 8, 1876, p. 1; and "Fatal Railroad Accidents," *Public Ledger*, June 26, 1876, p. 1. Grade crossings created numerous problems and expenses for the railroads. For example, the Reading on a three-mile stretch of its main line through the city had watchmen stationed at nineteen street crossings in 1881. J. E. Wooten from Henry G. Jones dated May 14, 1881, Reading collection (Hagley), box 227.

16. The concern over general safety is in John W. Royer to A. A. McLeod, November 23, 1886, and over lighting is in I. A. Sweigard to J. E. Wooten, November 20, 1883, both in the Reading collection (Hagley), box 1025.

17. *The Fourteenth Annual Report of the Philadelphia, Wilmington and Baltimore Railroad Company* (1851), p. 24, and *The Fifteenth Annual Report of the Philadelphia, Wilmington and Baltimore Railroad Company* (1853), p. 25; "History of the Philadelphia, Wilmington and Baltimore R. R. Co.," *American Railroad Journal*, February 24, 1855, pp. 120–24; Charles P. Dare, *Philadelphia, Wilmington and Baltimore Railroad Guide* (Philadelphia: Fitzgibbon & Van Ness, 1856); and *Baist's Atlas of the City of Philadelphia* (Philadelphia: Baist, 1873), plate 9.

18. *Eighteenth Annual Report of the Board of Directors of the Pennsylvania Rail Road Co.* (1865), p. 43, *Nineteenth Annual Report of the Board of Directors of the Pennsylvania Rail Road Co.* (1866), p. 56, and *Twenty-First Annual Report of the Board of Directors of the Pennsylvania Rail Road Co.* (1868), p. 51; and *Atlas of West Philadelphia including the 24th & 27th Wards* (Philadelphia: Hopkins, 1872), p. 8.

19. As to Prime Street, see *Thirty-ninth Annual Report of the Philadelphia, Wilmington and Baltimore Railroad Company* (1877), pp. 9–10, and "Preparations for the Centennial Travel over the Philadelphia, Wilmington and Baltimore Railroad," *Public Ledger*, May 8, 1876, p. 1. For West Philadelphia, see Burgess and Kennedy, *Centennial History of the Pennsylvania Railroad Company*, pp. 353–55; Pennsylvania Railroad board minute book no. 7 (January 26, 1876 meeting), p. 141; "Another Large Depot Improvement," *Public Ledger*, February 8, 1876, p. 1; "The New Depot of the Pennsylvania Railroad at Thirty-second and Market Streets," *Public Ledger*, April 22, 1876, p. 1; and *Atlas of the 24th & 27th Wards West Philadelphia*, p. 39.

20. *Smedley's Atlas of the City of Philadelphia* (Philadelphia: J. B. Lippincott, 1862), sec. 15; Pennsylvania Railroad board minute book no. 6 (May 1, 1873 meeting), p. 179; *Insurance Maps of the City of Philadelphia* (Philadelphia: Ernest Hexamer, 1879), vol. 8, p. 121; *Insurance Maps of the City of Philadelphia* (Philadelphia: Ernest Hexamer, 1879 [rev. 1889]), vol. 7, p. 121; and Campbell Collection, vol. 52, p. 113.

21. The resemblance to St. Pancras is probably more than coincidental. St. Pancras was the largest and newest of the London terminals (built 1863–76) when the PRR built Broad Street and the railroad may have used this well-known landmark as a model for its depot. At this time, Philadelphia was constructing its new City Hall (the "Public Buildings" to Victorian Philadelphians) in Centre Square, which, when completed, would be the largest office building in the world. Both structures were expressions of Philadelphia's continued competition with New York. For photographs and drawings of St. Pancras, see Grow, *Waiting for the 5:05*, p. 42; Meek, *The Railroad*

Station, figs. 40, 92, 109 and 110; and V. R. Anderson and G. K. Fox, *A Pictorial Record of L.M.S. Architecture* (Headington, England: Oxford Publishing, 1981), plates 111–20. See also Freeman, *Railways and the Victorian Imagination* for views of not just St. Pancras but other major London termini.

22. The details for these tours of the station are taken from "The New Broad Street Station of the Pennsylvania Railroad—Its Occupancy on Monday," *Public Ledger,* December 3, 1881, p. 1; Pennsylvania Railroad board minute book vol. 9 (December 28, 1881 meeting), pp. 389–90; and *Dictionary of Philadelphia and its Vicinity,* pp. 16–19. Entry for May 20, 1882, John L. Smith diary. The quote is from *Philadelphia and its Environs, Illustrated,* p. 9.

23. Entry for September 22, 1889, John L. Smith diary. Quote from *Dictionary of Philadelphia and its Vicinity,* p. 17. For the role of the matron, see E. F. Smith to Theodore Vorhees, April 26, 1902, Reading collection (Hagley), box 1032.

24. Entry for March 13, 1904, John L. Smith diary. Quote from *Dictionary of Philadelphia and its Vicinity,* p. 17. Walter G. Berg, *Buildings and Structures of American Railroads: A Reference Book* (New York: John Wiley & Sons, 1893).

25. Lost passengers wandering into railway offices is the subject of I. A. Sweigard to Theodore Voorhees, July 5, 1894, Reading collection (Hagley), box 1029. For the Reading's concerns over "bums" in the station, see I. A. Sweigard to Theodore Voorhees, February 26, 1897, box 1029, and E. F. Smith to Theodore Voorhees, March 6, 1899, Reading collection (Hagley), box 1030. The same company's problems with its Ladies' Waiting Room can be found in E. F. Smith to Theodore Voorhees, April 30, 1897, and Theodore Voorhees to Joseph S. Harris, October 1, 1898, Reading collection (Hagley), box 1030. For the creation of the Emigrant Waiting Room at Reading Terminal, see Theodore Voorhees to E. F. Smith, August 23, 1894, Reading collection (Hagley), box 1029. For a view of the Pennsylvania's immigrant facility, see the back cover of *Tariff of Immigrant Fares from Philadelphia* (Philadelphia: Immigrant Clearing House Committee, 1887), Balch Institute for Ethnic Studies.

26. For examples, see Ames, *Death in the Dining Room & Other Tales of Victorian Culture* (home interiors); Bluestone, *Constructing Chicago* (office buildings); Boyer, *Manhattan Manners* (city streets); and Kasson, *Amusing the Million* (urban space). Department stores and newspapers will be discussed in detail in subsequent chapters.

27. *The Philadelphia Inquirer,* December 9, 1890, p. 4. Reading Railroad System "News Item," October 6, 1893, Reading collection (Hagley), box 1028. *The Evening Bulletin,* March 27, 1897, p. 4. Theodore Voorhees to William H. Greene, March 31, 1897, and E. A. Smith to Theodore Voorhees, June 25, 1897, Reading collection (Hagley), box 1028.

28. None of the diaries that I examined even noted the creation of standard time, let alone commented on it. A few decades later, the start of Daylight Saving Time would cause a much greater stir; see Chapter 7. For examinations of the changing meanings of time in society, see Kern, *The Culture of Time and Space;* O'Malley, *Keeping Watch;* and Mark M. Smith, *Mastered by the Clock: Time, Slavery and Freedom in the American South* (Chapel Hill: University of North Carolina Press, 1996). An example of both a nod to other cities' time and the confusion local time could cause is included in the Pennsylvania railroad's listing in the *Travelers' Official Guide*

of the Railway and Steam Navigation Lines in the United States and Canada, April 1879 (Philadelphia: National Railway Publication Company, 1879), p. 87, where the company states: "Standard of Time.—On the Pennsylvania Railroad—*Main Line and Branches, and United Railroads of New Jersey Division*; Philadelphia & Erie R.R., and Northern Central R.W., from Baltimore to Williamsport, is PHILADELPHIA TIME, which is five minutes slower than New York time, and seven minutes faster than Harrisburg time, seven minutes faster than Williamsport time, thirteen minutes faster than Altoona time and nineteen minutes faster than Pittsburg time. On the Northern Central R.W., from Williamsport to Canandaigua, the standard is NEW YORK TIME."

29. Compare, for example, the train times in H. S. Tanner, *A New Picture of Philadelphia or the Stranger's Guide to the City and Adjoining Districts* (New York: T. R. Tanner, 1844), pp. 112–14, with the Philadelphia, Wilmington & Baltimore Railroad Time-table No. 6 effective June 26, 1881, library, Historical Society of Pennsylvania.

30. Entry for September 6, 1895, Leo G. Bernheimer diary.

31. Examples of all these timetables can be found in the collections of the California State Railroad Museum Library, the Hagley Museum and Library, the Historical Society of Pennsylvania, and the Railroad Museum of Pennsylvania.

32. The example is in the entry for May 20, 1882, John L. Smith diary. Other illustrations include the entries for January 1, 1888, May 6, 1888, September 22, 1889, November 24, 1889, October 28, 1894, and June 28, 1896. Examples of Smith's inattention to timetables include the entries for January 23, 1887, and January 1, 1888.

33. The example is from the entry for September 4, 1882, Edwin C. Jellett diary. Jellett's diary is filled with train times recorded to the minute; see, for example, the entries for January 4, 1880, August 25, 1881, and May 21, 1882. He took good care of his watch; see the entry for April 24, 1880.

34. Mary B. Smith and the members of her family seldom seemed to have problems with train times. She did not record them with quite the vigor of Edwin Jellett, but they appear upon occasion in the pages of her diary. See, for example, the entries for January 1 and 3, 1895, Mary B. Smith diary.

Chapter 3

1. Excerpt from chap. 5 of the memoirs of Eugenia L. Barnitz recalling the Wanamaker Grand Depot in the 1890s.

2. Herbert Adams Gibbons, *John Wanamaker*, 2 vols. (New York: Harper & Brothers, 1926), vol. 2, p. 196. One of the difficulties in tracing the creation of the department store is the lack of a good definition either at the time or more recently. See, for example, discussions in J. Russell Doubman and John R. Whitaker, *The Organization and Operation of Department Stores* (New York: John Wiley & Sons, 1927), p. 10; Hrant Pasdermadjian, *The Department Store: Its Origins, Evolution and Economics* (1954; reprint, New York: Arno Press, 1976), p. 916; and John William Ferry, *A History of the Department Store* (New York: Macmillan, 1960), pp. 9–10. The owners of the Philadelphia stores do not help resolve this issue. For example, John Wanamaker sel-

dom used the term "department store" to describe his firm; instead he preferred the awkward "a new kind of store." Gibbons, *John Wanamaker*, vol. 1, pp. 166–68. The evolution of the term will be discussed in more detail in Chapter 5. For the purposes of this work, a department store is a large urban retail establishment that sells both fashion and home merchandise and is divided administratively into multiple buying and selling departments.

3. Modern historians are as fascinated with the department stores as were the middle-class Victorians. My interest focuses on how the stores reflected the scientific worldview of the bourgeoisie, but recently other scholars have examined the retailers as a part of growing circuits of political and economic power (Leach, *Land of Desire*) and as windows to understanding changing gender roles (Elaine S. Abelson, *When Ladies Go A-Thieving: Middle-Class Shoplifters in the Victorian Department Store* [New York: Oxford University Press, 1989], and Benson, *Counter Cultures*). The most comprehensive work on the place of the department store in Victorian middle-class society remains Michael B. Miller, *The Bon Marché: Bourgeois Culture and the Department Store, 1869–1920* (Princeton, N.J.: Princeton University Press, 1981), which amply demonstrates the global nature of these changes by looking at Paris' leading merchant.

4. The comparison comes from *What We Look Like*, Strawbridge & Clothier collection. Although there is no comprehensive overview of all the Philadelphia retailers, there are histories of individual stores and biographies of their founders. Not surprisingly, John Wanamaker leads in coverage: the most detailed works on both man and store are Gibbons, *John Wanamaker*, and Joseph H. Appel, *The Business Biography of John Wanamaker Founder and Builder: America's Merchant Pioneer from 1861 to 1922* (New York: Macmillan, 1930); and the most recent are Herbert Ershkowitz, *John Wanamaker: Philadelphia Merchant* (Conshohocken, Pa.: Combined Books, 1999), and Zulker, *John Wanamaker*. For Strawbridge & Clothier, see Alfred Lief, *Family Business: A Century in the Life and Times of Strawbridge & Clothier* (New York: McGraw-Hill, 1968). Brief accounts of Wanamaker, Strawbridge & Clothier, Lit Brothers, Gimbel Brothers, and Snellenburg can be found in Ferry, *A History of the Department Store*, pp. 69–72 and 103–12. The biographies of the founding families of Gimbel Brothers and Lit Brothers are in Leon Harris, *Merchant Princes: An Intimate History of Jewish Families Who Built Great Department Stores* (1979; reprint, New York: Kodansha International, 1994). Howard Edwards memoirs, vol. 2, p. 51.

5. On the development of the mass market, see Strasser, *Satisfaction Guaranteed*. One illustration of the importance of the Wanamaker store to Victorian Philadelphia is that in papers of the middle-class guides the store accounts for 228 of the 736 nineteenth-century retail references. Strawbridge was a distant second with 34 and Gimbels third with 25 among the dry goods stores.

6. The relationship of the department store to the mass market has been examined by a number of scholars. See, for example, Leach, *Land of Desire*, chap. 1, and Pasdermadjian, *The Department Store*, chaps. 1 and 2. For John Wanamaker's explanation of his merchandising practices, see *Golden Book of the Wanamaker Stores* (Philadelphia: John Wanamaker, 1911), chaps. 10–12. Wanamaker's methods were not unique; based on their newspaper advertisements, the other major firms in Philadelphia developed along broadly similar lines. Entry for September 6, 1877, John L. Smith diary. Entry for December 20, 1878, Susan R. MacManus diary. Entry

for September 28, 1891, Leo G. Bernheimer diary. Entry for March 3, 1880, Susan R. MacManus diary.

7. "*Grand Depot (1876)—business principles—XXIII*," Gibbons Card File Number 1, John Wanamaker papers. *What We Look Like*, Strawbridge & Clothier collection. For details of the merchandise transfer system, see *The Wanamaker Store Directory* (1891), "Business Ephemera" scrapbook, pp. 4–5, John Wanamaker papers. A purchase and delivery can be found at the entries for December 12 and 17, 1888, Mrs. Tucker C. Laughlin diary. "*Restaurant—beginning of* (1883)," Gibbons Card File Number 1, John Wanamaker papers. *Public Ledger*, July 3, 1900. See, for example, the entry for April 3, 1893, Leo G. Bernheimer diary. A post office opened in the Grand Depot in 1884 and in Gimbel Brothers in 1900. Appel, *The Business Biography of John Wanamaker*, p. 106, and *Public Ledger*, July 2, 1900.

8. Entry for September 23, 1887, Edwin W. Lehman diary. Entry for December 28, 1891, Leo G. Bernheimer diary. Entry for March 8, 1894, Mary B. Smith diary. Appel, *The Business Biography of John Wanamaker Founder and Builder*, pp. 108–9. The Bon Marché in Paris also used bourgeois culture as a major part of its public persona. Miller, *The Bon Marché*, chap. 5. The Philadelphia merchants were well aware of their French counterpart. For example, John Wanamaker visited the Bon Marché in 1875 prior to opening his Grand Depot and established a buying office in Paris in 1881. Appel, *The Business Biography of John Wanamaker Founder and Builder*, pp. 78–79 and 401.

9. The Centennial annex remark is in the *Golden Book of the Wanamaker Stores*, p. 43. A recent work that also explores this link is Giberti, *Designing the Centennial*.

10. According to the middle-class guides, Wanamaker's was the leading destination for both men (79 out of 127 visits to department stores) and women (149 of 213). For women, Strawbridge's was clear second, but men preferred Gimbels' to Strawbridge's. The Marks Brothers quote comes from the *Public Ledger*, October 20, 1900. For an overview of gender in the late nineteenth-century department store, see Benson, *Counter Cultures* and Leach, *Land of Desire*.

11. Wanamaker's and Strawbridge's made overt attempts to reach the city's African American community in the late nineteenth century. An expression of John Wanamaker's racial attitudes during this period can be found in a city guidebook produced by the store: "Colored People of Philadelphia.—Very great changes in the social condition and general prosperity of the colored people of the city have taken place within twenty years, and they are at present very fully sustaining all the duties of citizens and receiving just and equal treatment in all the conditions of citizenship." *Dictionary of Philadelphia and its Vicinity*. Strawbridge & Clothier took advertisements in programs produced by bourgeois Black organizations. Jacob C. White, Jr. files, American Negro Historical Society Papers, Leon Gardiner Collection, box 6G, folder 13. With one exception, all the middle-class guides who recorded visits to Lits' or Snellenburg's in the Victorian era were Jewish.

12. 1876 First Floor Plan, Strawbridge & Clothier collection.

13. For Strawbridge's, see Lief, *Family Business*, pp. 18–25, 33–34, 46–47, 55–57, and 83–91. For Gimbel Brothers, see Cooper & Conrad Store drawings, Addison Hutton collection.

14. On growth in size, see Gibbons, *John Wanamaker*, vol. 1, p. 219; Appel, *The*

Business Biography of John Wanamaker, pp. 106 and 108; and *A Little Hand-book of Philadelphia: Together with Certain Annals of the Wanamaker System,* p. 23.

15. On the use of spectacle by department stores in general (with a strong focus on John Wanamaker), see Leach, *Land of Desire,* chaps. 1–3. Gibbons, *John Wanamaker,* vol. 1, pp. 214–15. Quotations and additional details are from an article in the *Evening Leader,* November 13, 1878, that can be found in Gibbons Card File Number 1, John Wanamaker papers. See also, "Wanamaker's Palace," *The Press,* March 13, 1877, p. 2.

16. For Wanamaker's layout in the 1880s, see *The Wanamaker Store Directory* (Philadelphia: John Wanamaker, n.d.), John Wanamaker papers. For Strawbridge & Clothier, see *What We Look Like,* Strawbridge & Clothier collection. For Gimbel Brothers, see Cooper & Conrad Store drawings, Addison Hutton collection. For an early twentieth-century look at department store layout, see Doubman and Whitaker, *The Organization and Operation of Department Stores,* chap. 7.

17. For the number of departments, see *Golden Book of the Wanamaker Stores,* p. 56; Appel, *The Business Biography of John Wanamaker,* p. 106; 1889 store guide, n.p., John Wanamaker papers; and *A Little Hand-book of Philadelphia,* p. 23, John Wanamaker papers. On the "science of merchandising," see Chapter 6.

18. Entry for December 22, 1887, Edwin C. Jellett diary. The information about the book department is from Gibbons, *John Wanamaker,* vol. 1, p. 202.

19. *The Wanamaker Directory,* "Business Ephemera" scrapbook, John Wanamaker papers.

20. For example, in 1886 one middle-class Philadelphian assumed the extended hours began earlier in December than they did. See the entry for December 2, 1886, Edwin C. Jellett diary. The advertisements announcing the extended hours are in the *Public Ledger* on the following dates: December 10, 1900 (Wanamaker), December 14, 1900 (Wanamaker), December 15, 1900 (Gimbels and Lits), and December 17, 1900 (Partridge & Richardson).

21. *Public Ledger,* December 15, 1900. For a similar conflict between the market and tradition at the Bon Marché, see Miller, *The Bon Marché,* chap. 3.

22. The Christmas retail season began in the antebellum period and predates the development of the department store, but department stores helped dramatically to expand this sales period. For the development of a consumer Christmas, see Leigh Eric Schmidt, *Consumer Rites: The Buying and Selling of American Holidays* (Princeton, N.J.: Princeton University Press, 1995), chap. 3. For example, in 1892 employment at Wanamaker's peaked at 4,800 but was only 3,000 during the summer months. "Phila. Store—number of employees in 1892," Gibbons Card File Number 1, John Wanamaker papers. Examples from Strawbridge & Clothier advertisements in the *Public Ledger* for March 29, 1881, and July 1, 1895. The *Public Ledger* throughout the late nineteenth century had an advertising index which makes it easy to track dry goods advertisements. It was also the most bourgeois of Philadelphia's newspapers and contained the most department store ads; see Chapters 4 and 5. Gimbel Brothers advertisement from the *Public Ledger,* January 3, 1898.

23. *Public Ledger,* January 2, 1900.

24. *Public Ledger:* January 4 (Strawbridge & Clothier and Partridge & Richardson) and January 5, 1900 (Gimbels).

25. *Public Ledger:* January 31 (Wanamaker) and February 5, 1900 (Gimbels).

26. *Public Ledger:* June 5 (Gimbels and Wanamaker), June 6 (Strawbridge & Clothier), and July 2, 1900 (Gimbels and Partridge & Richardson).

27. *Public Ledger:* July 2 (Gimbels and Wanamaker), July 3 (Gimbels), July 9 (Wanamaker and Gimbels), July 26 (Gimbels), and August 1, 1900 (Gimbels and Wanamaker).

28. Fall clothing advertisements were in the *Public Ledger* on September 4 (Strawbridge & Clothier and Darlington), September 10 (Strawbridge & Clothier), September 12 (Wanamaker), September 14 (Strawbridge & Clothier), September 17 (Wanamaker, Strawbridge & Clothier, and Gimbels), September 18 (Wanamaker and Gimbels), and September 26, 1900 (Partridge & Richardson). The sales were advertised in the *Public Ledger* on September 4 (Wanamaker, Darlington, Gimbels, and Strawbridge & Clothier), September 6 (Wanamaker), and September 14, 1900 (Gimbels).

29. *Public Ledger:* November 3 (Wanamaker's toy land), November 12 (Wanamaker's Swiss Village), and November 24, 1900 (Gimbels' toy land).

30. *Public Ledger:* November 26 (Darlington and Wanamaker), November 29 (Wanamaker), November 30 (Gimbels), December 1 (Gimbels), December 3, 1900 (Gimbels, Wanamaker, Partridge & Richardson, and Strawbridge & Clothier). Eugenia L. Barnitz memoirs, chap. 5.

31. *Public Ledger:* December 8 (Gimbels, Marks and Wanamaker), December 10 (Wanamaker, Gimbels, and Strawbridge & Clothier), December 11 (Gimbels), December 12 (Strawbridge & Clothier), and December 13, 1900 (Lits).

32. *Public Ledger:* December 18 (Gimbels), December 20 (Wanamaker's favor) and December 22, 1900 (Gimbels). Lilly Russell to Robert L. Sinclair, December 24, 1888, Robert L. Sinclair papers. Entry for December 19, 1891, Elizabeth B. Passmore diary.

33. *Public Ledger:* December 24 and 25 (Wanamaker and Gimbels), December 27 (Wanamaker) and December 28, 1900 (Gimbels).

Chapter 4

1. Entry for June 9, 1894, Albert J. Edmunds diary.

2. There is no adequate overview of the changing Philadelphia newspaper industry in the nineteenth century. Instead, one must rely on general histories of journalism that use Philadelphia examples (most often the *Public Ledger*) to illustrate national trends. See, for example, the brief entry in Frank Luther Mott, *American Journalism: A History, 1690–1960*, 3rd ed. (New York: Macmillan Company, 1962), pp. 450–51.

3. See note 29 below for a discussion of the study of newspaper design.

4. For the traditional typography of newspapers, see Mott, *American Journalism,* and for the entertainment/information dichotomy see Michael Schudson, *Discovering the News: A Social History of American Newspapers* (New York: Basic Books, 1978).

5. Based on my sampling of diaries and scrapbooks, bourgeois women and men read eleven of the seventeen dailies published in Philadelphia during this period but purchased (during the 1880s) these four in larger quantities than the overall market share of the papers would suggest. By 1900, the number of middle-class papers in the sampling had declined to three (the *Public Ledger*, *The Press*, and *The Times*), but the relationship between the leading titles and the bourgeoisie became stronger.

6. "The 'Ledger's' Half Century," *Public Ledger*, March 25, 1886, p. 8.

7. This is not an absolutely clean dichotomy as there are some newspapers that are difficult to categorize. *The Evening Bulletin*, prior to its purchase by William McLean in 1895, for example, was a survivor from the earlier period of the partisan press and existed almost solely to meet the needs of the Republican party. Others, such as *The Evening Star* and the broadsheet *Daily News*, were papers with low circulations, but they survived for long periods without adopting any of the norms of major city journals. All of the major newspapers, however, eventually can be placed comfortably in this dichotomy.

8. T. Chalkley Matlack memoirs, vol. 1, p. 90. For the importance of respectability to the bourgeoisie in the nineteenth century, see Halttunen, *Confidence Men and Painted Women*, and Kasson, *Rudeness & Civility*. Entry for June 9, 1894, Albert J. Edmunds diary. On the *Public Ledger's* self-conscious conservatism, see entries in the *Public Ledger Almanac* (Philadelphia: George W. Childs) for 1872, p. 49, and for 1875, p. 55.

9. *The Record Almanac 1885* (Philadelphia: The Philadelphia Record, 1885), n.p. McCabe, *The Illustrated History of the Centennial Exhibition*, p. 19.

10. Philadelphia and London were not the only Victorian cities to have a clustering of newspaper offices, Boston, too, had its "newspaper row." See Herbert A. Kenny, *Newspaper Row Journalism in the Pre-Television Era* (Chester, Conn.: Globe Pequot Press, 1987).

11. For an early example of "Chestnut Street" being used to refer to newspapers in general, see the entry for July 24, 1877, John L. Smith diary.

12. On the 1877 railroad strikes, see the entries for July 22–28, 1877, John L. Smith diary. Entry for November 8, 1881, Hinch family diary. Entry for June 23, 1888, Edwin C. Jellett diary. Howard Edwards memoirs, vol. 2, p. 185.

13. See, for example, entries for October 14 (Penn 54, Lehigh 0) and November 23, 1895 (the day he pronounced his judgment and Penn beat Howard 17 to 14), Leo G. Bernheimer diary.

14. *The Record Almanac 1885*, n.p.

15. Holm, *Sunday Best*, p. 111. T. Chalkley Matlack memoirs, vol. 1, p. 90. Hemsing, *The Diaries of William Souder Hemsing*, p. 5. Entry for December 28, 1886, Edwin W. Lehman diary. *Public Ledger Almanac 1875*, p. 52.

16. *Dictionary of Philadelphia and its Vicinity*, p. 99. On news boys (and girls) at Reading Terminal, see W. J. Bruehl to Theodore Voorhees, March 1, 1900, J. G. Haywood to W. J. Bruehl, February 13, 1901, and W. J. Bruehl to Theodore Voorhees, February 14, 1901, Reading collection (Hagley), box 1031. Howard Edwards memoirs, vol. 2, p. 209. See Horatio Alger, Jr., *Ragged Dick and Struggling Upward* (New York: Penguin, 1985), p. 38, for Ragged Dick's solution to a slow news day. For Bernheimer's confession, see the entry for December 28, 1896, Leo G. Bernheimer diary (in his defense, he was not a regular reader of *The Press*).

17. A. Edward Newton, "Introduction" to Christopher Morley, *Travels in Philadelphia* (1920; reprint, Philadelphia: J. B. Lippincott, 1937), p. xii. *Dictionary of Philadelphia and its Vicinity*, p. 99.

18. Entry for May 22, 1897, Septimus Winner diary. Entries for January 5, 1891; April 5, 1893; May 9, 1893; January 1, 1895; October 31, 1895; and April 14, 1896, Leo G. Bernheimer diary. Entry for June 27, 1881, Hinch family diary. Victorian editors had a rather gendered view of their readership: the primary subscriber was male and the women of the house were secondary readers (at best). *The Philadelphia Record* makes this assumption explicit when it refers to "the subscriber, his wife and mother-in-law." *The Record Almanac 1885*, n.p. The newspaper as a gendered space in the city will be considered in greater detail in Chapter 5.

19. Throughout the Victorian period, Philadelphia's morning papers dominated their evening counterparts in almost every way. Although most journals grew in length, the morning ones grew more rapidly. Between 1880 and 1900, the morning newspapers doubled in size, reflecting the circulation and advertising dominance these papers had over their afternoon counterparts at this time. In 1880, the combined circulation of the eight evening papers was smaller than that of the largest morning one. Although afternoon journals would become more competitive in circulation by 1900, morning editions still led in advertising content.

20. The use of "English-language" as a modifier for the term "daily newspaper" is necessary because of the presence of several non-English-language titles in the city. In 1885, for example, there were five German-language daily papers published in Philadelphia: *Abend Post, Demokrat, Freie Presse, Tageblatt,* and *Volksblatt.* The largest of these, the *Demokrat,* claimed a circulation of 20,000, which was greater than the sales of half of its English-language counterparts. *N. W. Ayer & Son's Newspaper Annual* (Philadelphia: N. W. Ayer, 1885), pp. 94–98. Ayer directories will be hereinafter cited as "*Ayer* (date)." The most complete source for tracing the various titles in Philadelphia is *A Checklist of Pennsylvania Newspapers,* vol. 1 (Harrisburg: Pennsylvania Historical Commission, 1944). Based on this work, the daily papers published in the city between 1880 and 1900 (using the title under which they are listed in the *Checklist,* as the exact wording of the names often changed) were: *The Call* (1883–1904); *The Daily News* (1879–1915[?]); *The Philadelphia Day* (1869–1881); *The Evening Bulletin* (1847–[1982]); *The Evening Herald* (1866–1912); *The Evening Republican* (1874–1880); *The Evening Star* (1866–1900); *The Evening Telegraph* (1864–1918); *The Item* (1847–1913); *The North American* (1771[sic]-1925); *The Philadelphia Inquirer* (1807–); *The Press* (1857–1920); *Public Ledger* (1836–1934); *The Philadelphia Record* (1870–[1948]); and *The Times* (1876–1902). This information was then verified by consulting the listings in *Ayer* and the holdings of the Free Library of Philadelphia. Circulation figures for this period are more an art than a science. The most complete source is the *Ayer* directory that was used by contemporary advertisers, but until the advent of audited circulation in the 1890s (in which not all papers participated), even the figures given in *Ayer* must be taken with a large degree of skepticism. They are, however, the best numbers historians have and probably are not wrong in order of magnitude, i.e., a 5,000 circulation paper may claim to sell 7,500 copies but not 25,000. Ayer (a Philadelphia-based advertising agency) refused to print circulation figures they thought were suspect, so there was a limit on how greatly newspaper

publishers could inflate their numbers. A brief discussion of period circulation figures can be found in Janet E. Steele, *The Sun Shines for All: Journalism and Ideology in the Life of Charles A. Dana* (Syracuse: Syracuse University Press, 1993), p. 143. For an interesting first-hand look at the fictive aspects of unaudited circulation figures in the early twentieth century, see J. David Stern, *Memoirs of a Maverick Publisher* (New York: Simon and Schuster, 1962), chaps. 7 and 8. Both of the neighborhood papers mentioned were read by the middle-class diarists. For West Philadelphia, see the entry for November 17, 1887, Edwin W. Lehman diary, and, for Germantown, see the clippings inserted in the 1896 and 1897 diaries of Edwin C. Jellett. For *The World*, see the entry for June 21, 1896, John L. Smith diary.

21. As there is no surviving readership data (other than gross numbers) for these Victorian papers, scholars have relied upon a number of ways to determine which segment of the market read the individual titles and I have used three of these methods. First is self description; the *Public Ledger*, for example, consistently highlighted its "proper" tone in period literature and regularly reflected upon its relationship with restrained middle-class values. A more modern example of this would be the modern tabloid *Daily News* of Philadelphia that proclaims its working-class identity through the appearance of the slogan "the people paper" in its masthead. Second is the data on middle-class reading patterns that I collected through examining the manuscript collections that contain entries mentioning specific titles or clippings from those papers. These collections contained a disproportionately high number of references to four titles—the papers I define as the "genteel metropolitan press"—and none to titles like the *Evening Item*. Finally, the advertisements placed in the various newspapers give a strong indication of the relative social class of the journal's readership. Bourgeois institutions like department stores placed their ads overwhelmingly in the genteel metropolitan press, to a far lesser extent in the general circulation press, and avoided altogether more working-class titles such as the *Evening Item* and the old *Daily News*.

22. The papers were *The Sunday Item* (circulation 184,009), *The Philadelphia Inquirer* (166,937), *The Philadelphia Record* (154,239), *The Sunday Press* (135,000), and *The Sunday Times* (50,000). *Ayer* (1901), pp. 1256–58.

23. *The Diaries of William Souder Hemsing*, p. 57. See, for example, the entries for June 18, 1882 and January 5, 1896, John L. Smith diary. For Smith's complaint about "so much trash," see his entry for December 11, 1898. Howard Edwards memoirs, vol. 2, p. 209.

24. For example, Sunday, January 8, 1888, was "Damp and disagreeable[,]" so William Hemsing stayed in and read "Rob Roy and The Press." *The Diaries of William Souder Hemsing*, p. 279.

25. An introduction to the changing newspaper market is contained in Schudson, *Discovering the News*. See also Gunther Barth, *City People: The Rise of Modern City Culture in Nineteenth-Century America* (New York: Oxford University Press, 1980), chap. 3. Although I disagree with his contentions regarding the egalitarian nature of the institutions he studies, Barth otherwise gives a nice summary of structural changes during the late nineteenth century in a human context. The story of *The New York World* is told in George Juergens' *Joseph Pulitzer and the New York World* (Princeton, N.J.: Princeton University Press, 1966); see p. 49 for a discussion of technology.

The link between maps and technology is explored in Mark Monmonier, *Maps with the News: The Development of American Journalistic Cartography* (Chicago: University of Chicago Press, 1989). A more recent account of the changing New York metropolitan press in the late nineteenth century links the rise of *The World* (and similar papers) to the emergence of the culture of consumption. See Steele, *The Sun Shines for All*, chap. 9. For Dana's own (largely negative) view of how technology allowed newspapers to print more photographs, see Charles A. Dana, *The Art of Newspaper Making: Three Lectures* (New York: D. Appleton, 1900), pp. 95–98.

26. *Philadelphia Record Almanac, 1899*, n.p.

27. *Philadelphia Record Almanac, 1899*, n.p. An announcement in the front of the almanac lists twenty "special departments" from "the Household" to "Women's Interests." *Public Ledger Almanac, 1900*, n.p. Willard Grosvenor Bleyer, *Main Currents in the History of American Journalism* (New York: Houghton Mifflin, 1927), p. 390. William Grosvenor Bleyer, *Newspaper Writing and Editing* (New York: Houghton Mifflin, 1932), p. 431.

28. The information on page length, news content, and design is derived from an examination of the surviving newspapers (primarily on microfilm at the Free Library of Philadelphia). Initially I looked at every title I could find every tenth year (1880, 1890, 1900, 1910, 1920). I would first pick issues at random during those years in order to develop a feel for how each paper varied in the course of the year. I then focused on two weeks of each year (the weeks in which May 21 and October 21 occurred, or, if those issues were not available, the closest weeks that were).

29. There has been almost no sustained analysis of changing newspaper design by scholars. For a traditional account of the changing newspaper industry that only discusses layout in passing, see Kenneth Stewart and John Trebbel, *Makers of Modern Journalism* (New York: Prentice-Hall, 1952). Some books targeted at newspaper design students do consider the topic but they take a rather "whiggish" view lacking often in any context other than technology; see, as an example, Harold Evans, *Newspaper Design* (London: Heinemann, 1972), chap. 2. Other, more popular, histories of the press present layout change in a very sweeping manner, again tending to emphasize the role of technology in the process; see, as an example, Alfred McClung Lee, *The Daily Newspaper in America* (New York: Octagon Books, 1973).

30. To guide me through the intricacies of page layout, I have used Evans, *Newspaper Design*, chaps. 1–2 and 4–5. See Chapter 2 for his history of design change and page 23 for "the tyranny of column rules." It is worth considering in passing how imbedded column rules are to the traditional look of newspapers even today when both *The New York Times* and *The Wall Street Journal* still use them on their front pages despite the conversion to computer typesetting.

31. Both the *Public Ledger* and *The Times* also led that day with the White murder. *The Times* indicated this by a bold three-column headline while the *Ledger* used its then standard six-deck headline (found on three other articles that morning) but signaled the story's importance by placing it in the far right column (which had become by then a convention in the paper).

32. The "Latest News" column in the 1880 *Public Ledger* is different from the page one news summary of the 1900 *Press* shown in figure 24. The latter gives a syn-

opsis of stories found elsewhere in the paper whereas the former groups short articles together that only appear in the column.

33. *The Daily News*, a four-page paper, did not use graphics or photographs but otherwise followed many of the conventions of the period. Its circulation numbers are not carried in the *Ayer* directory and all indications are it was a very minor, little-read journal. This broadsheet ceased publication around 1920 and is not the same publication as the twentieth-century tabloid of the same title.

34. The "stop press" or "late news" section was a portion of (usually) page one left blank when the paper first went to press. Upon the arrival of late news (often sports scores during this period), the paper was taken to a smaller press where the blank space was imprinted.

35. H. Sidney Smith scrapbook. See, for example, the Delaware County Scrapbook compiled by Anna E. Broomall, vol. 1. Entries for April 8 and May 28, 1886, William G. Armstrong diary. James Samuel Stemons papers, boxes 1 and 4.

36. An example of the first approach is Juergens, *Joseph Pulitzer and the New York World*; the second is Schudson, *Discovering the News*; and the third is Steele, *The Sun Shines for All*. For examples of the effects of changes in ownership in Philadelphia, see Robert L. Bloom, "The Philadelphia *North American*: A History, 1839–1925" (Ph.D. diss., Columbia University, 1952), pp. 444–45 and 467–507, and Stewart and Trebbel, *Makers of Modern Journalism*, chap. 21. The terms "informational" and "entertaining" are from Schudson, *Discovering the News*, chap. 3.

37. Based on my survey that examined in detail two randomly selected weeks, the percentage of the newspapers devoted to advertising fell from 41.37% in 1880 to 33.22% in 1890 to 31.73% in 1900.

38. The page shown in figure 25 is from *The Philadelphia Inquirer*, October 21, 1880, p. 5. The importance of newspaper advertisements to John Wanamaker is considered in Leach, *Land of Desire*, pp. 43–44 and 51–52; Lears, *Fables of Abundance*, pp. 200–201 and 205; and Zulker, *John Wanamaker*, chap. 7. For some of John Wanamaker's views on advertising, see Gibbons Card File Number 6, John Wanamaker papers. The same Wanamaker ad also appeared in *The Evening Bulletin, The Philadelphia Record, The Press*, and *The Times* that day. Similar announcements were in the *Public Ledger* and *The Evening Telegraph* and no display advertising from the firm was in *The North American* that day.

39. *The Evening Telegraph* had Wanamaker's ad (on p. 4) and one from Sharpless Brothers (p. 3); *The Press* contained V. E. Archambault (p. 2), Sharpless (p. 5), and Wanamaker and Granville B. Haines advertisements (both on p. 8); and *The Times* featured announcements from Archambault (p. 2), Marks Brothers and Haines (both on p. 3), Sharpless (p. 7), and Wanamaker (p. 8). The *Public Ledger* still contained no display advertising but did have announcements from most major department and dry goods stores in the city: on page one, Strawbridge & Clothier, and on page four, Wanamaker, Adolph Heller, B. F. Dewees, Haines, Sharpless, and Partridge & Richardson.

40. The following are ads that appeared in the May 19, 1890, editions. For Hood's see *The Call* (p. 2), *The North American* (p. 4), and *The Press* (p. 2); and for Royal see *The Call* (p. 7), *The Evening Telegraph* (p. 7), *The Philadelphia Inquirer* (p. 3), *The Press* (p. 3), and *The Times* (p. 3). The Model Coffee House ads were in *The*

Call (p. 7) and *The Philadelphia Inquirer* (p. 2); Caldwell's in *The Evening Telegraph* (p. 7) and *The Philadelphia Inquirer* (p. 3); and Smith's in *The Call* (p. 4). The carpet cleaning services were in *The Philadelphia Inquirer* (p. 5); and the Atlantic City hotels in *The Call* (p. 8), *The Philadelphia Inquirer* (p. 5), *The Press* (p. 6), and *The Times* (p. 7).

41. The dry goods ads on May 21, 1900, were as follows: in *The Times*, Gimbel Brothers took seven-eighths of page two, Strawbridge & Clothier one-quarter of page three, and John Wanamaker the entire back page for display advertisements; *The Press*, Gimbel's used two-thirds of page three, Strawbridge's one-quarter of page seven, and Wanamaker's again took the entire back page; the *Public Ledger* advertisers included Gimbel's with seven-eighths of page three, Marks Brothers with one-eighth of page five, Strawbridge's with one-third of page seven, Wanamaker's all of page eleven, and Partridge & Richardson with all of page thirteen, plus smaller ads from Joseph G. Darlington and V. E. Archambault (both p. 9) and B. F. Dewees (p. 10); *The Evening Bulletin* for Gimbel's (one-fifth of page two), Strawbridge's (one-third of page three), and Snellenburg's (seven-eighths of the back page); *The Evening Telegraph* for Mark's (one-tenth of page two), Strawbridge's (one-third of page three), Darlington's (one-tenth of page four), and Wanamaker's (all of page nine); *The North American* for Mark's (one-tenth of page five), Snellenburg's (six-sevenths of page seven), Partridge & Richardson (all of page nine), and Wanamaker's (all of page ten); *The Philadelphia Evening Item* for Strawbridge's (one-quarter of page four); *The Philadelphia Inquirer* for Mark's (one-third of page two); Gimbel's (seven-eighths of page three), Strawbridge's (one third of page seven), and Snellenburg's (two-thirds of the back page); and *The Philadelphia Record* for Gimbel's (three-quarters of page two), Lit Brothers (half of page three), Strawbridge's (one-third of page four), Mark's (one-third of page five), and Snellenburg's (half of page six).

42. The Gimbel advertisement is from *The Philadelphia Press*, May 21, 1900, p. 3.

Interlude

1. Edwin C. Jellet diary.

2. This narrative is derived from the entries for June 1, July 6, July 20, and August 5, 1901, Edwin C. Jellett diary; E. H. Rosenberger, *The Trolley Tourist: A Book of Trolley Routes in Eastern Pennsylvania, New Jersey and Delaware* (Philadelphia, 1905); and the *Public Ledger*, July 20 and 22, 1901.

The New Century

1. "Warm Greeting to New Century," *Public Ledger*, January 1, 1901, p. 1.

2. Elizabeth Robins Pennell, *Joseph Pennell's Pictures of Philadelphia* (Philadelphia: J. B. Lippincott, 1926), pp. 7–8.

3. A quick overview of the Philadelphia labor market for this period can be

found in Walter Licht, *Getting Work: Philadelphia, 1840–1950* (Cambridge: Harvard University Press, 1992), chaps. 1 and 2. Note, however, that Licht disagrees with the conclusion that working-class incomes increased significantly during this period; see pp. 240–41. The supporting data for the chart in figure 29 are from the following tables in U.S. Bureau of Census, *Historical Statistics of the United States: Colonial Times to 1970* (Washington, D.C.: Government Printing Office, 1975): "Consumer Price Indexes (BLS)" (series E 135), p. 211, and "Manufactures Summary: 1849–1970" (series P 4–5 and 8–9), p. 666. Because of methodological changes (the nature of which can be verified by examining the underlying published census data), these statistics must be used with caution but offer historians some reasonably concrete figures to work with. For the specifics of Philadelphia, the figures on wages and salaries are drawn from the published data from the census of manufactures. In 1899, the Census Bureau changed the definition of factory (effectively excluding many smaller facilities) that makes an exact comparison between pre- and post-1899 data difficult. Support for the broad contention that members of the working classes made real wage gains throughout the Europeanized world during this period can be found in David Hackett Fischer, *The Great Wave: Price Revolutions and the Rhythm of History* (New York: Oxford University Press, 1996), pp. 179–91.

    4. On the expansion of the market, see, in general, Strasser, *Satisfaction Guaranteed*; for department stores, Benson, *Counter Cultures*; amusement parks, Kasson, *Amusing the Million*, and Schlereth, *Victorian America*, pp. 77–85.

Chapter 5

    1. John Cecil Holm recalling the early twentieth century in *Sunday Best*, p. 231.

    2. Morley, *Kitty Foyle*, p. 142. David G. Wittels, "The Paper That Was Tailored to a City," *The Saturday Evening Post* (April 7, 1945).

    3. On the rise of mass amusement in general, see Nasaw, *Going Out*. Even if one does not accept Nasaw's argument regarding the egalitarian nature of these institutions, the book illustrates the increased options available to the leisure-minded consumer. Entry for September 25, 1915, Clair Wilcox diary.

    4. Almost every middle-class person in my sampling either mentioned reading "the papers" (plural) or had clippings from multiple journals in their collections.

    5. *A Checklist of Pennsylvania Newspapers*, pp. 259, 268–69, 295, and 299. The papers Curtis acquired were *The Evening Telegraph* in 1918, *The Press* in 1920, and *The North American* in 1925. Stewart and Trebbel, *Makers of Modern Journalism*, pp. 348–49. The remaining broadsheets were *The Philadelphia Inquirer*, *The Philadelphia Record*, and the *Public Ledger* in the morning, and *The Evening Bulletin*, *The Evening Public Ledger*, and *The Evening Star* in the afternoon. The two tabloids were *The Daily News* and *The Illustrated Sun*.

    6. *The Diaries of William Souder Hemsing*, p. 433. T. Chalkley Matlack memoirs, vol. 1, p. 85.

    7. Henrietta Ulman Newmayer collection. The 1890 daily circulation for the genteel metropolitan press was 227,806 out of total sales of 628,193. By 1920 total daily

circulation had risen to 1,130,642, but the middle-class press accounted for no more than 90,000 copies. By 1920, Curtis combined the sales figures of the morning and evening *Ledgers*, so it is impossible to be more precise.

8. Holm, *Sunday Best*, p. 104.

9. *The Philadelphia Inquirer* so dominated the classified market in the morning that David Stern, later publisher of *The Philadelphia Record* and *The New York Post*, described it as a virtual monopoly. Stern, *Memoirs of a Maverick Publisher*, p. 83. Entry for November 21, 1902, Albert J. Edmunds diary. Holm, *Sunday Best*, pp. 199–200. 1919 was the first year that the *Ayer* directory included a notation that the newspaper accepted mats.

10. See the introduction of the next chapter for this vignette in more detail. Holm, *Sunday Best*, p. 231. See Leach, *Land of Desire*, pp. 42–43, for another look at this interdependence between newspapers and department stores. For the changing role of advertising in magazines at approximately the same time, see Ellen Gruber Garvey, *The Adman in the Parlor: Magazines and the Gendering of Consumer Culture, 1880s to 1910s* (New York: Oxford University Press, 1996). Both Lears, *Fables of Abundance*, and Roland Marchand, *Advertising the American Dream: Making Way for Modernity, 1920–1940* (Berkeley: University of California Press, 1985), offer broader settings for this shift in advertising to a mass market.

11. The book was *One Day* (Philadelphia: The Evening Bulletin, 1929), and the data on reading matter comes from pp. iii-iv.

12. There is no biography of McLean nor adequate history of *The Evening Bulletin*. This story, however, can be found in both the *Dictionary of American Biography* and my entry on McLean in the *American National Biography*. Both biographic entries list other sources.

13. This overview of Curtis' failure with the *Public Ledger* is based largely on Stewart and Trebbel, *Makers of Modern Journalism*, chap. 13 (the quote comes from pp. 348–49). Their account, in turn, is drawn from Oswald Garrison Villard, *The Disappearing Daily: Chapters in American Newspaper Evolution* (New York: Alfred A. Knopf, 1944), chap. 22. Villard had been an editor at *The New York Evening Post* (another of Curtis' excursions into journalism) and his critique is somewhat more biting than mine. The title of his chapter on Curtis became more vitriolic over time: from "The Philadelphia *Public Ledger*, a Muffed Opportunity" in 1926 to "Cyrus H. K. Curtis, a Total Failure" in 1944. Compare Oswald Garrison Villard, *Some Newspapers and Newspapermen* (New York: Alfred A. Knopf, 1926), chap. 9, with Villard, *The Disappearing Daily*, chap. 22. References to *The Guardian* can be found in contemporary *Public Ledger* advertising and Stewart and Trebbel, *Makers of Modern Journalism*, p. 214.

14. Katherine Bingham, *The Philadelphians* (Boston: L. C. Page, 1903), p. 25. Morley, *Kitty Foyle*, p. 11.

15. Kitty Foyle on the *Public Ledger*: "I'd read [father] the sleepiest things I could find in the *Ledger*, where there was plenty to choose from." Morley, *Kitty Foyle*, p. 85.

16. Stern, *Memoirs of a Maverick Publisher*, p. 91. McLean's quote is from an article in the final edition of the paper. McLean reacted well to changing market conditions in the early twentieth century, but his successors failed to do so decades later. "God bless you and farewell," *The Bulletin*, January 29, 1982, p. F10.

17. For the argument that all space in the nineteenth-century British press was gendered see Laurel Brake, "Gendered Space and the British Press," in *Studies in Newspaper and Periodical History, 1995 Annual* (Westport, Conn.: Greenwood Press, 1997), pp. 99–110.

18. Eugenia L. Barnitz memoirs, p. 101.

19. For a review of the literature and an argument about the limits of the separate spheres as applied to middle-class magazines, see Helen Damon-Moore, *Magazines for the Millions: Gender and Commerce in the* Ladies' Home Journal *and the* Saturday Evening Post, *1880–1910* (Albany: State University of New York Press, 1994), pp. 1–13. John L. Given, *Making a Newspaper* (New York: Henry Holt & Co., 1907), p. 3.

20. See, for example, the *Public Ledger*, May 29, 1880, p. 5, *The North American*, May 19, 1890, p. 5, and *The Philadelphia Inquirer*, May 19, 1890, p. 4.

21. The five journals with explicitly denominated gendered space (and the columns' titles) were *The Evening Telegraph* ("Woman and Her Ways"), *The Philadelphia Inquirer* ("Happening in Women's World"), the *Public Ledger* ("Woman's Interests"), *The Press* ("Women as They Pass"), and *The Times* ("In Women's Realm"). The one paper not to have even an implicitly defined female space in 1900 was the minor *Daily News*. Given, *Making a Newspaper*, p. 3.

22. Three papers surveyed used explicitly denominated pages (page numbers are from May 16, 1910 editions): *The Evening Star* ("Fads, Fashions and Home Topics"), p. 7, *The North American* ("Of Interest To Women"), p. 12, and *The Press* ("Women as They Pass"), p. 10. The two papers that never developed a regular section for women's news were *The Daily News* and *The Philadelphia Evening Item*. The *Public Ledger* had dropped its daily women's column but did regularly group together articles aimed at female readers. By 1920, only *The Philadelphia Inquirer* and *The Press* had explicitly titled "women's" pages daily, but the others had unlabeled groupings of articles on a regular basis. It should be noted, however, that the relationship between editorial and advertising matter could still be somewhat imperfect. See, for example, the ad for a man's "rupture" cure on the "Woman and Her Ways" page of *The Evening Telegraph*, May 21, 1900, p. 5.

23. For classified advertising, see, as an example, the *Public Ledger*, May 17, 1880, p. 3. See, as examples, the *Public Ledger*, May 21, 1900, p. 18, for "Sports" and Anheuser Busch beer, and *The Evening Bulletin*, May 21, 1900, p.7, for an all-sports page with a plethora of male-targeted advertising. On attendance at sporting events, see Barth, *City People*, chap. 5. For examinations of the development of gendered space (including targeted advertising) on the pages of middle-class magazines during this period, see Damon-Moore, *Magazines for the Millions*, and Garvey, *The Adman in the Parlor*.

Chapter 6

1. John Cecil Holm recalling the early-twentieth century in *Sunday Best*, p. 231.

2. The annual sales figure can be found in the John Wanamaker papers, box 37, folder 19. Holm, *Sunday Best*, p. 134. For another example ("To Wanies for spats"), see

the entry for November 7, 1914, Margaret Moffat diary. Unlike in New York City, the retail area in Philadelphia did not move; the hub remained at Eighth and Market streets (where there were still three department stores as late as the 1970s) with the other two large stores a little further west on Market Street. For developments in New York City, see Robert A. M. Stern, Gregory Gilmartin, and John Montague Massengale, *New York 1900: Metropolitan Architecture and Urbanism 1890–1915* (New York: Rizzoli International Publications, 1983), pp. 190–94, and Ferry, *A History of the Department Store*, chap. 3, especially pp. 35–39.

3. These same five stores (with their suburban branches) would dominate Philadelphia retailing for almost the entire twentieth century. Snellenburg would be the first to close in 1961, followed by Lits in 1976, and Gimbels in 1986. The May Department Stores Company purchased John Wanamaker and Strawbridge & Clothier in 1995 and 1996, respectively, ending the period of locally owned department stores in Philadelphia.

4. *Oxford English Dictionary*, p. 472. See also Benson, *Counter Cultures*, chap. 1. Gibbons, *John Wanamaker*, vol. 1, p. 179. This discussion, of course, begs the question: What merchandise did a traditional (read mid nineteenth-century) dry goods store carry? In modern terms, dry goods stores began by selling textiles and related goods used to convert those fabrics into clothing, sheets, and draperies (such as buttons and decorations). The term "dry goods" is a North American one; the British equivalent is draper. See the *Oxford English Dictionary*, pp. 474 and 482.

5. Gimbel Brothers advertisement, *Public Ledger*, October 6, 1902, pp. 2 and 6. *A Book About the Gimbel Store Philadelphia: The Largest Retail Store in the World* (Philadelphia: Gimbel Brothers, July 1905), n.p. "Largest Retail Store in the World Opened," *Public Ledger*, October 7, 1902, p. 3. See also an article about Marks Brothers that uses the term, *Public Ledger*, October 20, 1900.

6. *The Great Department Store of Strawbridge & Clothier.*

7. *Boyd's Philadelphia City Directory* (Philadelphia: C. E. Howe, 1911–15).

8. For examples of John Wanamaker explicitly calling retailing a science, see *Golden Book of the Wanamaker Stores*, pp. 3, 100, 143, 160, and 175. John Wanamaker, "The Evolution of Mercantile Business," *Annals of the American Academy of Political and Social Science* (1900 annual meeting), pp. 123–35.

9. Wanamaker, "The Evolution of Mercantile Business," pp. 124–25.

10. Gimbel Brothers advertisement, *Public Ledger*, October 6, 1902, pp. 4 and 5. Snellenburg advertisement, *The Evening Bulletin*, May 16, 1910, p. 16. *A Friendly Guide-Book To the Wanamaker Store, Philadelphia 1913* (Philadelphia: John Wanamaker, 1913), p. 3. Like Snellenburg, the other major stores often used streets in their advertisements to illustrate the size of their buildings. Strawbridge & Clothier gave the following address in newspaper announcements: "Market Street, Eighth Street, Filbert Street," and Lit Brothers headed their ads "Market, Filbert, Seventh, Eighth." *The Evening Bulletin*, May 16, 1910, pp. 5 and 11.

11. *A Book About the Gimbel Store Philadelphia: The Largest Retail Store in the World*, n.p. *The Great Department Store of Strawbridge & Clothier*, p. 4. *A Friendly Guide-Book To the Wanamaker Store, Philadelphia 1913*, pp. 3 and 38, and *A Friendly Guide Book to Philadelphia and the Wanamaker Store* (Philadelphia: John Wanamaker, 1926), pp. 38–39. Wanamaker (and the other department stores) kept their ex-

isting structures open as they built around them. Wanamaker broke ground for the new store in 1902 and built it in three sections, dedicating the structure in 1911. Appel, *The Business Biography of John Wanamaker Founder and Builder*, p. 138.

12. *A Book About the Gimbel Store Philadelphia*. Announcement from Strawbridge & Clothier June 1910 catalogue and an undated flyer, Strawbridge & Clothier collection. *A Friendly Guide-Book To the Wanamaker Store, Philadelphia 1913*, pp. 10–11 and 36. *A Friendly Guide Book to Philadelphia and the Wanamaker Store*, (1926) p. 46. By 1927, all the major Philadelphia stores (except for Snellenburg) operated their own radio stations. Doubman and Whitaker, *The Organization and Operation of Department Stores*, p. 61.

13. *A Book About the Gimbel Store Philadelphia: The Largest Retail Store in the World*, n.p. *The Great Department Store of Strawbridge & Clothier*, p. 21. *Store Chat* 10 (September 15, 1916), p. 178.

14. *A Friendly Guide Book to Philadelphia and the Wanamaker Store*, pp. 56–58.

15. Entry for December 28, 1916, Mary B. Smith diary. Entry for December 28, 1917, Margaret Moffat diary, John Wanamaker papers. Other examples of shopping combined with lunch (often going with or meeting friends) include the entries for August 28, 1911; October 25, 1922; April 21, 1923; and October 30, 1923, Mary B. Smith diary; and the entries for June 27, 1914, and June 26, 1915, Margaret Moffat diary, John Wanamaker papers.

16. See, for example, the entry for January 26, 1907, and January 14, 1909, John L. Smith diary. Entry for December 20, 1924, Cyril Hingston Harvey diary.

17. Entry for January 7, 1904, John L. Smith diary. See Chapter 2 for a discussion of gendered space at train stations. The breakdown by gender of retail sales is found at "*Customers, women—percentage of in different lines*," Gibbons Card File Number 8, John Wanamaker papers (the card is undated but given the context, most likely describes the 1920s). The information on the facilities at Wanamaker comes from *What To See in Philadelphia* (Philadelphia: John Wanamaker, 1911), pp. 20–21, and *A Friendly Guide Book to Philadelphia and the Wanamaker Store* (1926), pp. 56–57. John Wanamaker did more explicit gendering of space than did most department stores. In New York, for example, when it built an addition to the old A. T. Stewart store, Wanamaker left all the women's departments in the original structure and declared it to be "exclusively a Women's Store." *Golden Book of the Wanamaker Stores*, pp. 296–97. When Strawbridge & Clothier opened its new restaurant in 1916, the firm also provided a special smoking room explicitly aimed at attracting a male clientele.

18. *The Great Department Store of Strawbridge & Clothier*, p. 29. *A Book About the Gimbel Store Philadelphia*. For the vast array of services at the John Wanamaker store, see *A Friendly Guide-Book To the Wanamaker Store, Philadelphia 1913*, p. 38. "*Phila. Store—playgrounds for children (1909–21)*," Gibbons Card File number 6, John Wanamaker papers.

19. "Went in town in afternoon. Finished 'The Vindication' in Wanamaker's Waiting room." Entry for July 13, 1916, Margaret Moffat diary, John Wanamaker papers. For phone calls, see the entry for July 13, 1916, Edith Shelhom (Garwood) diary. For an example of a tired "country" shopper relaxing in the Wanamaker waiting room, see the entry for April 5, 1906, Mary Roberts diary.

20. Gimbels introduced charge accounts in 1894, and both Lit and Snellenburg

offered them by 1899. In 1901, Strawbridge adopted charge tokens. "Business Ephemera" scrapbook, folder 2, John Wanamaker papers. For budget accounts, see *A Friendly Guide Book to Philadelphia and the Wanamaker Store* (1926), pp. 51–52, and Lief, *Family Business*, p. 148. On the rise of consumer credit generally, see Lendol Calder, *Financing the American Dream: A Cultural History of Consumer Credit* (Princeton: Princeton University Press, 1999).

21. For delivery in the 1870s, see *Store Chat* 12 (June 15, 1918), pp. 102–3; for 1912, see *Store Chat* 6 (June 15, 1912), p. 150, and 7 (August 15, 1913), p. 212. The information about the components of Wanamaker's delivery service can be found in the margins of an undated print (evidence within the print suggests it was made between 1911 and 1915), "Shops, Stores" file, Philadelphiana Collection, Print and Picture Collection, Free Library of Philadelphia. *Gift Suggestions for Christmas, 1912* (Philadelphia: John Wanamaker, 1912), John Wanamaker papers, box 70, folder 4.

22. For his niece Emma's 1916 non-delivery, T. Chalkley Matlack memoirs, vol. 1, p. 342; for her 1918 mistaken one, see vol. 1, p. 425. Wanamaker experimented with issuing pre-printed shipping stickers to regular delivery customers in 1904. "Business Ephemera" scrapbook, folder 3, John Wanamaker papers. For some examples of delivery and charge instructions directed at employees, see "Reminder For the Betterment of the Service, December, 1905," Strawbridge & Clothier collection; *Store Chat* 3 (February 15, 1909), pp. 50–51; and *Store Chat* 7 (November 15, 1913), pp. 287–89.

23. This is not to say that the working classes and the aristocracy never shopped at the Victorian department stores but only that the merchants targeted the largely middle-class mass market. Some of the wealthy shopped down and the working classes up, but the Victorian stores concentrated on their middle-class market. See Benson, *Counter Cultures*, p. 113.

24. The number of selling departments can be found in store directories, such as *Guide to Philadelphia and the Wanamaker Store* (Philadelphia: John Wanamaker, 1908) and *A Friendly Guide-Book To the Wanamaker Store, Philadelphia 1913*, pp. 39–40. The "bargain basement" can be found in *A Book About the Gimbel Store Philadelphia: The Largest Retail Store in the World*, n.p., and the "London Shop" at *What To See in Philadelphia*, p. 17. A good overview of twentieth-century selling departments can be found in Susan Porter Benson, "Palace of Consumption and Machine for Selling: The American Department Store, 1880–1940," *Radical History Review*, 21 (1979), pp. 199–221, 208–13.

25. The quotation is from the Gimbel Brothers advertisement, *Public Ledger*, October 6, 1902, p. 6. See also *A Book About the Gimbel Store Philadelphia*, n.p. A description of basement merchandising policy during the 1920s can be found in Doubman and Whitaker, *The Organization and Operation of Department Stores*, pp. 128–31. Advertisements for the bargain basements can be found in the May 17, 1920 editions of *The Evening Bulletin*, pp. 12 (Gimbels), 15 (Snellenburg), and 21 (Lits); and *The Evening Public Ledger*, pp. 9 (Gimbels) and 13 (Wanamaker). The first "true" bargain basement in Philadelphia was created by Gimbel Brothers in 1902. Before that, John Wanamaker and others had used parts of their below-ground floors from time to time as clearance centers but never as a separately constituted organization with its own departments. The use of the term "Subway Store" by Lits and Gimbels was an intriguing link between modernity (Philadelphia's subway had just opened) and

physical location. All five major Philadelphia department stores had underground entrances to the city's subway so people like the Holms could walk directly from the trains to the stores without ever having to go to the surface.

26. For an example of Wanamaker's assurance of how fresh the Subway Floor's air was in 1910, see *What To See in Philadelphia*, p. 11. Holm, *Sunday Best*, p. 231.

27. On the development of chain stores and their challenges to department stores, see Doubman and Whitaker, *The Organization and Operation of Department Stores*, pp. 6–8 and 287–95. On the development of Woolworth, see Karen Plunkett-Powell, *Remembering Woolworth's: A Nostalgic History of the World's Most Famous Five-and-Dime* (New York: St. Martin's Press, 1999) and John K. Winkler, *Five and Ten: The Fabulous Life of F. W. Woolworth* (New York: R. M. McBride, 1940). Entry for September 21, 1916, Albert J. Edmunds diary. Examples of other visits to five-and-tens can be found at the entries for June 16, 1910, Edith Shelhom (Garwood) diary; September 28, 1911, John L. Smith diary; and November 19, 1915, Margaret Moffat diary, John Wanamaker papers. For the Woolworth locations, see *Gopsill's Philadelphia City Directory for 1897* (Philadelphia: James Gopsill's Sons, 1897), p. 2177, and *1908 Boyd's Co-Partnership and Residence Business Directory of Philadelphia City* (Philadelphia: C. E. Howe, 1908), p. 1074*l*.

28. The quotations come from "*Department store—can be too rich in its furnishings*," Gibbons Card File number 8, John Wanamaker papers. The note card is undated, but given the context, is most likely from the mid 1920s. For information on Kensington, see Jamie Catrambone and Harry C. Silcox, *Kensington History: Stories and Memories* (Philadelphia: Brighton Press, 1996), especially chap. 2.

29. The description of the London Shop comes from *What To See in Philadelphia*, p. 17, and that of the Little Gray Salons, from *A Friendly Guide-Book To the Wanamaker Store, Philadelphia 1913*, pp. 17–19.

30. *Guide to Philadelphia and the Wanamaker Store*, n.p.

31. On efficiency in layout, see "Revolution Toward Efficiency" advertisement, *The Wanamaker Diary, 1912*, p. 31; *The Great Department Store of Strawbridge & Clothier*, pp. 3–4 and 29–30; Doubman and Whitaker, *The Organization and Operation of Department Stores*, especially chap. 7; and Paul H. Nystrom, *Retail Selling and Store Management* (New York: D. Appleton, 1919), chap. 13.

32. See Chapter 4 for a discussion of the creation of the annual retail calendar. For Gimbels' annual shirt sale, see the advertisement in the *Public Ledger*, May 16, 1920, pp. 18–19. The 12/12/12 card is in the William E. Stokes scrapbook, 1911–21. For a reproduction of the first Clover Day advertisement, see Lief, *Family Business*, p. 110. The quote is from Nystrom, *Retail Selling and Store Management*, p. 243.

33. The quotation comes from the T. Chalkley Matlack memoirs, vol. 1, p. 468 (Tuesday, April 29, 1919). The other Clover Day references are at vol. 1, p. 331 (Tuesday, August 29, 1916) and p. 363 (Wednesday, March 28, 1917).

34. Examples of these daily specials appear in advertising in the *Public Ledger* on the following dates: May 6, 13, and 20, 1910, pp. 6–7 (Gimbels' and Lits' Friday sales); May 10 and 17, 1910, p. 7 (Lits' Tuesday specials); May 7 and 21, 1920, p. 14 (Lits' Friday bargains); and May 4 and 18, 1920, p. 22 (Gimbels' Subway Store Tuesday).

35. "Mr. Wanamaker's Address To the Aisle Managers of the John Wanamaker Store Philadelphia In relation to the Saturday closing during July and August, May 27,

1914," John Wanamaker papers, box 73, folder 1. The store statistics come from *A Friendly Guide-Book To the Wanamaker Store, Philadelphia 1913*, pp. 10 and 35.

36. The literature on "scientific racism" can be quite frustrating as there is no one source that weaves together the scholarship in intellectual history, the history of science, cultural history, immigration history, and African-American history. I find the most useful starting point is Cotkin, *Reluctant Modernism*, chap. 3. Two other good recent works are Hawkins, *Social Darwinism in European and American Thought, 1860–1945*, and Degler, *In Search of Human Nature*.

37. None of Philadelphia's department stores placed ads in *The Philadelphia Tribune*, a leading African-American weekly paper, during the period 1912 to 1920. For a Strawbridge advertisement in an African-American musical program in 1893, see Jacob C. White, Jr. files, American Negro Historical Society papers, Leon Gardiner collection, box 6G, folder 13. DuBois, *The Philadelphia Negro*, p. 132.

38. *Public Ledger*, December 1, 1900, p. 3. *The Philadelphia Tribune*, December 14, 1912, p. 5. *Store Chat* (June 15, 1912), p. 164. James S. Stemons to Henry W. Wilbur, March 24, 1914, James Samuel Stemons papers, box 2, folder 3. On the portrayal of blacks in advertising in general in the period, see Marilyn Kern-Foxworth, *Aunt Jemima, Uncle Ben, and Rastus: Blacks in Advertising, Yesterday, Today, and Tomorrow* (Westport, Conn.: Greenwood Press, 1994), and M. M. Manring, *Slave in a Box: The Strange Career of Aunt Jemima* (Charlottesville: University of Virginia Press, 1998).

39. Gibbons, *John Wanamaker*, vol. 2, pp. 264–65.

Chapter 7

1. Holm, *Sunday Best*, pp. 133–34.

2. Holm, *Sunday Best*, pp. 5–6. *Visitors' Guide Book to Philadelphia* (Philadelphia: J. B. Lippincott, 1916), pp. 41–42.

3. Department of City Transit, *Report of Transit Commissioner, City of Philadelphia, July 1913* (Philadelphia: City of Philadelphia, 1913).

4. Holm, *Sunday Best*, p. 133.

5. For a brief history of the PRT and its predecessors, see Harold E. Cox, *Early Electric Cars of Philadelphia, 1885–1911* (priv. pub., 1969), pp. 2–3. For a more detailed, contemporary account, see W. W. Wheatly, "The Philadelphia Rapid Transit System," *Street Railway Journal*, 21: 472–77, 502–7, 555–60, and 588–95. See also Mervin E. Borgnis, *The Near-Side Car and the Legacy of Thomas E. Mitten* (priv. pub., 1994). The lines operated by the PRT can be found in the *PRT Route Guide and Owl Car Time-Table* (Philadelphia: Philadelphia Rapid Transit, 1920).

6. On the P&WC, see Ronald DeGraw, *Red Arrow: The First Hundred Years 1848–1948* (Glendale, Calif.: Interurban Press, 1985), chaps. 2–5. For Public Service, see James C. G. and Richard Conniff, *The Energy People: A History of PSE&G* (Newark, N.J.: Public Service Electric and Gas Company, 1978); William J. Coxey, "Camden Area Trolleys" in William J. Coxey, ed., *West Jersey Rails* (Oaklyn, N.J.: West Jersey Chapter, National Railway Historical Society, n.d.), pp. 30–33; and Edward T. Francis, "The Camden Trolley Lines," *The Marker*, 24 (January 1952). Examples of minor lines

can be found in Harry Foesig and Harold E. Cox, *Trolleys of Montgomery County, Pennsylvania* (priv. pub., 1968).

7. For a brief history of the subway-elevated, see Harold E. Cox, *The Road From Upper Darby: The Story of the Market Street Subway-Elevated* (priv. pub., 1967).

8. *The Official Guide of the Railways and Steam Navigation Lines of the United States, Porto Rico, Canada, Mexico and Cuba* (New York: National Railway Publication Company, 1906).

9. Similar cuts in service could be found on the Reading's Mullica Hill (New Jersey) and Chester (Pennsylvania) lines. Compare the *Travelers' Official Guide of the Railway and Steam Navigation Lines in the United States and Canada* (New York: National Railway Publication Company, 1893), with *The Official Guide of the Railways and Steam Navigation Lines of the United States, Porto Rico, Canada, Mexico and Cuba* (1906). Information on the Newtown Square branch can be found in Philip W. Klaus, Jr., "The Newtown Square Branch," *The High Line*, 7 (Winter 1986–87), pp. 3–15. "Report of the Committee on Conducting Transportation, in Co-operation with the Passenger Department, on the Subject 'How Should We Treat Trolley Competition?'," p. 5, Penn Central Railroad collection (MG 286), Association of Transportation Officers files, box 3, Pennsylvania State Archives.

10. The story of the PRR electrification can be found in Michael Bezilla, *Electric Traction on the Pennsylvania Railroad, 1895–1968* (University Park: The Pennsylvania State University Press, 1980), chap. 3, and George Gibbs, "The Philadelphia-Paoli Electrification of the Pennsylvania Railroad Company," *The Electric Journal*, 13 (February 1916), pp. 68–78. Townsend, *The Old "Main Line,"* p. 106.

11. Conniff and Conniff, *The Energy People.*

12. The concept of an elite borderland as something different from a typical middle-class suburb is from John R. Stilgoe, *Borderland: Origins of the American Suburb, 1820–1939* (New Haven, Conn.: Yale University Press, 1988).

13. See the introduction to Part II for a discussion of rising working-class wages in the early twentieth century. On the evolving nature of West Philadelphia, see the following works by Margaret S. Marsh: "The Transformation of Community: Suburbanization and Urbanization in Northern West Philadelphia, 1880–1930," (Ph.D. diss., Rutgers University, 1975) and "The Impact of the Market Street 'El' on Northern West Philadelphia: Environmental Change and Social Transformation, 1900–1930," in Cutler and Gillette, *The Divided Metropolis*, pp. 169–92.

14. A map illustrating this pattern of development can be found in *The Atlas of Pennsylvania* (Philadelphia: Temple University Press, 1989), pp. 232–33.

15. Entry for January 27, 1899, John L. Smith diary. Entry for December 30, 1904, Mary B. Smith diary.

16. Entry for April 14, 1901, John L. Smith diary. Howard Edwards memoirs, vol. 2, p. 355, (entry written in 1904).

17. These excursions were so common, virtually any week picked at random from the Mary B. Smith diary will contain at least one.

18. *1912 Wanamaker Diary*, pp. 12–26, Edith Shelhom (Garwood) collection.

19. Because of racial discrimination in housing, the African-American bourgeoisie continued to live in and around Center City in large numbers. The final section of this chapter will look at this subject in more detail.

20. On the rise of "cheap amusements" nationally (both focus on New York City), see Kathy Lee Peiss, *Cheap Amusements: Working Women and Leisure in New York City, 1880 to 1920* (Philadelphia: Temple University Press, 1986) and Nasaw, *Going Out.* Most of Philadelphia's "cheap amusements" were located on the fringes of Center City and can be plotted using city directories and advertisements in the general circulation press.

21. On amusement parks, see Schlereth, *Victorian America,* pp. 237–41. A contemporary article that puts the park in a national context is "Street Railway Parks and Pleasure Resorts," *Street Railway Journal,* June 1, 1901, 27: 662–65. A short book that looks at some of the New Jersey parks is Bailey and Parkhurst, *Early South Jersey Amusement Parks.*

22. Although people from the suburbs and the hinterland visited these amusement parks, they never did so as frequently as did their city counterparts. Members of the suburban and rural middle class went to the parks very occasionally to see the attractions, to try new rides, and to hear the music, while their urban brothers and sisters used the parks a number of times a week in July and August to escape the summer heat. On the People's Traction Company's (a corporate predecessor of the PRT that initially developed the park) plans for the park, see the *Public Ledger,* August 6, 1895, p. 2. For trolley service to the park see Foesig and Cox, *Trolleys of Montgomery County, Pennsylvania,* pp. 82–87. For an article on the new terminal, see "Improved New Car Terminal at Willow Grove, Philadelphia Rapid Transit," *Street Railway Journal,* August 27, 1904, 24: 297–98.

23. On respectability at the park see Thompson, *Willow Grove Park.* For the view that Coney Island was a more liminal place, see Kasson, *Amusing the Million.* Barnitz memoirs, p. 67.

24. Barnitz memoirs, p. 67. Entry for July 22, 1897, Mary B. Smith diary. Entry for August 21, 1897, Mary Roberts diary. Entries for September 2, 1897, and June 27, 1898, Septimus Winner diary.

25. In 1899, the average wage for a factory worker in Philadelphia was $441.10. See note 2 to the introduction of Part II for the source of this data.

26. Diarists in my sampling recorded seven visits to Woodside Park during the nineteenth century, compared with three during the twentieth. All three of the twentieth-century visits were made by poorer members of the bourgeoisie. See the entries for August 26, 1897, Mary Roberts diary; June 14 and August 28, 1897, Mary B. Smith diary; April 30, 1899, John L. Smith diary; June 8 and August 15, 1899, Septimus Winner diary; August 19, 1899, Edwin C. Jellett diary; August 23, 1910 and August 31, 1913, Albert J. Edmunds diary; and August 6, 1918, Margaret Moffat diary. On the Fairmount Park trolley, see Harold E. Cox, *The Fairmount Park Trolley: A Unique Philadelphia Experiment* (priv. pub., 1970).

27. For train service, see 1906 and 1915 *Official Guides.* Entry for August 5, 1917, John L. Smith diary. A (perhaps overly romantic) description of an excursion train ride can be found in Holm, *Sunday Best,* pp. 69–70. For examples of Sunday excursion train memories from people raised in south Jersey, see "Memories of Mildred Schwaemmle," p. 45, and Clemens Titzck, Jr., "Seventy Years Ago," p. 18, *Haddon Heights Remembered* (Haddon Heights, N.J.: Haddon Heights Historical Society,

1990). The 1904 figure comes from Samuel Rea to Theodore Voorhees, January 16, 1905, Reading Company collection (Hagley), box 941, folder 4.

28. Holm, *Sunday Best*, p. 50. See, for example, the *Public Ledger Summer Resort Directory Section 1914*, Library, Historical Society of Pennsylvania. Entries for July 21, July 24, July 31, August 8, August 11, August 14, August 19, August 31, September 4, September 7, and September 15, 1908, Mary B. Smith diary. In 1919 the Smith family spent most of the summer at Island Heights and used the Pennsylvania Railroad to stay in contact with the city; see, for example, the entry for July 21, 1919, Mary B. Smith diary. Two years later, they summered at Wildwood Crest; see the entries June 25, June 28, July 3, July 6, July 14, July 18, August 11, and September 7, 1921, Mary B. Smith diary. Edwin Jellett's friend Clara spent a few weeks at the religious resort of Ocean Grove (near Asbury Park) in the summer of 1907 and Edwin visited her by train. Entries for July 6 and July 21, 1907, Edwin C. Jellett diary. Edith Shelhom (then a teenager living in suburban New Jersey) spent a few weeks in Asbury Park with relatives in 1913; see the entries for July 3, July 7, and July 12, 1913, Edith Shelhom (Garwood) diary. Margaret Moffat (while a high school student) went to Ocean Grove by train for two weeks in 1914. Entries for August 8 and August 22, 1914, Margaret Moffat diary. While a college student, Moffat made a similar trip a few years later; see the entries for August 10 and August 23, 1917, Margaret Moffat diary.

29. *Official Guide June 1906* and *Official Guide January 1915*. For relative passenger load, see "Comparative Statement of Easter Business to Seashore Points," Reading Company collection (Hagley), box 943 (data for 1906 and 1907). A. M. Heston, *Heston's Hand Book Atlantic City Illustrated* (Philadelphia: A. M. Heston, 1902), pp. 30–31.

30. Bessie Newburger Rothchild memoirs. Heston, *Heston's Hand Book Atlantic City Illustrated* (1902), p. 30.

31. Entry for July 19, 1908, John L. Smith diary. Entry for August 31, 1920, Albert J. Edmunds diary.

32. It was tracing this route through the park on city maps, taken in whole or in part quite often by the West Philadelphia Smiths and other diarists, that helped me realize how easy it was for middle-class Philadelphians to blur the image of "their" city—Holm's "great big stretch of middle class"—with the physical reality of the heterogeneous metropolis. The houses on the main streets on which the trolleys operated would have been overwhelmingly middle class, with the working-class homes largely hidden on smaller side streets.

33. *Visitors' Guide Book To Philadelphia*, p. 41. "Thirty Miles Around Philadelphia on the Lines of the Pennsylvania Railroad" (Philadelphia: Pennsylvania Railroad, 1916), Library, Historical Society of Pennsylvania. Historians have closely linked Philadelphia with the development of railroad suburbs. See, as examples, Jackson, *Crabgrass Frontier*, pp. 90–92; Robert Fishman, *Bourgeois Utopias: The Rise and Fall of Suburbia* (New York: Basic Books, 1987), chap. 5; Marsh, *Suburban Lives*, and Gary R. Hovinen, "Suburbanization in Greater Philadelphia 1880–1941," *Journal of Historical Geography* (April 1985), pp. 174–95.

34. According to 1920 population data derived from published census figures, the total population of suburban municipalities with large middle-class populations was 253,451 compared with 851,855 in identifiable middle-class wards in the city.

While both numbers clearly contain some non-middle-class people, they can serve as reasonable surrogates as there is no reason to suspect that they are wrong by order of magnitude.

35. Townsend, *The Old "Main Line,"* p. 106. *Report of Transit Commissioner, City of Philadelphia, July 1913,* vol. 1, p. 115.

36. Howard Edwards memoirs, vol. 2, p. 405. Entry for June 6, 1903, John L. Smith diary. The next year, Smith again took the trolley to explore the new construction in West Philadelphia, May 21, 1904. *Report of Transit Commissioner, City of Philadelphia, July 1913,* vol. 1, p. 118. A booster publication claimed that this type of construction was typical of the 9,000 homes built each year. Frank H. Taylor and Wilfred H. Schoff, *The Port and City of Philadelphia* (Philadelphia, 1912), p. 77.

37. For information on the Smith house, see *Atlas of the City of Philadelphia* (Philadelphia: G. W. Bromley, 1910), plate 24, and the survey for policy number 7959, Mutual Assurance Company collection (for a similar home at 4504 Pine Street). For both Germantown residences, see *Atlas of the City of Philadelphia* (Bromley, 1910), plate 36.

38. "Thirty Miles Around Philadelphia on the Lines of the Pennsylvania Railroad," pp. 41–42. On the opening of the line, see Burgess and Kennedy, *Centennial History of the Pennsylvania Railroad Company,* pp. 413–14. Because Cynwyd, like many of Philadelphia's suburban communities, is and was not an independent municipality (in Cynwyd's case it is part of Lower Merion Township), charting population growth can be difficult. The 1900 figure comes from the manuscript census, which lists 103 households with 399 family members and total population (including servants and boarders) of 505 for the area around Cynwyd train station and roughly what the local civic association would later define as Cynwyd in its 1909 and 1912–13 directories. The *1912–1913 Neighborhood Club Directory* (Bala-Cynwyd, Pa.: The Neighborhood Club, 1912) lists 396 households with 1094 family members in Cynwyd. Extrapolating from the manuscript census data, I would estimate there were at least 200 servants and boarders not listed in the directory.

39. "Thirty Miles Around Philadelphia on the Lines of the Pennsylvania Railroad," pp. 5, 90, and 141. On the importance of non-rail infrastructure for suburbanization, see Warner, *Streetcar Suburbs,* pp. 29–31.

40. *Cynwyd: Modern Suburban Homes* (Cynwyd, Pa.: Lower Merion Realty Company, [1910]), pp. 2 and 8, "Bala-Cynwyd II" file, Lower Merion Historical Society. Entry for June 17, 1906, Albert J. Edmunds diary. On street paving in Lower Merion, see *The Government of Lower Merion Township, Pennsylvania: A Report of a Survey by the Bureau of Municipal Research of Philadelphia* (Ardmore, Pa.: Lower Merion Township, 1922). The complaint about dust comes from a typescript of a 1966 address on the history of Bala-Cynwyd by William J. Phillips in the "Bala-Cynwyd" file, Lower Merion Historical Society.

41. *The Government of Lower Merion Township, Pennsylvania* gives a good overview of Cynwyd's infrastructure in the 1920s. Additional information (particularly about non-governmental entities) can be found in the *Bala-Cynwyd Directory 1912–1913.*

42. Entry for October 27, 1918, Mary B. Smith diary. Entry for March 30, 1919, John L. Smith diary.

43. The timetable can be found in the Reading collection, library, Historical Society of Pennsylvania. At least one more observation can be drawn from this little booklet: the importance of railroad time to members of the bourgeoisie. The initials "A. J. E." on the cover belong to Albert J. Edmunds, who was the librarian at the Historical Society and is one of the diarists I used in this study. Edmunds, a regular user of the Reading, asserted ownership over this timetable through these initials. The press run is encoded in small type on the folder.

44. Jellett's diary makes fascinating reading on this issue because he habitually recorded his trips in great detail. The details of one of many Schwenksville trips can be found at the entry for June 1, 1902.

45. Pennsylvania Railroad Form 40, Philadelphia, West Chester, and Phoenixville, effective June 13, 1886.

46. Droege, *Passenger Terminals and Trains*, p. 328. Baltimore & Ohio Railroad T.T. 8, Royal Blue Trains, effective April 1, 1910. *Official Guide June 1906*, pp. 333 and 415. *Official Guide January 1915*, p. 327.

47. Entries for July 6, 1902 and February 15, 1906, John L. Smith diary. For Chinatown visits, see, for example, the entries for September 18, 1910, John L. Smith diary, and April 17, 1916, Clair Wilcox diary.

48. James Samuel Stemons to his sister, September 2, 1912, James Samuel Stemons Papers, box 1, folder 18. Stemons' observation is supported by DuBois' 1897 study of the city; see DuBois, *The Philadelphia Negro*, secs. 29 and 44–47. Section 46 also includes a brief discussion of social class. Entries for May 18 and 30, 1917, Albert J. Edmunds diary. For a less heated (but still quite clear) expression of housing discrimination, see James Dobson to C. Gordon Stafford, July 10, 1918, James Dobson letterbook, p. 219.

49. Howard Edwards memoirs, vol. 2, p. 355.

50. 1900 Manuscript Census. Entries for October 16 and November 26, 1923; February 24, 1925; January 17, January 26, January 27, January 29, January 31, February 21, April 17, April 29, June 20, September 24, and October 15, 1926; May 7 and October 15, 1927; May 17 and October 15, 1930; May 14 and October 15, 1932; and November 3 and November 29, 1951, Mary B. Smith diary. For an article on the 1923 zoning meeting, see "West Phila calls for improvement," *Public Ledger*, November 20, 1923, p. 2.

51. For a similar movement from private to public action by the elite in New York City, see Gregory F. Gilmartin, *Shaping the City: New York and the Municipal Art Society* (New York: Clarkson Potter, 1995), chap. 11.

52. This brief overview of city planning in Philadelphia has been greatly influenced by Warner, *The Private City*, pp. 205–10. A work that gives an overview of the City Beautiful movement nationally is William H. Wilson, *The City Beautiful Movement* (Baltimore: Johns Hopkins University Press, 1989). A recent collection of essays that explores planning more generally is Robert Fishman, ed., *The American Planning Tradition: Culture and Policy* (Washington: The Woodrow Wilson Center Press, 2000).

53. *The Government of Lower Merion Township, Pennsylvania*, p. 361. See also pp. 308–10 for a discussion of zoning and the city. A brief account of Philadelphia's tentative first steps toward zoning can be found in Cutler and Gillette, *The Divided Metropolis*, pp. 256–66. On the 1923 battle for zoning, see "Growing need seen for

zoning in city," *Public Ledger*, April 27, 1923, p. 2; "Ask quick action on the zoning bill," *Public Ledger*, October 17, 1923, p. 2; "Urge limit here for skyscrapers," *Public Ledger*, October 23, 1923 ; "Council keeping hands off zoning," *Public Ledger*, October 26, 1923, p. 2; "Board of Zoning created for city" and "Zoning issue pressed," *Public Ledger*, November 2, 1923, p. 2; and "Housing experts advocate zoning," *Public Ledger*, December 8, 1923, p. 2. For an early report of the Philadelphia Zoning Commission containing a wonderful taxonomy of space along with the logic behind it, see the *Third Annual Report of Hary A. Mackey, Mayor of Philadelphia* (Philadelphia: City of Philadelphia, 1930), pp. 775–82.

Postlude

1. Cyril Hingston Harvey diary.

2. This narrative is derived from the entries for April 19, 1925, April 15, April 17, June 10, June 14, July 15, July 17, and August 23, 1926, Cyril Hingston Harvey diary; *Public Ledger*, August 23 and 24, 1926; "Mills Explains Traffic Signals," *Public Ledger*, November 16, 1923, p. 2; "Highway Safety," *The Haddon Gazette*, April 17, 1924, p. 2; "New Parking Regulations on King's Highway," *The Haddon Gazette*, July 15, 1926; "Aged Woman Seriously Hurt When Struck by Automobile," *The Haddon Gazette*, July 29, 1926, p. 1; "New Traffic Regulations on King's Highway Satisfactory," *The Haddon Gazette*, August 5, 1926, p. 1; *The Wanamaker Diary 1924* (Philadelphia: John Wanamaker, 1923), pp. 141–42; and the Sesquicentennial Collection, Free Library of Philadelphia.

Conclusion

1. Entry for August 6, 1911, John L. Smith diary.

2. On the need for integrating political and social history, see William E. Leuchtenburg, "The Pertinence of Political History: Reflections on the Significance of the State in America," *The Journal of American History*, 73 (December 1986), pp. 585–600.

3. The use of the concept of a paradigm to explain sudden shifts in thought originally came from the history of science. See Thomas S. Kuhn, *The Structure of Scientific Revolutions* (Chicago: University of Chicago Press, 1962). Subsequently, scholars in other fields have borrowed the concept; see, for example, Robert L. Beisner, *From the Old Diplomacy to the New, 1865–1900* (Arlington Heights, Ill.: AHM Publishing, 1975).

Bibliography

Secondary sources are listed in the notes. This bibliography consists of both the published and unpublished primary sources I consulted in the course of this study.

Manuscripts, Oral Histories, and Archives

American Negro Historical Society Papers. Historical Society of Pennsylvania.

Armstrong, William G. Diary, 1880–88. Historical Society of Pennsylvania.

Askew, Mary Brown. Diary, 1880–85. Historical Society of Pennsylvania.

Bailey, Gilbert S. Papers. Historical Society of Pennsylvania.

Bala-Cynwyd file. Lower Merion Historical Society.

Barnitz, Eugenia L. Memoirs. Historical Society of Pennsylvania.

Bascom (Warley) Sons Upholsterers. Financial Records, 1903–10. Balch Institute for Ethnic Studies.

Bernheimer, Leo G. Diary, 1890–98. Philadelphia Jewish Archives Center.

Broomal, Anna E. Scrapbooks. Delaware County Historical Society.

Burlington County Vertical File. Burlington County Free Library.

Caravelli, Fred. Oral history transcript. Haddonfield Public Library.

Centennial Ephemera Collection. Historical Society of Pennsylvania.

Central High School files. Library. Historical Society of Pennsylvania.

Chew, Robert B. Oral history transcript. Haddonfield Public Library.

Cleary, James. Papers. Balch Institute for Ethnic Studies.

Crothers Family Collection. Historical Society of Pennsylvania.

Deering, Laurence A. Diary, 1909. Delaware County Historical Society.

Dobson, James. Papers. Historical Society of Pennsylvania.

Dow, J. William. Oral history transcript. Haddonfield Public Library.

Edmunds, Albert J. Diary, 1885–1920. Historical Society of Pennsylvania.

Edwards, Howard. Memoirs. Historical Society of Pennsylvania.

Evans, William B. Scrapbook. Delaware County Historical Society.

Garwood, W. E. Oral history transcript. Haddonfield Public Library.
Geary, A. B. Scrapbooks. Delaware County Historical Society.
Gilbert, Mrs. Bennett H. R. Oral history transcript. Haddonfield Public Library.
Greenfield, Albert M. Papers. Historical Society of Pennsylvania.
Harvey, Cyril Hingston. Diary, 1924–26. Historical Society of Haddonfield.
Heston Room. Atlantic City Public Library.
Hinch Family. Diary, 1881, 1897. Society Collection. Historical Society of Pennsylvania.
Jellett, Edwin C. Diary, 1876–1917. Historical Society of Pennsylvania.
Krause, William Augustus. Oral history transcript. Haddonfield Public Library.
Laughlin, Mrs. Tucker C. Diary, 1888–90. Historical Society of Pennsylvania.
Lehman, Edwin W. Diary, 1886–87. Historical Society of Pennsylvania.
Local history room. Collingwood Free Public Library.
Local history room. Haddonfield Public Library.
Local history room. Haddon Heights Public Library.
Local history room. Lansdowne Public Library.
Lockwood, William E. Diary, 1881–89. Chester County Historical Society.
Long, Sylvia Smith. Oral history transcript. Haddonfield Public Library.
MacManus, Susan R. Diary 1877–81. Historical Society of Pennsylvania.
Magee, Paul V. Oral history transcript. Haddonfield Public Library.
Main Line History Collection. Ludington Library (Bryn Mawr, Pa.).
Map Collection. Free Library of Philadelphia.
Matlack, T. Chalkley. Memoirs. Historical Society of Pennsylvania.
McMichael, Clayton. Papers. Historical Society of Pennsylvania.
Mills, Charles K. Scrapbooks. Historical Society of Pennsylvania.
Mills, Maude Frisby. Collection. Afro-American Historical and Cultural Museum.
Moore Tatem Brigham. Scrapbooks. Historical Society of Haddonfield.
Morley, Katie. Scrapbook. Delaware County Historical Society.
Music Department. Free Library of Philadelphia.
Mutual Assurance Company surveys. Historical Society of Pennsylvania.
Name files. Delaware County Historical Society.
Newmayer, Henrietta Ulman. Papers. Balch Institute for Ethnic Studies.
Ocean Grove annual reports, 1880–96. Collingwood Free Public Library.
Parry, George T. Diary, 1880, 1886. Historical Society of Pennsylvania.
Passmore, Elizabeth B. Diary, 1891–95. Chester County Historical Society.
Penn Central Railroad Collection. Pennsylvania State Archives. Pennsylvania Historical and Museum Commission.
Penn Central Railroad Collection. Railroad Museum of Pennsylvania. Pennsylvania Historical and Museum Commission.
Pennsylvania Railroad. Annual reports. 1852–81. Library. Historical Society of Pennsylvania.
Pennsylvania Railroad. Timetables. Library. Historical Society of Pennsylvania.
Pennsylvania Railroad Collection. Hagley Museum and Library.
Pennsylvania Room. Gladwyne Free Library.
Pennypacker, James A. Oral history transcript. Haddonfield Public Library.
Philadelphia & Reading Railroad. Annual reports, 1877–82. Library. Historical Society of Pennsylvania.

Philadelphia & Reading Railroad. Timetables and Brochures. Library. Historical Society of Pennsylvania.

Philadelphia, Germantown and Norristown Railroad. Annual reports, 1851–64. Library. Historical Society of Pennsylvania.

Philadelphia Rapid Transit Company. Brochures. Library. Historical Society of Pennsylvania.

Philadelphia, Wilmington & Baltimore Railroad. Annual reports, 1839–81. Library. Historical Society of Pennsylvania.

Philadelphia, Wilmington & Baltimore Railroad. Timetables and brochures. Library. Historical Society of Pennsylvania.

Railroad file. Lower Merion Historical Society.

Railway & Locomotive Historical Society Collection. California State Railroad Museum Library.

Reading Company Collection. Hagley Museum and Library.

Roberts, Mary. Diary, 1894–1911. Chester County Historical Society.

Rothchild, Bessie Newburger. Memoirs. Philadelphia Jewish Archives Center.

Schecter, Minnie. Memoirs. Philadelphia Jewish Archives Center.

Sellers, Sarah P. Scrapbooks. Delaware County Historical Society.

Shelhom, Edith. Diary, 1910–16, 1924. Historical Society of Haddonfield.

Shelton, Bernice Dutrieuille. Papers. Balch Institute for Ethnic Studies.

Smith, A. Lewis. Papers. Historical Society of Pennsylvania.

Smith, H. Sidney. Scrapbook. Delaware County Historical Society.

Smith, John L. Diary, 1876–1921. Historical Society of Pennsylvania.

Smith, Mary B. Diary, 1894–1953. Historical Society of Pennsylvania.

Stackhouse, David Ludlow. Oral history transcript. Haddonfield Public Library.

Stemons, James Samuel. Papers. Balch Institute for Ethnic Studies.

Stokes, William E. Scrapbooks. Historical Society of Pennsylvania.

Strawbridge & Clothier Collection. Hagley Museum & Library.

Timetable Collection. California State Railroad Museum Library.

Township file. Delaware County Historical Society.

University of Pennsylvania files. Library. Historical Society of Pennsylvania.

Waite, Laura Virginia Touchstone. Memoirs. Delaware County Historical Society.

Wallin, Anna. Scrapbook. Balch Institute for Ethnic Studies.

Wanamaker, John. Papers. Historical Society of Pennsylvania.

West Chester & Philadelphia Railroad. Annual reports, 1860–78. Library. Historical Society of Pennsylvania.

Wilcox, Clair. Diary, 1915–17. Delaware County Historical Society.

Wilson, John A. Diary, 1876–96. Historical Society of Pennsylvania.

Winner, Septimus. Diary. 1880–1901. Historical Society of Pennsylvania.

Pictures and Graphics

Airplane Photographic Studies. Print and Picture Collection. Art Department. Free Library of Philadelphia.

Ballinger Company Collection. Athenaeum of Philadelphia.
Campbell Collection. Historical Society of Pennsylvania.
Castner, Samuel. Collection. Free Library of Philadelphia.
Centennial Collection. Print and Picture Collection. Art Department. Free Library of Philadelphia.
Centennial Railroad Depot Collection. Athenaeum of Philadelphia.
Detrieuille Family Photographs. Balch Institute for Ethnic Studies.
Dixon Collection. Athenaeum of Philadelphia.
Evans, Benjamin R. Collection. Historical Society of Pennsylvania.
Furness, Frank. Collection. Historical Society of Pennsylvania.
Heston Room. Atlantic City Public Library.
Historic American Buildings Survey microfilm. Free Library of Philadelphia.
Hutton, Addison. Papers. Athenaeum of Philadelphia.
Kennedy, David J. Collection. Historical Society of Pennsylvania.
Local history room. Collingwood Free Public Library.
Local history room. Haddonfield Public Library.
Local history room. Haddon Heights Public Library.
Local history room. Lansdowne Public Library.
Main Line History Collection. Ludington Library (Bryn Mawr, Pa.).
Map Collection. Free Library of Philadelphia.
Morron and Meigs Collection. Athenaeum of Philadelphia.
Naef Collection. Historical Society of Pennsylvania.
Penn Central Railroad Collection. Pennsylvania State Archives. Pennsylvania Historical and Museum Commission.
Penn Central Railroad Collection. Railroad Museum of Pennsylvania. Pennsylvania Historical and Museum Commission.
Pennsylvania Railroad Collection. Hagley Museum and Library.
Perkins Collection. Historical Society of Pennsylvania.
Philadelphiana Collection. Print and Picture Collection. Art Department. Free Library of Philadelphia.
Philadelphia Photographs. Temple University Urban Archives.
Philadelphia Railroad Photographs. Historical Society of Pennsylvania.
Phoenix Bridge Company Collection. Athenaeum of Philadelphia.
Photograph and Lantern Slide Collection. Atlantic County Historical Society.
Postcard Collection. Pennsylvania State Archives. Pennsylvania Historical and Museum Commission.
Postcard Collection. Print and Picture Collection. Art Department. Free Library of Philadelphia.
Print and Picture Collection. Free Library of Philadelphia.
Reading Company Collection. Hagley Museum and Library.
Reading Railroad Collection. Railroad Museum of Pennsylvania. Pennsylvania Historical and Museum Commission.
Sesquicentennial Collection. Print and Picture Collection. Art Department. Free Library of Philadelphia.
Smith, John Gibb, Jr. Collection. Print and Picture Collection. Art Department. Free Library of Philadelphia.

Society Print Collection. Historical Society of Pennsylvania.
Strawbridge & Clothier Collection. Hagley Museum & Library.
Suburban Photographs. Temple University Urban Archives.
Wanamaker, John. Papers. Historical Society of Pennsylvania.

Newspapers

The Advertising Gazette. Haddonfield, N.J. 1900.
American Railroad Journal. New York. 1834–36, 1855, 1862, 1865, 1867, 1868, 1875–77.
The Basket. Haddonfield, N.J. 1876, 1888–90.
The Call. Philadelphia. 1900.
The Daily News. Philadelphia. 1900, 1910, 1920.
The Evening Bulletin. Philadelphia, 1880, 1890, 1893, 1895, 1900, 1910, 1920, 1926, 1931, 1982.
The Evening Public Ledger. Philadelphia. 1920.
The Evening Star. Philadelphia. 1910.
The Evening Telegraph. Philadelphia. 1880, 1890, 1900, 1910.
The Evening Times. Philadelphia. 1910.
The Haddonfield News. Haddonfield, N.J. 1893–94.
The Haddon Gazette. Haddonfield, N.J. 1902, 1909, 1913–20, 1923–1924, 1926.
The Haddon Monthly. Haddonfield, N.J. 1901.
The North American. Philadelphia. 1880, 1890, 1900, 1910, 1920.
The Philadelphia Evening Item. 1910, 1920.
The Philadelphia Inquirer. 1876, 1880, 1890, 1893–95, 1900, 1910, 1920.
The Philadelphia Record. 1880, 1890, 1900, 1910, 1920, 1926.
The Philadelphia Tribune. 1912–20.
The Press. Philadelphia. 1880, 1890, 1894, 1900, 1910, 1920.
Public Ledger. Philadelphia. 1875–78, 1880–83, 1890, 1893–1905, 1910, 1914–15, 1920, 1923–24, 1926.
The Street Railway Journal. New York. 1888–90, 1905–09.
The Times. Philadelphia. 1880, 1890, 1900.
The Tricity Sun. Westmont, N.J. 1925.
The Tribune. Haddonfield, N.J. 1898, 1904, 1906, 1910.

Other Published Period Works

Appendix to the Journal of the Proceedings of the United States Centennial Commission, at Philadelphia, 1872. Philadelphia: E. C. Markley, 1872.
Appleton's Railway and Steam Navigation Guide. New York: D. Appleton & Co., 1869, 1872.
Atlas of 6th 9th & 10th Wards, Philadelphia. Philadelphia: Elvino V. Smith, 1921.
Atlas of the City of Philadelphia: Complete in One Volume. Philadelphia: G. W. Bromley & Co., 1895, 1910.
Atlas of the 24th & 17th Wards West Philadelphia. Philadelphia: J. D. Scott, 1878.

Atlas of West Philadelphia including the 24th & 27th Wards. Philadelphia: G. M. Hopkins, 1872.

Authorized Visitors Guide to the Centennial Exhibition and Philadelphia, 1876. Philadelphia: J. B. Lippincott, 1876.

Auto Road Map of Philadelphia and Vicinity. Philadelphia: W. Nuneviller Co., 1915.

Backstage with a Great Newspaper. Philadelphia: The Philadelphia Record, 1936.

Baist's Atlas of the City of Philadelphia. Philadelphia: Baist, 1888.

Bala-Cynwyd Directory 1912–1913. Bala-Cynwyd, Pa.: The Neighborhood Club, 1912.

Berg, Walter G. *Buildings and Structures of American Railroads: A Reference Book.* New York: John Wiley & Sons, 1893.

A Book About the Gimbel Store Philadelphia: The Largest Retail Store in the World. Philadelphia: Gimbel Brothers, 1905.

Boyd's Philadelphia City Directory. Philadelphia: C. E. Boyd, 1900, 1908–15, 1918.

Bullitt, William C. *It's Not Done.* New York: Harcourt, Brace, 1926.

Burlington Directory 1910. Burlington, N.J.: Enterprise Company, 1910.

Catalogue of the Central High School of Philadelphia, 1898–1899. Philadelphia, [1898].

Catalogue of the University of Pennsylvania, 1897–98. Philadelphia: University of Pennsylvania, 1897.

Centennial City: Syckelmoore's Illustrated Hand Book of Philadelphia. Philadelphia: Calxton, Remsen & Haffelfinger, 1874.

The Centennial Exhibition and the Northern Central and Pennsylvania Railroads. Philadelphia: Pennsylvania Railroad, 1876.

Childs, George W. *Recollections.* Philadelphia: J. B. Lippincott, 1890.

Combination Atlas Map of Burlington County, New Jersey. Philadelphia: J. D. Scott, 1876.

Crawford, Andrew Wright. "The Interrelationship of Housing and City Planning." *Annals of the American Academy of Political Science.* 51 (January 1914), pp. 162–71.

Cyclers' and Drivers' Best Routes in and around Philadelphia. Philadelphia: Frank H. Taylor, 1896.

Cynwyd: Modern Suburban Homes. Cynwyd, Pa.: Lower Merion Realty Company, [1910].

Cynwyd-Bala Directory 1909. Bala-Cynwyd, Pa.: The Neighborhood Club, 1909.

d'Apery, Tello J. *Overbrook Farms.* Philadelphia: Magee Press, 1936.

Dare, Charles P. *Philadelphia, Wilmington and Baltimore Railroad Guide.* Philadelphia: Fitzgibbon & Van Ness, 1856.

Department of City Transit. *Report of Transit Commissioner, City of Philadelphia, July 1913.* Philadelphia: City of Philadelphia, 1913.

Dictionary of Philadelphia and its Vicinity. Philadelphia: John Wanamaker, 1887.

Directory of the Borough of Lansdowne, East Lansdowne and Vicinity, 1910. Lansdowne, Pa.: Henry S. Barker, 1910.

Dreiser, Theodore. *The Financier.* New York: Boni & Liveright, 1927.

Edmonds, Franklin Spencer. *History of the Central High School of Philadelphia.* Philadelphia: J. B. Lippincott, 1902.

A Facsimile of Frank Leslie's Illustrated Historical Register of the Centennial Exposition 1876. 1877. Reprint, New York: Paddington Press, 1974.

"Features of Pennsylvania Electrification at Philadelphia." *The Electric Review,* 67 (November 13, 1915), pp. 923–28.

Frazier's Pocket Guide To Philadelphia and Travellers' Time Table. Philadelphia: John
    W. Frazier, August 1875.
A Friendly Guide-Book to Philadelphia. Philadelphia: John Wanamaker. 1913.
A Friendly Guide Book to Philadelphia and The Wanamaker Store. Philadelphia: John
    Wanamaker, 1926.
Gibbs, George. "The Philadelphia-Paoli Electrification of the Pennsylvania Railroad
    Company." *The Electric Journal,* 13 (February 1916), pp. 68–78.
Golden Book of the Wanamaker Stores. Philadelphia: John Wanamaker, 1911.
Gopsill's Atlantic City Directory for 1885. Philadelphia: James Gopsill's Sons, 1885.
Gopsill's Philadelphia City Directory. Philadelphia: James Gopsill's Sons, 1876–77,
    1880–81, 1884, 1887, 1889, 1890–1905.
*The Government of Lower Merion Township, Pennsylvania: A Report of a Survey by the
    Bureau of Municipal Research of Philadelphia.* Ardmore, Pa.: Lower Merion
    Township, 1922.
*Guide Book and Industrial Journal of the Philadelphia, Wilmington and Baltimore
    Railroad.* West Chester, Pa.: Andrew S. Brown, 1877.
Guide-Book to the West Chester and Philadelphia Railroad. Philadelphia, 1869.
A Guide on the North Pennsylvania Rail Road, Between Philad'a & Fort Washington.
    Philadelphia: Ringwalt, 1859.
Guide to Philadelphia: Its Public Buildings, Places of Amusement, Churches, Hotels, &c.
    Philadelphia: John Dainty, 1868.
Guide to Philadelphia and the Wanamaker Store. Philadelphia: John Wanamaker, 1908.
Heston, A. M. *Heston Hand Book Atlantic City Illustrated.* Philadelphia: Franklin
    Printing House, 1895.
———. *Heston's Hand Book Atlantic City Illustrated.* Philadelphia: A. M. Heston, 1902.
———. *Illustrated Hand-book of Atlantic City, New Jersey.* Philadelphia: Franklin
    Printing House, 1887.
History of the Baldwin Locomotive Works from 1831 to 1897. Philadelphia: J. B. Lippin-
    cott, 1897.
Illustrated Guide To Fairmount Park and the Centennial Exhibition. Philadelphia: J. B.
    Lippincott, 1876.
Insurance Maps of the City of Philadelphia. Philadelphia: Ernest Hexamer, 1879.
Insurance Maps of the City of Philadelphia. Philadelphia: Ernest Hexamer & Son,
    1887, 1898.
Jackson, Joseph. *Market Street: The Most Historic Highway in America.* Philadelphia:
    The Public Ledger Company, 1918.
Jenkins, Charles F. *The Guide Book to Historic Germantown.* Germantown [Philadel-
    phia]: The Site & Relic Society, 1902.
Johnson, George C. *Lansdowne Past and Present, 1888–1908.* Privately published, 1908.
*Journal of the Proceedings of the United States Centennial Commission, at Philadelphia,
    1872.* Philadelphia: E. C. Markley, 1872.
*A Little Hand-book of Philadelphia: Together with Certain Annals of the Wanamaker
    System.* Philadelphia: John Wanamaker, 1899.
N. W. Ayer & Son's Newspaper Annual. Philadelphia: N. W. Ayer & Son's, 1880, 1885,
    1887, 1890, 1896, 1900, 1910, 1915–16, 1918, 1921, 1926.

1901 Street, Business, and General Directory of Haddonfield, Camden County, N. J., and Vicinity. Camden, N.J.: Chas. L. Hoopes & Co., 1901.

1921 Haddonfield Directory including Batesville Camden County N.J. Haddonfield, N.J.: Haddonfield Boosters, 1921.

The Official Guide of the Railways and Steam Navigation Lines of the United States, Porto Rico, Canada, Mexico and Cuba. New York: National Railway Publication Company, 1901, 1906, 1915, 1925.

The Official Street Directory for Philadelphia. Philadelphia: The Central News Co., 1898.

The Official Street Directory for Philadelphia. Philadelphia: E. S. Hartranft, 1902.

Official Street Railway Map and Guide Book of Philadelphia. Philadelphia: E. P. Noll, 1886.

Our City Guide. Philadelphia: W. D. Reichner, April 1875.

Pennell, Elizabeth Robins. *Joseph Pennell's Pictures of Philadelphia.* 2nd ed. Philadelphia: J. B. Lippincott, 1926.

——— and Joseph Pennell. *Our Philadelphia: Described by Elizabeth Robins Pennell Illustrated with One Hundred & Five Lithographs by Joseph Pennell.* Philadelphia: J. B. Lippincott, 1914.

Philadelphia and Its Environs. 2nd ed. Philadelphia: J. B. Lippincott, 1873.

Philadelphia and Its Environs Illustrated. Philadelphia: J. B. Lippincott, 1876, 1887.

Philadelphia and Its Places of Interest. Philadelphia: William Mann, 1876.

The Philadelphia Colored Directory, 1910. Philadelphia: Philadelphia Colored Directory Co., 1910.

Philadelphia Monthly Diary: March 1896. Philadelphia: American Diary, 1896.

The Philadelphia Record Almanac. Philadelphia: The Philadelphia Record, 1889–1901.

Polk's—Boyd's Combined City and Business Directory of Philadelphia, 1926. Philadelphia: R. L. Polk, 1926.

The Port of Philadelphia: Second in the United States. Philadelphia: City of Philadelphia, 1926.

Public Ledger Almanac. Philadelphia: George W. Childs, 1870–75, 1883, 1895–1901.

The Public Ledger Building, Philadelphia: With an Account of the Proceedings Connected with Its Opening June 20, 1867. Philadelphia: George W. Childs, 1868.

Quaint Corners in Philadelphia. 2nd ed. Philadelphia: John Wanamaker, 1899.

Rand McNally & Co.'s Handy Guide to Philadelphia and Environs, Including Atlantic City and Cape May. New York: Rand, McNally, 1900.

The Record Almanac 1885 Illustrated. Philadelphia: Philadelphia Record, 1885.

Repplier, Agnes. *Philadelphia: The Place and the People.* New York: Macmillan Company, 1909.

Sanborn Map Company, Haddon Heights, Camden County, New Jersey. New York: Sanborn Map Company, 1909, 1914, 1922.

Sanborn Map Company, Haddon Heights Including Mt. Ephraim, Camden County, New Jersey. New York: Sanborn Map Company, 1927.

Smedley's Atlas of the City of Philadelphia. Philadelphia: J. B. Lippincott, 1862.

Strangers and Citizens Hand Book and Official Guide to Railroads, Steamship and Steamboat Lines, Business Houses, and Places of Interest in Philadelphia, September 1880. Philadelphia: Burk & McFetridge, 1880.

Suburban and Rural Homes on the Pennsylvania Railroad. Philadelphia: Pennsylvania Railroad, 1875.

Suburban Homes. Philadelphia: Philadelphia, Wilmington & Baltimore Railroad, 1875.

Summer Excursion Routes, 1901, Pennsylvania Railroad. Philadelphia: Pennsylvania Railroad, 1901.

Summer Excursion Routes, Pennsylvania Railroad, 1884. Philadelphia: Pennsylvania Railroad, 1884.

System of Steam/Street Railroads/Railways of Philadelphia: A Complete Guide with Maps. Philadelphia: Allen, Lane & Scott, 1887.

Tanner, H. S. *A New Picture of Philadelphia or the Stranger's Guide to the City and Adjoining Districts.* New York: T. R. Tanner, 1844.

Third Annual Report of Harry A. Mackey, Mayor of Philadelphia. Philadelphia: City of Philadelphia, 1930.

Thirty Miles Around Philadelphia on the Lines of the Pennsylvania Railroad. Philadelphia: Pennsylvania Railroad, 1913.

The Times Almanac. Philadelphia: Philadelphia Times, 1895–1901.

Townsend, J. W. *The Old "Main Line."* Privately printed, 1922.

Trautwine, Jr., John C. *The Philadelphia and Columbia Railroad of 1834.* Philadelphia: City History Society, 1925.

Travelers' Official Guide of the Railway and Steam Navigation Lines in the United States and Canada. Philadelphia: National Railway Publication Company, 1875, 1879.

Travelers' Official Guide of the Railway and Steam Navigation Lines in the United States and Canada. New York: National Railway Publication Company, 1881, 1884, 1888, 1893.

Travelers' Official Railway Guide for the United States, Canada and Mexico. New York: National Railway Publication Company, 1897.

Twining, Robert S. *A Study and Review of the Problem of Passenger Transportation in Philadelphia by a United System of Lines.* Philadelphia: City of Philadelphia, 1916.

Visitors' Guide Book To Philadelphia. Philadelphia: J. B. Lippincott, 1916.

West Chester and Philadelphia Railroad Guide Book and Industrial Journal. Cheyney, Pa.: A. S. Brown, 1876.

What To See in Philadelphia. Philadelphia: John Wanamaker, 1911.

What We Look Like. Philadelphia: Strawbridge & Clothier, [1887].

Where to Live—Why? Philadelphia: Haddonfield Manor Realty Company, [1920s].

Index